AF688504

PRINCIPLES OF FEDERAL CONSTRUCTION CONTRACTING

Written by Stan Uhlig

Certificate of Registration

This Certificate issued under the seal of the Copyright Office in accordance with title 17, *United States Code*, attests that registration has been made for the work identified below. The information on this certificate has been made a part of the Copyright Office records.

United States Register of Copyrights and Director

Registration Number
TXu 2-451-657
Effective Date of Registration:
October 10, 2024
Registration Decision Date:
October 18, 2024

Title

Title of Work: Principles of Federal Construction Contracting: 2nd Edition

Completion/Publication

Year of Completion: 2024

Author

- **Author:** Stan Uhlig
  Author Created: text, artwork
  Citizen of: United States

Copyright Claimant

Copyright Claimant: Stan Uhlig
16911 SE 144th St., Renton, WA 98059, United States

Rights and Permissions

Name: Stan Uhlig
Email: fcconsultants.stan@gmail.com
Telephone: (425)241-1792

Certification

Name: Ian Tanner
Date: October 03, 2024

About the Author

Stan Uhlig, founder and owner of Federal Construction Consultants is a leading expert who began his extensive career as a Seabee in Vietnam. A veteran and graduate civil engineer, his experience spans from teaching civil engineering technology to working in federal construction contracting around the world. During his 40 years as a contractor to the Department of Defense (DoD) and other federal agencies, Stan worked as a chief engineer, project manager, senior project manager, and general manager of operations. The founder of a multi-million-dollar construction business, Stan has successfully completed some of the biggest and most complex government contracts ever conceived at home or abroad. These include underground aircraft hangars, nuclear weapons storage facilities, fire stations, air traffic control towers, operations facilities, barracks, dining facilities, high-rise bridges, historic renovations (including the first YMCA building west of the Mississippi River) Visitor Centers such as Ash Meadows National Wildlife Refuge Visitor Center (shown on book cover), rebuilding dry docks (the West Coast's largest), and an underground hospital (again, the world's largest at the time).

These projects not only presented unique engineering challenges, but also involved intricate contractual complexities and operational difficulties. Stan has expertise in successfully managing such contracts in a way that not only delivers quality and on-time results but also avoids lawsuits, delays, added costs, and loss of credibility. Stan has managed an average of forty projects and up to 1,500 employees. He has also taught construction contracting at the college level and mentored a large general contractor. He is an engaging speaker in his interactive workshops.

Table Of Contents

About the Author iii

Preface xi

Chapter:1 Finding and Understanding the Solicitation 1

1.0 Chapter Description and Use 1

1.1 Finding Federal Projects to Bid On 2

1.1.1 Using SAM 3

1.1.1.1 Unique Entity ID: 3

1.1.1.2 Registration: 4

1.2 Understanding the Solicitation 18

1.2.1 Basic Statutory and Regulatory Provisions 19

1.2.2 Acquisition Methods 20

1.2.2.1 Sealed Bidding 20

1.2.3 Parts of a Solicitation 22

1.2.3.1 Part I – The Schedule 23

1.2.3.2 Part II – Contract Clauses 27

1.2.3.3 Part III – List of Documents, Exhibits, and Other Attachments 28

1.2.3.4 Part IV – Representations and Instructions 28

1.2.4 Amendments 29

1.2.5 Submitting Questions 29

Chapter 2 Building a Strategy and Developing a Proposal 30

1.0 Chapter Description and Use 31

2.0 The Strategy 31

2.1 Resources and Capabilities: 31

2.2 Size, Type, and Location of the Project: 32

2.3 Evaluation Criteria: 33
3.0 Risk Management 33
3.1 Risk Management Review Process 33
3.1.1 The Review Process: 34
3.2 Risk Management Listing 35
3.2.1 External Risks: 35
3.2.2 Management Risks 37
3.2.3 Operational Risks 47
4.0 RFP Requirements/Proposal Preparation 70
4.1 Bidder Eligibility: 70
4.2 Bid Feasibilty: 71
4.3 Self-Assessment: 71
4.4 Competition: 72
4.5 Preparing the Proposal: 73
5.0 Protest after Award 76
6.0 Surety Bonds 79
7.0 Insurance 81
8.0 Taxes 83
9.0 Utilization of Small Business Concerns 83

Chapter 3 Contracts 88

1.0 Chapter Description and Use 88
2.0 Types of Contracts 88
2.1 Fixed-Price Contracts 90
2.2 Cost-Reimbursement Contracts 91
2.3 Incentive Contracts 92
2.4 Indefinite-Delivery Contracts 93
2.5 Time-and-Materials, Labor-Hours, and Letter Contracts 94

3.0 Types of Contracting Officers 94
4.0 Contracting Officer's Representative 96

Chapter 4 Design....97

1.0 Chapter Description and Use:....98
2.0 Requirements for Registration of Designers 98
3.0 Correlating Design to RFP and Proposal:....99
4.0 Shop Drawings: 99
5.0 Specifications and Drawings:....100
5.1 Partnering and Project Progress Processes:....101
5.2 Stages of Designs Submittals: 101
5.3 Specifications: 104
5.4 Drawings:....104
5.5 Design Analysis: 104
6.0 Design Quality Control: 108
6.1 Acceptance of Plan: 108
6.2 Notification of Changes:....108
6.3 DQC PLAN: 109
7.0 DrChecks Design Review and Checking System: 126
7.1 Procedures: 126
7.2 Tracking Design Review Comments:....127
8.0 Preliminary Construction/Design Progress Schedule: 127
9.0 Fast – Tracking: 128
9.1 Why the Government Uses Design – Build: 128
9.2 Fast – Track Construction:....128
10.0 Understanding Military Specific Codes: 129
11.0 Anti-Terrorism/Force Protection (AT/FP) Requirements:....130
12.0 Leed: 130

13.0 Procedure for Obtaining Variance after Design is Complete: 131

Chapter 5 Quality Control 133

1.0 Chapter Description and Use 133

2.0 Contractor Quality Control Requirements 134

3.0 Contractor Quality Control Plan (CQCP) 134

4.0 Preconstruction Submittals 137

5.0 Submittal Register 137

6.0 Three-Phase Quality Control Program 138

6.1 Preparatory Phase 138

6.2 Initial Phase 139

6.3 Follow-up Phase 140

6.4 Additional Preparatory and Initial Phases 140

7.0 Quality Control Manager Qualifications and Certification 140

8.0 Inspector Qualifications 141

9.0 RMS/QCS 142

Chapter 6 Safety 144

1.0 Chapter Description and Use 144

2.0 Safety Program and Safety Plans 145

3.0 Accident Prevention Plan 151

4.0 EM 385-1-1 Safety Manual 152

5.0 Contractor and Subcontractor Safety Training Requirements 152

6.0 Activity Hazard Analysis (AHA) 153

7.0 Environmental Protection Plan 154

Chapter 7 Contract Clauses 155

1.0 Chapter Description and Use 157

2.0 FAR Clauses by Reference vs. Full Text 158

3.0 Professional and Consultant Service Costs 159
4.0 Security 161
5.0 Liquidated Damages 166
6.0 Order of Precedence 166
7.0 Price Evaluation Preferences 168
8.0 Small Business Subcontracting Plan 170
8.1 Clause Inclusion and Flowdown 171
8.2 Recordkeeping 171
9.0 Davis-Bacon Act (Prevailing Wages) 199
9.1 General FAR Requirements 199
9.2 Who is allowed to work? 200
9.3 Site of the Work 200
9.4 Wage Determination 200
9.5 Pay Determination 201
9.6 Work Hours 201
9.7 Payrolls and Basic Records 201
9.8 Apprentices and Trainees 203
9.9 Withholding of Funds 204
9.10 Contract Flowdown 205
10.0 Contract Flowdown 208
11.0 Buy American Act 210
12.0 Prompt Payment Act 250
12.1 Progress Payments 251
12.2 Final Payments 251
12.3 Payment Requests – U.S. Army Corps of Engineers 252
12.4 Interest Penalty 253
12.4.1 Computing Penalty Amount 253
12.4.2 Additional Interest Penalty 253

12.5 Prompt Payment for Subcontractors 254
13.0 Disputes 268
14.0 The Miller Act 271
14.1 Requirements 271
14.2 Alternatives to Payment Bonds 272
14.3 Who is Covered by the Miller Act? 272
14.4 Who is Not Covered by the Miller Act? 272
14.5 Getting a Copy of the Contractor's Bond 272
14.6 Non-payment Recourse under the Miller Act 273
14.7 Waiver of Right to Civil Action 274
14.8 Coverage for Taxes in the Performance Bond 274
15.0 Work by the Contractor 276
16.0 Differing Site Conditions 279
17.0 Site Investigations and Conditions Affecting the Work 280
18.0 Use and Possession Prior to Completion 283
19.0 Schedules 283
20.0 Suspension of Work 285
21.0 Changes 287
22.0 Government Furnished Property (GFP) 289
23.0 Inspection of Construction 290
24.0 Warranty of Construction 293
25.0 Value Engineering 295
26.0 Default 300
27.0 Indian Incentive 306
28.0 Government Rights 309
29.0 Levies on Contract Payments 310

Chapter 8 Modification Proposals 312

1.0 Chapter Description and Use 312

2.0 Modifications 313

2.1 Modification Price Guidelines 313

2.2 Modification Format and Profit Calculation 313

3.0 Indirect Cost Allowability 315

4.0 Equipment Pricing for Modifications 315

5.0 Subcontractor Cost or Pricing Data—Modifications 316

6.0 Modification Markup Meeting 319

7.0 Guidelines for Pricing Modifications 323

8.0 Schedules (FRAGNET) 326

Chapter 9 Claims 327

1.0 Chapter Description and Use 327

2.0 Requests for Equitable Adjustment 328

3.0 Documentation Required for a Claim 330

4.0 Notifications 330

5.0 Contracting Officer's Final Decision 333

6.0 Armed Services Board of Contract Appeals 336

Commonly Used Government Acronyms 337

Government Contracts Glossary 342

Index 348

Preface

Principles of Federal Construction Contracting (2nd edition) has been updated to include the changes made in the Federal Aquisition Regulations (FAR) clauses, processes, and procedures that the federal government has made. Some have simplified the processes, e.g., the System for Award Management (SAM) and some have made it more complicated. I was once asked "why would you want to do business with the federal government" and my answer was" because the money is always there and is guaranteed". This is because an agency must have the funds "in hand" before it can sign a contract. In commercial construction the owner may only have a promise from a bank or investors before they sign a contract. In other words, you do not have to "chase" the money you are owed.

Many construction companies want to enter the federal government construction contracting market but because the laws and processes are vastly different from the commercial and state and local construction sectors, a knowledge of these laws and processes is essential to success. Companies today are bidding on projects without a clear understanding of what it takes to do work for the government; as a result, many are encountering serious financial difficulties.

Opportunities abound in federal construction contracting. The DoD has a budget of 30 billion dollars each year for construction, maintenance and repair and the other agencies have about the same, but the devil is in the details. Federal government construction contracting requires that management systems be set up to deal with mandated everyday processes and the inherent risk associated with those processes. You cannot just do business in the same old way if you want to do business with the federal government.

Effective construction operations management requires that a company manage its risk. *Principles of Federal Construction Contracting* has a "risk management" chapter intended to be used in your decision-making process. Companies performing work for the federal government must plan and operate based on the realities of having a business relationship with the federal government. You might need to change your management systems to incorporate the required federal government processes.

You will also need to set up management systems to identify and monitor the additional costs inherent in federal construction contracting. *Principles of Federal Construction Contracting* will guide you in understanding and interpreting the various federal government rules, regulations, processes, and procedures. For example, general conditions costs are higher for federal government construction contracting than for commercial construction contracting because additional staff members are needed to handle the various additional federal government required tasks. The timeliness of actions such as notifications must be tracked and forms and procedures must be developed to provide adequate documentation that the federal government's rules and regulations, specifically the Federal Acquisition Regulations (FAR), have been addressed. Quality control systems must be established. The home office and the field office staff will have more work to do and could face severe penalties if some of that work - such as meeting Davis-Bacon Act (prevailing wages) and Small Business Subcontracting Plan documentation requirements – is not done properly. Reviewing your management systems early on will help you to succeed in federal government construction contracting.

In developing *Principles of Federal Construction Contracting,* I have drawn on my 40 years working directly on federal government contracts. The discussions and advice I offer in this book are not academic or theoretical – based on the reality of what it takes to perform successfully in the federal government construction contracting marketplace.

What This Book Will Do for You

Principles of Federal Construction Contracting is designed to be your complete reference for the rules, regulations, procedures, and processes of doing business with the federal government in construction contracting. This book has been designed around the U.S. Army Corps of Engineers' operating methods and their rules, processes, and procedures. Although other federal government agencies operate under the same laws and regulations, they may have slightly different processes and requirements. This book will help all levels of construction firms, architect/engineer firms, subcontractors, and vendors that want to do business with the federal government; it will also help firms that are already in the field become more effective and, thus, more profitable. It will empower firms with the knowledge of the processes, rules, regulations, and procedures needed to be successful in federal construction contracting.

This book will serve as a ready reference to all federal government construction requirements, rules, regulations, and procedures. It will save your company precious time, effort, money, and frustration and will put you in a position to challenge the federal government on issues instead of succumbing to its every demand. You will understand when a demand must be met and how to deal with it and when a demand is inappropriate and unenforceable.

***Principles of Federal Construction Contracting* is your complete guide to:**

Finding federal construction projects to bid on

Understanding federal government solicitations and contracts

Understanding what constitutes a winning proposal

Building a strategy for your firm that meets your goals and enhances your business plan

Understanding federal government rules, regulations, and procedures for producing project designs for both design-bid-build and design-build contracts

Preparing quality control and safety programs that comply with federal regulations and processes

Understanding the FAR and knowing when and how to use it for your benefit and protection

Determining when a change order is required and how to price and properly process it

Identifying a claim and knowing how to process it

Each chapter is designed to provide you with:

An in-depth guide to how the process works

A complete understanding of how to use the process, regulation, or procedure for your benefit and protection

Checklists, where appropriate, that help you decipher requirements

Recommendations and tips to help you through the process and protect you from potential claim situations

Knowledge so that the federal government must deal with you as an equal

I hope that this book will provide you with the tools and knowledge you need to succeed in the federal construction contracting marketplace. Please be in touch with your success stories, or I can help you with your efforts.

Stan Uhlig

www.contractingguru.com

Chapter:1
Finding and Understanding the Solicitation

1.0	Chapter Description and Use
1.1	Finding Federal Projects to Bid On
1.1.1	Using SAM
1.1.1.1	Unique Entity ID
1.1.1.2	Registration
1.2	Understanding the Solicitation
1.2.1	Basic Statutory and Regulatory Provisions
1.2.2	Acquisition Methods
1.2.2.1	Sealed Bidding
1.2.2.2	Negotiation
1.2.3	Parts of a Solicitation
1.2.3.1	Part I – The Schedule
1.2.3.2	Part II – Contract Clauses
1.2.3.3	Part III – List of Documents, Exhibits, and Other Attachments
1.2.3.4	Part IV – Representations and Instructions
1.2.4	Amendments
1.2.5	Submitting Questions

1.0 Chapter Description and Use

The objectives of this chapter are to determine what types of federal projects there are to bid on, how to use the System for Award Management (SAM.GOV) to search for projects, how to read and understand the solicitation and acquisition methods, find the pertinent information from the

SF form 1442, how to register with the federal government in order to be able to bid on a project, and how to complete the online SAM.GOV registration. This section will walk you through these processes, and after using this section, you should be able to find projects, understand the solicitation, where to find any information you will need from it, and be able to get registered with the federal government to perform work with them.

1.1 Finding Federal Projects to Bid On

The federal government uses three different methods of construction contracting. For very minor works, such as repairing a boiler, that are less than $2,500 in cost, they have the option of purchasing the service using the federal government VISA credit card. Not all government personnel have this card, but there are many at each site that do. For construction over $2,500 but less than $25,000, the local contracting office can let out the contract. Federal government construction projects having an estimated value of over $25,000 are posted on the official federal government website, WWW.SAM.GOV.

Using the Federal Government VISA Credit Card:

This method allows local federal government users to get items repaired and maintained in an expeditious manner. The requirements to follow FAR regulations are minimized, so there is very little paperwork involved, and it allows the contractor/vendor to be paid immediately and upfront. It is as simple as giving a written quote, agreeing with the user on the work and price, and then just running the card through your credit card machine. You will have to have your system set up to accept the VISA card, but this is usually done very quickly. It is highly recommended that you get to know the personnel at each office or base who have access to the VISA card and develop a close relationship with them to get work from them. You can get this information from the local office or base and from the regional contracting office. Most department heads are the ones who have access to a VISA card for their specific trade, such as HVAC Shop or Electrical Shop. The advantage is that each agency/office or base has an operations and maintenance fund that they can draw from, and there is always a need to get repairs or maintenance done quickly. The profit margins are normally very good. Another advantage is that by building personal relationships with these people it can also lead to other larger projects as they are always asked to give their recommendations.

Federal Projects up to $25,000:

Federal government construction projects that are estimated to be more than $2,500 but less than $25,000 are normally contracted by the local contracting office. Again, the strict FAR requirements are relaxed somewhat to allow time frames to be compressed and firms are invited to bid based on a local bidders list without having to be advertised. Normally, the contracting office wants at least three bids for each project as that determines the "fair market value" of the project. Although there is still competition for the contract, the margins can be quite high. Your firm should make a point of meeting with the local contracting office to get on the bidders' list. Each contracting office has a website where you can locate the right person to talk to.

Federal Projects over $25,000:

All federal government projects over $25,000 that are to go out for bid must be advertised on the SAM.GOV website. It is imperative that any contractor, subcontractor, vendor, or architect/engineer firm use this website with the federal government through this website to do business with it. A firm can look up opportunities and view the plan holders list without fully registering, but to be able to bid on a project as a prime contractor, you must be fully registered through this site. Every project from every agency (except NASA) will have their projects advertised through this website.

1.1.1 Using SAM

SAM.gov is the official site used by the federal government to document and track the eligibility of an individual or entity to receive federal funds. You must register with the federal government before you can do business with any federal agency. This includes bidding on projects, getting on GSA schedules, consulting services, etc. I highly recommend subcontractors also register, as this will allow you to review projects that you may be interested in and see the list of prime contractors bidding on the project. The SAM registration must be renewed each year, but it is much simpler than the initial one.

1.1.1.1 Unique Entity ID:

On April 4, 2022, the DUNS number requirement changed to the Unique Entity Identifier, which is now used across all federal government agencies. This Unique Entity Identifier is generated through the SAM.GOV website and is the first thing that you must do, as it will be used anytime you want to get into SAM.GOV. Entity registration, searching, and data entry in SAM.GOV now requires the use of the Unique Entity ID. The Unique Entity ID is a 12-character alphanumeric ID assigned by SAM.GOV and needs to be used by all contractors, subcontractors and vendors. Firms with multiple offices and/or locations can set up a separate Unique Entity ID for each location.

1.1.1.2 Registration:

Registering on SAM.GOV is a laborious and time-consuming process and needs to be renewed once each year. There is no fee for this registration. The renewal process will only require that you verify and update any information previously submitted. Prior to starting the registration process, I highly recommend that you review the following SAM.GOV Entity Registration Checklist and gather all the documents required to complete it.

Unique Entity ID:

After you select your purpose of the registration (All Awards) and your entity type, you will enter the following information to get a Unique Entity ID:

Legal Business Name

Physical Address (A post office box may not be used as your physical address)

Date of Incorporation

State of Incorporation (Entities outside the U.S. may need to provide alternate information)

National Provider Identifier (NPI) (Non-U.S. entities only)

Your entity name and address will be validated by SAM.gov. If SAM.gov cannot validate your entity, you can create a help ticket with the Federal Service Desk from the page. Once you receive your Unique Entity ID, you can continue the registration.

You will also select whether you want your entity to be visible in public search results:

> Note: Publicly viewable entity records display your record status, legal business name, and physical address on SAM.gov. You can restrict the public viewing of your record by deselecting the checkbox. If you restrict your information, it will not be visible to other non-federal entities or state and local governments who may wish to do business with you. However, your non-sensitive entity information remains available to federal government users and those who download the SAM public data file.

MPIN:

Marketing Partner Identification Number. A number created by you when you register in SAM. It is a personal code that allows you to access other government applications such as the Past Performance Information Retrieval System (PPIRS) and SAM. The MPIN acts as your password in these other systems, and you should guard it as such. You must know your MPIN to update your SAM. If you are uncertain about whether you can update it, make sure to write it down.

Core Data:

Core data includes the following information:

Business Information:

Organization start date

Date on which your company's fiscal year ends

Organization's division name and number (optional)

Organization's website URL (optional)

Marketing Partner Identification Number (MPIN) (You will create this when you register.)

Physical address (auto filled from Unique Entity ID section)

Mailing address (You can copy your physical address or enter a different address.)

Taxpayer Identification Number (TIN) (U.S. entities only)

IRS Consent:

IRS Consent Form (taxpayer name and address) (U.S. entities only)

CAGE or NCAGE Code:

CAGE Code (U.S. entities only) (If you do not have a CAGE code, select "No" and one will be assigned to your entity after you submit your registration.) NCAGE Code (Non-U.S. entities) (If your entity is based outside of the U.S., you must go to the NCAGE Request Tool and request an NCAGE code before starting a SAM.gov registration.)

Ownership Details:

Is your entity owned or controlled by another entity? (yes or no)

If yes, is your immediate owner located outside the U.S. and its territories? (yes or no)

If yes, enter your immediate owner's NCAGE Code. (Required for non-U.S. entities to start a registration)

Predecessor Details:

Is your entity a successor to a predecessor entity that held a federal contract or grant within the last three years? (yes or no)

If yes, provide your three most recent predecessors in reverse chronological order (newest to oldest). Start by entering your most recent predecessor's CAGE or NCAGE Code.

General Information:

Country of Incorporation

State of Incorporation (U.S. entities only)

Company Security Clearance (optional)

Highest Employee Security Clearance Level (optional)

Institution Type (e.g., foundation, hospital, educational, if applicable)

Disadvantaged Business Enterprise (must be certified by a federal agency)

Native American Entity Type (if applicable)

Organization Factors (e.g., S corporation, LLC, foreign owned)

Entity Structure (e.g., Corporate Entity-Not Tax Exempt, Corporate Entity-Tax Exempt, Sole Proprietorship)

Profit Structure (e.g., for-profit, non-profit)

Socioeconomic Categories (e.g., veteran-owned, minority-owned)

Financial Information:

Accept credit cards as a method of payment (yes or no)

Electronic Funds Transfer (optional for non-U.S. entities)

Account type

Routing number

Account number

Automated Clearing House

U.S. phone number

Remittance Address

Name and address

Executive Compensation Questions:

Answer yes if in the last fiscal year:

80% or more of your organization's revenue come from federal sources (e.g., contracts, grants, loans, etc.);

Your total revenue from federal sources exceeded $25 million.

Does the public have access to information about the compensation of the senior executives in your business or organization? (yes or no)

If yes to the first two questions and no to the third question:

Provide names, titles, and total compensation values of your top five executive compensated employees

Proceedings Questions:

Is your organization responding to a federal procurement opportunity that contains the provision at FAR 52.209-7?

Is your organization subject to the clause in FAR 52.209-9 in any current federal contracts?

Is your organization applying for a federal grant opportunity that contains the award term and condition described in C.F.R. 200 Appendix XII?

If yes to all of the previous questions, answer the following questions:

Does your organization have current federal contracts or grants with a total value (including any exercised or unexercised options) greater than $10 million?

Within the last five years, has the organization or any of its principals, in connection with the award to or performance by the business or organization of a federal contract or grant, been subject of a federal or state:

Criminal proceeding resulting in a conviction or other acknowledgment of fault

Civil proceeding resulting in a finding of fault with a monetary fine, penalty, reimbursement, restitution, and/or damages greater than $5,000, or other acknowledgment of fault, and/or

Administrative proceedings resulting in a finding of fault with either a monetary fine or penalty greater than $5,000 or reimbursement, restitution, or damages greater than $100,000, or other acknowledgment or fault?

If you answer yes to all three above questions, you must provide the following detailed information about each current proceeding against your entity:

Instrument

State

Instrument Number

Type of Proceeding

Disposition

Description of the Proceeding

Assertions:

Assertions include the following information:

Goods and Services

North American Industry Classification System (NAICS) codes

Go to https://www.census.gov/naics/ to lookup NAICS codes for your organization

Product Service Codes (PSCs) (optional)

Go to https://www.acquisition.gov/content/product-and-service-code-manual to lookup PSCs for your organization

Size Metrics

Worldwide (organizational size information according to 13 CFR 121)

Annual receipts

Number of employees

Locations (optional)

Annual receipts

Number of employees

Electronic Data Interchange (EDI)

Do you wish to enter EDI Information for your non-government entity? (yes or no)

Disaster Response Information

Do you wish to be included in the Disaster Response Registry? (yes or no)

If yes, does your company require bonding to bid on contracts? (yes or no)

If yes, provide in whole dollars:

Construction bonding level, per contract

Construction bonding level, aggregate

Service bonding level, per contract Service bonding level, aggregate

Geographical area served (any state, one state, or multiple states)

Representations and Certifications

Representations and Certifications include the following information:

FAR Response 1

(1) Name and title of person(s) responsible for determining prices offered in bids and proposals for your entity.

(2) Does your entity have other plants or facilities at different addresses routinely used to perform on contracts? (yes or no) If yes, enter the place of performance address, owner name, and owner address for each facility.

(3) TIN is on file (This is usually entered as a part of Core Data. If not, you can enter it here.)

(4) Is your entity following the guidelines established by the Environmental Protection Agency (EPA) for recovered material? (yes, no, or vendor will provide information with specific offers to the government)

FAR Response 2

(5) Is your entity a small business concern and qualifies as a labor surplus area (LSA) concern? (yes or no) (If your entity is not a small business based on the size metrics data provided in the Assertions section, you will not be able to answer this question.) If yes, indicate the LSA in which the manufacturing or production costs amount to more than 50% of contract price.

(6) Is your entity owned or controlled by a common parent that files its Federal Income Tax returns on a consolidated basis? (yes or no) If yes, provide the company name and tax identification number.

(7) Is your entity or any of its principals currently debarred, suspended, proposed for debarment, or declared ineligible for the award of contracts by any federal agency? (yes or no)

(8) (part 1) In the past three years, has your entity, or any of its principals, been

convicted or had a civil judgment rendered against it for commission of fraud or a criminal offense in connection with obtaining, attempting to obtain, or performing a public (federal, state, or local) contract or subcontract; violation of federal or state antitrust statutes relating to the submission of offers; or commission of embezzlement, theft, forgery, bribery, falsification or destruction of records, making false statements, tax evasion, violating federal criminal tax laws, or receiving stolen property? (yes or no)

(8) (part 2) In the past three years, has your entity been notified of any delinquent federal taxes in an amount that exceeds $3,000 for which liability remains unsatisfied? (yes or no)

(9) Is your entity, or any of its principals, presently indicted for, or otherwise criminally or civilly charged by a governmental entity with, commission of any of the offenses enumerated in either part of Question 8? (yes or no)

(10) Within the past three years, has your entity been terminated for cause? (yes or no)

(11) List the name of any HUBZone small businesses participating in a HUBZone Joint Venture with your entity. If your entity is not participating in a HUBZone Joint Venture, select "None."

(12) Reserved (no answer required)

(13) If you indicated that you are a Joint Venture Women Owned Small Business on the General Information page in the Core Data section, provide the name of the company participating in the Joint Venture with your entity.

(14) If you indicated that you are a Joint Venture Economically Disadvantaged Women Owned Small Business on the General Information page in the Core Data section, provide the name of the company participating in the Joint Venture with your entity.

(15) Does your entity provide any data to the government that qualifies as limited rights data or restricted computer software? (yes, no, or vendor will provide information with specific offers to the government)

If yes, please list limited rights data or restricted computer software

FAR Response 3

(16) Your structure type and how your business or organization is defined by the IRS will be pre-filled based on your answers on the General Information page of the Core Data

section. If you selected "Other" as your type, you will be provided with a box to enter more information.

(17) Is your entity a small, disadvantaged business concern? (yes or no) (If your entity is not a small, disadvantaged business based on the size metrics data provided in the Assertions section, you will not be able to answer this question.)

(18) Reserved (no answer required)

(19) Does your entity deliver any end products (from the corresponding country of origin) that are listed on the List of Products Requiring Federal Contractor Certification as to Forced or Indentured Child Labor under Executive Order No. 13126? (yes or no)

(20) Has your entity held previous contracts/subcontracts subject to Federal Acquisition Regulation (FAR) 52.222-26 (Equal Opportunity)? (yes or no)

(21) Are any end products delivered to the Government by your entity foreign (non-domestic) end products? (yes, no, or vendor will provide this information with specific offers to the government)

If yes, list the products and their corresponding country of origin.

(22) Has your entity filed all required Equal Employment Opportunity compliance reports? (yes or no)

(23) Choose the statement that best applies to your entity's affirmative action programs. The statements you may choose from are:

Your entity has developed and has on file affirmative action programs required by Secretary of Labor Regulations

Your entity does not have developed and does not have "on file affirmative action programs" required by Secretary of Labor Regulations

Your entity has not had previous contracts subject to written affirmative action program requirements from Secretary of Labor Regulations

(24) Does your entity provide maintenance, calibration, and/or repair of information technology, scientific and medical and/or office and business equipment? (Yes, No, or vendor will provide information with specific offers to the government.)

If yes, you need to answer additional questions about who services your equipment, if your equipment is used regularly outside of government purposes, if it is sold or traded to the general public, if your service prices are based on an established catalog or on market prices, and if your entity uses wage and fringe benefits plans for all service employees performing work under government contracts, as it uses for equivalent employees servicing the same equipment for commercial customers.

FAR Response 4

(25) Does your entity provide services as described in FAR 22.1003-4(d) (1) (Service Contract Labor Standards), FAR 52.212-3 (Commercial Products and Commercial Services), and FAR 52.222-52 (Service Contract Labor Standards to Contracts for Certain Services-Certification)? (Yes, No, or vendor will provide information with specific offers to the government.)

If yes, you need to answer additional questions about whether your services are offered and sold regularly to non-government customers in substantial quantities in the course of normal business operations, if your service prices are based on an established catalog or on market prices, whether you can ensure each service employee will spend less than 20% of their time servicing the government contract, and if your entity uses wage and fringe benefits plans for all service employees performing work under government contracts, as it uses for equivalent employees servicing the same equipment for commercial customers.

(26) If any of the PSCs you entered in the Goods and Services page in the Assertions section are Federal Supply Codes (FSC), you need to provide whether the place of manufacture for each FSC code is in the U.S. or outside the U.S.

(27) Is your entity an inverted domestic corporation? (yes or no)

(28) Is your entity a subsidiary of an inverted domestic corporation? (yes or no)

(29) Reserved (no answer required)

(30) Is your entity a corporation with a delinquent tax liability? (yes or no)

(31) In the last 24 months, has your entity been convicted of a felony criminal violation under a federal law? (yes or no)

(32) Did your entity receive $7.5 million or more in federal contracts during the previous federal fiscal year, requiring it to publicly disclose greenhouse gas emissions and reduction goals, or did your entity receive less than $7.5 million federal contracts during the previous federal fiscal year and still want to publicly disclose greenhouse

gas emissions and reduction goals? (yes or no)

If yes, add a URL to a publicly accessible website to access the results of a greenhouse gas inventory.

Additionally, does your entity, through itself or its immediate owner or highest-level owner, publicly disclose a quantitative greenhouse gas emissions reduction goal? (yes or no)

If yes, add a URL to a publicly accessible website to access the target to reduce absolute emissions or emissions intensity by a specific quantity or percentage.

(33) (part 1) Does your entity provide covered telecommunications equipment or services as a part of its offered products or services to the Government in the performance of any contract, subcontract, or other contractual instrument? (yes or no)

(33) (part 2) Does your entity use covered telecommunications equipment or services, or any equipment, system, or service that uses covered telecommunications equipment or services? (yes or no)

Architect-Engineer Response

(34) If you did not enter a NAICS code connected to architect and engineer activities, you will see the following text "Our records indicate that has not selected NAICS 541310, 541320, 541330, 541360, 541370, 541410 or 541620. SF 330, Part II information is not applicable." You will not be asked any additional questions on this page.

If you did enter one of the applicable NAICS codes, you can provide additional information to complete your SF 330 Part II.

Are you interested in applying for Federal Architect-Engineer contracts under FAR Part 36 and want to enter an SF 330, Part II for this entity? (yes, no, or vendor will provide information with specific offers to the government)

If yes, then you will be required to enter additional information.

List any former firm names and the year established, used by the entity in the past six years. If there are no other names, select "None."

Enter the number of employees for the entity by function code and discipline. If you have more than one discipline within your firm, you will need to create a new table for each discipline by selecting, "Add New Discipline Details."

List the profile codes, experience, and annual average revenue for the last five years.

List the professional services revenues for the entity in the last three years.

Enter the name and title of the person certifying the Architect-Engineer information.

Defense Response

(35) Does your entity wish to bid on or currently hold any Department of Defense (DOD) issued or DoD-funded contracts? (yes or no)

If yes, you must answer Questions 36–42. If no, the answers to questions 36–42 will be answered as "Not Applicable."

(36) Do you anticipate that supplies will be transported by sea in the performance of any contract or subcontract resulting from this solicitation? (yes or no)

(37) Are prices set forth in contracts that are based on the wage rate(s) or material price(s) established and controlled by a foreign government and do not include contingency allowances to pay for possible increases in wage rates or material prices? (yes or no)

If yes, provide the name of the host country.

(38) Is your entity effectively owned or controlled by a foreign government? (yes or no)

If yes, provide the name and contact information for someone at your entity who can answer questions about disclosure. You must also provide the name and address of the entity/entities controlled by a foreign government, description of interest, ownership percentage, and the foreign government country.

(39) Is your entity a foreign entity in which the government of a covered foreign country has an ownership interest that enables the government to affect satellite operations? (yes or no)

(40) Is your entity foreign and if so, does it plan to provide or use launch or other

satellite services under the contract from a covered foreign country? (yes or no)

(41) Is your entity offering commercial satellite services provided by a foreign entity in which the government of a covered foreign country has an ownership interest that enables the government to affect satellite operations? (yes or no)

42) Is your entity offering commercial satellite services provided by a foreign entity that plans to or is expected to provide or use launch or other satellite services under the contract from a covered foreign country? (yes or no)

Financial Assistance Response

Do you wish to apply for a federal financial assistance project or program, or is your entity currently the recipient of funding under any federal financial assistance project or program? (yes or no)

If yes, the financial assistance representations and certifications will be displayed. You must read and certify your entity attests to the accuracy of the representations and certifications listed. Go to Appendix I to review the financial assistance representations and certifications.

Points of Contact (POCs)

POCs include the following information:

Mandatory POCs

Enter the first and last name, email, phone number, and address (if applicable) for these mandatory POCs:

Accounts Receivable POC

Electronic Business POC

Government Business POC

Optional POCs

Enter the first and last name, email, phone number, and address (if applicable) for these optional POCs:

Past Performance POC

Past Performance Alternate POC

Electronic Business Alternate POC

Government Business Alternate POC

Additional Optional POCs as Needed

Small Business Certification

Small Business Association (SBA) Profile

If you have selected at least one small business NAICS code, you will be provided a link to the SBA Supplemental Page. If you would like to provide additional information for market research or are applying for SBA's HUB zone or 8(a) programs, use that link to complete the SBA profile. A new window will open and take you to the SBA page. Make sure to go back to the SAM.gov window to submit your registration.

Some of the information you will be asked to provide is mandatory, and some is optional. Your TIN is either your Employer Identification Number (EIN) or your Social Security Number (SSN), if you are a sole proprietorship. If you need an EIN, then you should get this from the IRS before proceeding any further because the registration process requires that your EIN be active, and it can take the IRS two to five weeks to activate a newly issued EIN. SAM will forward the name and TIN to the IRS to confirm that both match their records. Other information you will need to enter into the SAM registration will be statistical, such as location information, worldwide organization, NAICS codes, and electronic funds transfer (EFT) information etc.

Your information from your registration will be submitted to the Small Business Administration (SBA) to determine the official size of your business. The information for receipts will be for the last three years because the business size is determined using a three-year average. SAM includes an SBA link to help you with this. If you are determined by the SBA to be a small business, then this opens up additional opportunities as government agencies have small business "set aside" goals that they have to meet. This means that there are many solicitations that only small businesses can bid on.

The **North American Industrial Classification System (NAICS)** is the standard used by federal statistical agencies in classifying business establishments for the purpose of collecting, analyzing, and publishing statistical data related to the U.S. business economy. You will have to determine which NAICS codes your business corresponds to and enter these into SAM. Choose as many as you see fit. You should choose quite a number of these because in order for you to bid on a project, you will have to have a NAICS code that matches the one(s) listed in the solicitation. The SAM website will direct you to a Census Bureau website that gives definitions for each NA- ICS code.

SAM requires that you include your electronic funds transfer (EFT) information. This will be used by the government to pay invoices. This method has proven to be effective, and the required information is simple to enter. The EFT substantially speeds up the payment process.

Now that you are registered and have a Unique Entity ID, you can search for solicitations and view the attached documents. This is a simple process. The SAM website has a user guide and a video demonstration that will walk you through this process. The site has many handy features to help you limit the time required to search for solicitations. Using the "Opportunities" navigation, you can use the "search" and "advanced search" modes that will limit the solicitations to only those you are interested in.

I found that the easiest and quickest way to find projects I'm interested in is to set up my search using the "advanced search" tab and put in the states and NAICS codes that match where and what I'm looking for.

You can use the "Watch List" to list solicitations that you want to follow. Vendors receive a daily e-mail that outlines any changes impacting a notice on their "watch list" target list. Vendors can also set up "search agents" based on selected detailed search elements. This can be set up on an ad hoc or scheduled basis, allowing you to receive solicitations that align with the designated search criteria. These search tools will help you target specific types of solicitations and make better use of your time.

1.2 Understanding the Solicitation

The solicitation is the process by which the federal government advertises a project for bid. The advertising can appear either on SAM or other methods. SAM is the government's preferred method, but many small contracts are advertised locally through the local agency contracting offices.

As the contractor, you need to understand that the solicitation and bidding process for each project has different requirements. Some projects may be unrestricted, meaning that the bidding is open to all contractors regardless of size or designation. Some projects will be set asides, meaning that only firms meeting specific sizes and/or types, such as small businesses, women-owned, service-disabled/veteran-owned, small disadvantaged, or HUBZONE businesses, may be allowed to bid. You must formulate a business strategy that will put you in a position to win the contract. This will be discussed later in the manual.

Contracting with the federal government is a highly regulated and structured process that, unlike commercial contracting, is ordinarily governed by the Uniform Commercial Code and common law. Federal government contracting is governed by a complex set of statutes and regulations. These statutes and regulations determine what method or process an agency must use to solicit a contract; how the agency is to negotiate or award a contract; and under certain circumstances, what costs the government will reimburse and how a contractor must account for those costs.

You must also be aware that the U.S. government imposes a host of socio-economic requirements through its contracts, including requirements related to affirmative action, drug-free workplace, subcontracting, and minimum employee wages, etc. You must understand the federal government's contracting process if you are going to be successful.

1.2.1 Basic Statutory and Regulatory Provisions

The Armed Services Procurement Act of 1947 (ASPA), the Federal Property and Administrative Services Act of 1949 (FPASA), and the Competition in Contracting Act (CICA) are the three statutes that form the federal acquisition process. The ASPA governs the acquisition of all property (except land), construction, and services by defense agencies while the FPASA governs similar civilian agency acquisitions.

The CICA, applicable to both defense and civilian acquisitions, requires federal agencies to seek and obtain "full and open competition" wherever possible in the contract award process. A federal agency cannot award a contract using a sole source contractor or "other than full and open competition" except in specific cases.

The Federal Acquisition Regulation (FAR) contains uniform policies and procedures for acquisitions by all federal agencies. It implements or addresses nearly every procurement-related statute or executive order. The FAR affects every stage of the acquisition process. The FAR's publication in 1984 reflected Congress' efforts to create a uniform structure for Executive Branch federal contracting. This replaced defense services and civilian agencies regulations dating back to the late 1940s. Even though there are still numerous agency-specific supplements that were implemented after the creation of the FAR, these supplements may not conflict with or supersede relevant FAR clauses.

1.2.2 Acquisition Methods

The ASPA, FPASA, and CICA established two basic methods of obtaining "full and open competition": (1) sealed bidding and (2) competitive negotiation. Sealed bidding is characterized by a rigid adherence to formal procedures. Those procedures aim to provide all bidders an opportunity to compete for the contract on an equal footing. In a sealed bidding acquisition, the agency must award to the responsible bidder who submits the lowest responsive bid (price). In contrast, competitive negotiation is a more flexible process that enables the agency to conduct discussions, evaluate offers, and award the contract using price and other factors.

1.2.2.1 Sealed Bidding

Once a federal agency identifies a need and decides to proceed with an acquisition, it must solicit sealed bids if (1) time permits the solicitation, submission, and evaluation of sealed bids; (2) the award will be made on the basis of price and other price-related factors; (3) it is not necessary to conduct discussions with the responding offerors about their bids; and (4) there is a reasonable expectation of receiving more than one sealed bid.

The agency's contracting officer (CO) initiates a sealed bidding acquisition by issuance of an "Invitation for Bids" (IFB). The IFB must describe the government's requirements clearly, accurately, and completely. The agency publicizes the IFB through display in a public place, announcement in newspapers or trade journals, publication in the Commerce Business Daily (CBD), on the federal government's website SAM.GOV, and by mailing the IFB to those contractors on the agency's solicitation mailing list.

It is critical that you submit your bids by the deadline stated in the IFB. A late bid will not be considered for award except where: (1) the bid was sent to the CO by registered or certified mail at least five days before the bid receipt date; (2) the government mishandled the bid after receipt; (3) the bid was sent to the CO by "Postal Service Next Day Service" two days prior to the bid receipt date; or (4) the bid was transmitted electronically and received by 5:00 p.m. one working day prior to the bid receipt date.

All bids received by the time and at the place set for opening are publicly opened and read aloud by the CO. The bids are then recorded on an "Abstract of Offers" (Standard Form 1049) and examined for mistakes. If no mistakes are found, the CO awards the contract to that responsible bidder who submitted the lowest responsive bid.

A responsive bid is one that contains a definite, unqualified offer to meet the material terms of the IFB. Conditions, informalities, or defects in the bid that affect the price, quantity, quality, or delivery of the items being acquired by the agency will result in the rejection of the bid. Prior to awarding the contract to the lowest bidder, the FAR also requires the prospective awardee to be determined to be responsible by having the ability and capacity to fulfill the contract. More specifically, the FAR requires a prospective contractor to (1) have adequate financial resources to perform the contract; (2) be able to comply with the required or proposed delivery or performance schedule; (3) have a satisfactory performance record; (4) have a satisfactory record of integrity and business ethics; (5) have the necessary organization, experience, accounting and operational controls, and technical skills; (6) have the necessary production, construction, and technical equipment and facilities; and (7) be otherwise qualified and eligible to receive an award under applicable laws and regulations.

Beyond responsiveness and responsibility, the CO may only consider price and price-related factors during evaluation of the bids. Price-related factors include costs or delays to the government resulting from differences in inspection, locations of supplies, and transportation; taxes; and changes made or requested by a bidder in any provision of the IFB. After evaluating price and price-related factors, the CO awards the contract to the responsible bidder whose bid is most advantageous to the government—i.e., the lowest price. Award is made by furnishing a properly executed award document to the successful bidder. Under sealed bidding procedures, only two types of contract price methods may be used: (1) firm-fixed-price or (2) fixed price with economic price adjustment.

1.2.2.2 Negotiation

If one of the four conditions for use of sealed bidding is not present, the CO will award the contract using competitive negotiation. Contracting by negotiation allows more flexibility in awarding the contract. Unlike sealed bidding, the CO may engage in discussions with offerors and, in evaluating proposals, may also consider non-cost factors (such as managerial experience, technical approach, and/or past performance).

The negotiating process begins when the CO issues a "Request for Proposal" (RFP). As in sealed bidding, if the procurement is over $25,000, the CO will synopsize a notice of the proposed contract action in SAM.GOV. An RFP must, at a minimum, state the agency's need, anticipated terms and conditions of the contract, information the contractor must include in the proposal, and factors and significant sub-factors that the agency will consider in evaluating the proposals and awarding the contract. All interested parties may then submit proposals.

Evaluation of the proposals includes an assessment of the proposals' relative qualities based upon the factors and sub-factors specified in the solicitation. Typically, the CO will evaluate (a) the offeror's cost or price proposal; (b) the offeror's past performance on government and commercial contracts; (c) the offeror's technical approach; and (d) any other identified factors for award. During the evaluation period, the CO and source selection team may communicate with the offerors to clarify ambiguous proposed terms.

The CO may award a negotiated contract without any further negotiations, called "discussions." However, if the CO intends to conduct discussions, he or she will preliminarily identify the offerors that fall within the "competitive range." The competitive range is comprised of all the most highly rated proposals. To assist in determining the competitive range, the CO may engage in limited communications with all offerors. After establishing the competitive range, the CO will notify each excluded offeror and proceed to conduct "discussions" with the remaining offerors. According to the FAR, the "primary objective" of discussions is to maximize the agency's ability "to obtain best value, based on the requirement and the evaluation factors set forth in the evaluation." During the discussions, the CO must indicate to each offeror the significant weaknesses, deficiencies, or other aspects of the proposal that could be altered to enhance the proposal's potential for award. However, the CO must not (1) engage in conduct that favors one offeror over another; (2) reveal an offeror's technical solution;(3) reveal an offeror's price without permission; (4) disclose the names of persons providing information about the offeror's past performance; or (5) furnish sensitive source selection information.

After discussions begin, the CO may eliminate from consideration any offeror originally in the competitive range but no longer considered among the most highly rated offerors. Further, the CO may request that offerors revise their proposals to clarify any compromises reached during negotiation. At the conclusion of the discussions, the CO will request a final proposal revision from each offeror still in the competitive range.

Finally, the CO will undertake a comparative analysis of the final offers in accordance with the evaluation procedures set forth in the RFP and select the offeror whose proposal is most advantageous to the government. The documented award decision should contain an analysis of the trade-offs accomplished by negotiations and the reasons why the awardees' proposal represents the best value to the agency. The CO always has the discretion not to award any contract if he or she deems that course to be in the government's best interests. If requested by an unsuccessful offeror, the CO will conduct a post-award debriefing during which the basis for the selection decision is explained.

1.2.3 Parts of a Solicitation

The standard parts of a solicitation are determined by the "Uniform Contract Format" and are generally listed alphabetically but may be listed numerically or by the form number. For instance, Part A of a solicitation is the solicitation/contract form but for Department of Defense contracts it will usually be shown as SF 1442. The parts of a solicitation are:

Part I – The Schedule

A. Solicitation/Contract Form

B. Supplies or Services and Prices/Costs

C. Description/Specifications/Work Statement

D. Packaging and Marking

E. Inspection and Acceptance

F. Deliveries and Performance

G. Contract Administration Data

H. Special Contract Requirements

Part II – Contract Clauses

I. Contract Clauses

Part III – List of Documents, Exhibits, and Other Attachments

J. List of Documents, Exhibits, and Other Attachments

Part IV – Representations and Instructions

K. Representations, Certifications, and other Statements of Bidders

L. Instructions, Conditions, and Notices to Bidders

M. Evaluation Factors for Award

1.2.3.1 Part I – The Schedule

Section A – Solicitation/Contract Form

The Standard Form 1442 (SF 1442) is the "Solicitation, Offer, and Award" form that is used by the federal government to solicit bids and to award a contract for construction, alteration, or repair. It is the basic part of the contract whereby the federal government, through the contracting officer, consummates the contract award. This form is used for the solicitation and will also be used to make the award.

Page 1 contains the SOLICITATION section and Page 2 contains the OFFER and AWARD sections. The government completes the SOLICITATION section when it issues the package. The contractor completes the OFFER section when it submits its bid or proposal. Upon acceptance of the bid or proposal by the government, the CO completes the AWARD section.

Block 1 contains the SOLICITATION NUMBER

Block 2 contains the TYPE OF SOLICITATION, SEALED BID (IFB), or NEGOTIATED (RFP)

Block 3 contains the DATE ISSUED

Block 4 contains the CONTRACT NUMBER. This block will be completed when the government awards the contract.

Block 5 contains the REQUISITION/PURCHASE REQUEST NUMBER. This is sometimes left blank but may contain a number that is issued by the installation.

Block 6 contains the PROJECT NUMBER. This may be left blank but may be completed by the installation, especially for small contracts.

Block 7 is the ISSUED BY block. This contains the name and address of the issuing agency and contains a block labeled CODE. The CODE is the installation identifier that identifies the installation where the work will be accomplished.

Block 8 is the ADDRESS OFFER TO block. This will contain the address to which the offer will be sent.

Block 9 is the FOR INFORMATION CALL block. Part a. NAME contains the name of the contact person and Part b. contains the TELEPHONE NUMBER of that contact person.

Solicitation

Block 10 is titled THE GOVERNMENT REQUIRES PERFORMANCE OF THE WORK

DESCRIBED IN THESE DOCUMENTS (Title, identifying number, date). This is where a brief description of the work will be shown.

Block 11 tells the contractor when the work must begin, how many days to complete the work, and from when, such as award or notice to proceed.

Block 12a is titled THE CONTRACTOR MUST FURNISH ANY REQUIRED PEFORMANCE AND PAYMENT BONDS. It will be either "yes" you have to or "no" you don't have to.

Block 12b is titled CALENDAR DAYS and shows how many days after award the contractor has to submit the required bonds.

Block 13 contains ADDITIONAL SOLICITATION REQUIREMENTS: This section shows the number of copies of the proposal to be submitted, the date and time for receipt of proposals, whether an offer guarantee is or is not required, and how many days it must be good for.

Offer

Block 14 contains the NAME AND ADDRESS OF OFFEROR (include zip code). This must be the full name and address and should also include the firm's DUNS, TIN, and the e-mail address of the contractor's point of contact. CODE and FACILITY CODE are left blank unless inserted later by the government.

Block 15 requires the TELEPHONE NUMBER of the contractor's point of contact.

Block 16 requires the REMITTANCE ADDRESS of the contractor.

Block 17 requires that the offered price be inserted or reference made to a schedule of prices if included in the solicitation documents. The contractor must also either insert a period of time that this price will hold or be bound to hold it for the time period shown in Block 13D. Very often, the time shown in Block 13D is mandatory and cannot be changed.

Block 18 states that the offeror agrees to furnish any required performance and payment bonds.

Block 19 contains the ACKNOWLEDGEMENT OF AMENDMENTS. It is critical that all amendments issued under this solicitation be acknowledged here. The amendment number and date must be shown.

Block 20a requires the typed NAME AND TITLE OF PERSON AUTHORIZED TO SIGN OFFER.

Block 20b requires the SIGNATURE of the person authorized to make the offer.

Block 20c requires the OFFER DATE.

Award

Block 21 contains ITEMS ACCEPTED and shows the prices the offeror proposed, and that the government has accepted. The specific line items will be shown here.

Block 22 contains the AMOUNT the government has accepted. This should equal the sum of the line items the government accepted in Block 21.

Block 23 contains the ACCOUNTING AND APPROPRIATION DATA that the government will use to charge all contract expenses. The government will add this.

Block 24 indicates where to SUBMIT INVOICES TO ADDRESS SHOWN IN. Normally this will show Block 26.

Block 25 is the OTHER THAN FULL AND OPEN COMPETITION PURSUANT TO Block that the CO will check if the solicitation is a sole source negotiated contract.

Block 26 contains ADMINISTERED BY information. This will be the office and address of the group that will administer the contract.

Block 27 shows the name and address of the unit that the PAYMENT WILL BE MADE BY.

Block 28 is used only when there is a NEGOTIATED AGREEMENT. If the C0 checks this box, then the contractor must sign and date the document and return the required copies to the CO.

Block 29 is used when the CO is making an AWARD based upon an accepted proposal.

Blocks 30a, 30b, and 30c are used only when Block 28 has been checked by the CO and must be signed by the contractor.

Blocks 31a, 31b, and 31c are used only when Block 29 has been checked and signed by the CO.

Section B – Supplies or Services and Prices/Costs

Following the solicitation/contract form will be a brief description of the acquisition and required pricing. This will be composed of at least one line item for the base bid and, quite often, line items for options. These are called "Contract Line Item Numbers" or CLINs. These descriptions need to be very carefully read as they can be either "Additive" or "Deductive" and understood as they can overlap. The performance period is also included in the CLINs, and options may allow additional time or may deduct performance time. The type of acquisition will also be denoted such as "Firm Fixed Price" (FFP) or "Unit Price" contract. If it is an FFP, then the unit will always be 1, and the Unit Price will be the total for the line item.

Section C – Description/Specifications/Statement of Work

The description of what the project is, any specifications, and the statement of work are included in this section.

Section D – Packaging and Marking

This section contains requirements for packaging, packing, preservation, and marking. It is very seldom used in construction contracts but is used by the government when purchasing supplies and materials.

Section E – Inspection and Acceptance

This section includes inspection, acceptance, quality assurance, quality control, and reliability requirements.

Section F – Deliveries or Performance

The requirements for the time, place, and method of delivery and/or performance are specified here. The statement of work will normally detail these requirements.

Section G – Contract Administration Data

The government must include any required accounting and appropriation data and any required contract administration information or instructions here. This is in addition to the information shown on the SF 1442 form.

Section H – Special Contract Requirements

This section will include special contract clauses that are not included in Section I, Contract Clauses, or in other sections of the solicitation. Most federal agencies add their own supplemental clauses, which regard their specific way of doing business.

1.2.3.2 Part II – Contract Clauses

Section I – Contract Clauses

This section includes clauses required by law and any additional clauses expected to be included in any resulting contract if these clauses are not required in any other section. An index may be inserted if this section's format is particularly complex. The FAR clauses in this section may be "Clauses by Reference" or "Clauses by Full Text." The "Clauses by Reference" carry just as much importance as the "Clauses by Full Text", so I recommend that you read and try to understand the reference clauses as well as the full-text clauses.

1.2.3.3 Part III – List of Documents, Exhibits, and Other Attachments

Section J - List of Documents, Exhibits, and Other Attachments

The solicitation shall list the title, date, and number of pages for each attached document, exhibit, and other attachments. Cross-references to material in other sections may be inserted as appropriate.

1.2.3.4 Part IV – Representations and Instructions

Section K – Representations, Certifications, and other Statements of Bidders

Included in this section are those solicitation provisions that require representations, certifications, or the submission of other information by bidder. These will be in addition to what you have already imputed into the SAM.GOV.

Section L – Instructions, Conditions, and Notices to Bidders

This section includes solicitation provisions and other information and instructions not required elsewhere to guide offerors or respondents in preparing proposals or responses to requests for information. Prospective bidders may be instructed to submit proposals or information in a specific format or severable parts to facilitate evaluation. The instructions may specify further organization of proposal or response parts, such as:

1.) Administrative

2.) Management

3.) Technical

4.) Past performance

5.) Cost or Pricing Data or Other Information

Section M – Evaluation Factors for Award

The solicitation must identify all significant factors and any significant sub-factors that will be considered in awarding the contract and their relative importance. This section is where you either "win" or "lose" the bid. The factors normally are "weighted" to show what the Government considers the most important criteria to them. These need to be well thought through, and a strategy needs to be determined on how best to respond to them.

1.2.4 Amendments

Amendments are issued by the CO during a solicitation to "amend" or change the requirements of the solicitation. This can be done for any reason and happens with almost every solicitation. You, as the contractor, can usually use SAM.GOV to sign up for automatic notification of any amendments that have been issued. Pay special attention to the changes included in the amendment and develop a system to track all changes. I highly recommend that you use a "living document" system to keep the solicitation up to date. The date for submittal of the proposal quite often changes with an amendment, so this should be watched very carefully.

The contractor must acknowledge all amendments in **Block 19, ACKNOWLEDGE OF AMENDMENTS**. This is extremely important because if ALL amendments are not acknowledged, the CO will not consider the proposal, and this could cost you a project.

1.2.5 Submitting Questions

The contractor usually will have questions after reviewing the solicitation. This is a normal part of the review process, but you should make a determination early in the process as to whether or not the questions should be submitted for government clarification. Develop a strategy that clarifies concerns but does not give an advantage to your competitors. You need to make sure that the questions "level the playing field" for all the competing contractors but do not give away any competitive advantage you may have.

Questions must be submitted in the manner (such as e-mail, fax, etc.) prescribed in the solicitation to the office/person specified and no later than the cut-off date and time shown in the solicitation. Questions submitted that do not follow these guidelines may be disallowed by the CO. All questions sent to the Government by the time prescribed in the solicitation are answered and posted for all the bidders to review.

Chapter 2
Building a Strategy and Developing a Proposal

1.0 Chapter Description and Use

2.0 The Strategy

2.1 Resources and Capabilities

2.2 Size, Type, and Location of the Project

2.3 Evaluation Criteria

3.0 Risk Management

3.1 Risk Management Review Process

3.1.1 The Review Process

3.2 Risk Management Listing

3.2.1 External Risks

3.2.2 Management Risks

3.2.3 Operational Risks

4.0 RFP Requirements/Proposal Preparation

4.1 Bidder Eligibility

4.2 Bid Feasibility

4.3 Self – Assessment

4.4 Competition

4.5 Preparing the Proposal

5.0 Protest after Award

6.0 Surety Bonds

7.0 Insurance

8.0 Taxes

9.0 Utilization of Small Business Concerns

1.0 Chapter Description and Use

This chapter's purpose is to help you develop a strategy that will set you up to win projects that you have a chance to win instead of competing with all the other construction firms going after federal work. This is done by helping you understand your capabilities and resources and being able to determine through the federal government's evaluation process whether or not you should compete for the project. The risk management section will help you determine whether a project is within your risk tolerance level. The risk management section should be used after you have picked out a potential project to bid on, so that you can look more closely at the specifics of the project, and determine if the project has risks that are unacceptable to you.

Once you have determined that going after a project to bid on is part of your strategy then you will have to evaluate the RFP requirements and prepare a proposal that can win the project. This section will help you to prepare and submit a winning proposal to the federal government. The section on small business utilization will help you to determine which firms may be good to use to meet the small, disadvantaged business concerns requirement if this is required by the solicitation. You will also learn how to protest an award if you feel that it was either solicited or awarded improperly.

The federal government requires bonds and insurance and there are specific requirements for each. The bonding requirement is straightforward, but the insurance requirement is minimal. So I have shown in this section the differences between what the government requires, what would normally be provided by the owner, and what you should provide for your own protection.

2.0 The Strategy

A "Winning Strategy":

To put together a "winning" strategy, you must first perform a thorough analysis of your resources and capabilities; determine which type and size of project you want to bid on; and determine whether or not you will be able to score high enough according to the evaluation criteria. In today's economic environment, the bidding will be very competitive, so picking the right project for your firm to bid on will save you time and money. It makes no sense to bid on projects that you have very little chance of winning.

2.1 Resources and Capabilities:

You must decide what resources you have. These may include access to money such as a line of credit, cash flow, bonding capacity, home office organization and personnel, offices and/or personnel in various locations, field personnel, tradesmen (union/non-union), equipment, etc.

Evaluating your company's capabilities will help you define whether or not you will be able to perform the work. Items such as the type of work you perform well, such as remodeling, new construction, vertical construction, horizontal construction, specialty trade, etc., must be defined. Ability to joint venture and/or team with another company must be determined and considered. Type of contract capability such as design-build, design-bid-build, negotiated, cost plus fixed fee, indefinite delivery/indefinite quantity must be determined. Will your cash flow allow for the preparation of a detailed and thus a potentially costly proposal? Can you bond the project and, if so, will it use up all of your bonding capacity?

2.2 Size, Type, and Location of the Project:

Part of your strategy must include determining the size, type, and location of the project you want to bid on. This should be based on your resources, capabilities, risk review, and competition.

Size should be based on your bonding capability and your resources to perform the work on time. Picking a project that uses all of your bonding capacity could keep you from bidding on projects that could be more lucrative and will use up more of your resources. Also, the ability to manage a larger project could be daunting.

The type of project selected must be in line with your capabilities. A design-build project will require the general contractor to partner with an architect-engineer firm, and the evaluation criteria will require that the partners have worked together in the past. Unless you can score high on this, you could be wasting a great deal of time and money preparing a proposal. A specialty trade contractor needs to pick a project that is primarily in his or her trade but could have a minor amount of general contracting. Thought must be given to picking a type of project that will allow you the best opportunity to win the bid.

Risk assessment has become a major component of the decision-making process. This process should include evaluating areas such as external risks, i.e. soil/subsurface conditions, project site; management risks, i.e. financial and human resources; operational risks, i.e. quality of plans and specifications, environmental concerns, phasing, etc. Corporate policy will have to determine what acceptable risk is, and again, this needs to be part of your strategy. Only projects that meet those criteria should be picked to bid on.

Knowing your competition is of great importance and should be a key factor in determining whether to bid on a project. If you don't know the bidders, then take the time to find out about them. Go to their website, check with the Department of Labor and Industries or whichever department issues business licenses in your state, check the local trade organizations, etc. Learning your competition needs to be part of your strategy.

2.3 Evaluation Criteria:

Section M of the solicitation package contains the "Evaluation Factors for Award." These factors can be very simple, such as only requiring you to list how long you have been doing this type of work, to very complex and time consuming, such as requiring detailed plans, schedules, past history, architectural drawings, etc. The evaluation criteria must be read very carefully, and your team must decide early on whether the criteria can be met and combined with the other parts of your strategy. Meeting some of these criteria can be very expensive and may keep you from bidding on other projects that you are more suited for. Some evaluation factors, such as the past history or strength of your management team, may require that you build up a resume.

I recommend that you pick projects to bid on that contain evaluation criteria you can easily meet, that may limit your competition, and that will not be expensive to prepare.

3.0 Risk Management

Risk management can be considered the identification, assessment, and prioritization of risks followed by coordinated and economical application of resources to minimize, monitor, and control the probability and/or impact of unfortunate events or to maximize the realization of opportunities. Risks can come from uncertainty in financial markets, management failure, project failures, unforeseen conditions, legal liabilities, credit risk, accidents, natural causes and disasters, as well as many other areas. Risk and subsequent mitigation must be managed before, during, and after the project has been won. Failure to do so could prove disastrous and cause severe financial loss.

The strategies to manage risk include transferring the risk to another party, avoiding the risk, reducing the negative effect of the risk, and accepting some or all of the consequences of a particular risk.

3.1 Risk Management Review Process

This Risk Management Review Process is provided as a generic federal government project-focused review process for risk and other likely management questions. This process is intended to identify risks and mitigation of those risks. You should use this process after you have identified a potential project to bid on but before you start preparing a proposal. Some firms, I have worked for, have developed numerical systems that rate the different areas of the various risks and then assign a numerical grade to the risk before the firm can bid on the project. This has the advantage of identifying high-risk projects along with mitigation methods, allowing the firm to calculate these methods into the price and possibly the proposal. You should set up a system specifically tailored to your company.

3.1.1 The Review Process:

- Generate and review a business risk bid/no bid form prior to the review.
- Understand the basic prospect analysis, i.e. contract terms, bid partners, and payment terms to set the context for the remainder of the review.
- Understand thoroughly the scope of the work, project requirements, the type of contract and its documentation requirements, and what innovative changes/additions and or exclusions will be done to be more competitive.
- Review the project schedule, looking especially for comparisons with similar project durations, clear illustration and timing of government responsibilities, presence of minimum float requirement or definition of who owns the float, clear definition of what constitutes the completion and completion date, illustration of the completion date that the cost estimate is based upon as well as any liquidated damages and/or penalty dates.
- Review the estimate tools and methodology used to verify appropriateness for the purpose.
- Prepare an execution plan that shows offices involved, key personnel to be proposed, self-performed work, and subcontracted work.
- Review the risk listing and mitigation plan and how this is reflected in the solicitation/contract questions and responses, proposal clarifications, and pricing.
- Review the estimate itself beginning with the general conditions first, material quantities, unit prices for material, construction labor hours, productivity, labor posture if applicable, labor costs per work unit with backup from subcontractors if applicable, or in-house estimators' recommendation including hours to be worked, per diems, etc. Compare with other similar projects using actual finals where possible.
    - Buy Down – Review buy down projections compared to history and how they will be used: profit or contingency.
    - Indirect – Review construction management staffing plan, use of local temporary labor, tools, consumables, equipment, etc. and compare with regional data for similar past projects. Review insurance cost basis against planned prime contract terms.
    - Engineering – Review hours and costs estimated versus past history, also office work split and local rates if partner or JV is used.
  - Cash Flow – Review the use of the schedule and estimate data versus the billing plan for the contract or proposal.

• Contingency – Review for proper methods, risk range parameters, and underrun probability.

• Fee/Margin – Review for minimum recommended margin consistent with risk profile, market opportunity, and strategic importance.

• Review the solicitation/clarification statements for adequacy in presenting lowest costs and protecting your position.

• Inspect the pricing model to determine consistency with the estimate.

• Review the most likely highest and lowest profit/margin cases.

3.2 Risk Management Listing

3.2.1 External Risks:

• Project Site Risk

These risks relate to the actual construction site:

• Population in the area is too small to either provide the necessary labor or to support the project with sufficient lodging, restaurants, police, fire, security, medical facilities, utilities, potable water, telephone, internet service, or other infrastructure.

• Tourist/local population interferences (attitude toward project, client, or contractor) and local economic, social, political, or labor posture conditions.

• Access to ports, railroad, highways, altitude, remoteness, or congestion, dimensional or weight restrictions on the transport of construction equipment or components.

• Severe winters, difficult topography, restricted trafficability or drainage.

• Access to rights-of-way, easements, utility connections, and other site elements.

• Noise, dust, night lighting, labor congestion, parking, or travel to site restrictions.

• Soil/Subsurface Conditions Risk

• Risk arising from subsurface "unknowns." Examples such as voids due to mining operations either current or past; obstructions such as large rocks, operational or abandoned equipment, electrical cabling or trenching, piping or foundations that aren't shown on drawings; sinkholes; shallow water table; burial sites; or sites of paleontological or archeological value.

• Risk of unevenly compressed or expansive soil (soil studies performed by the client often fail to reveal relevant site soil conditions because the borings are too far apart, or were done in an area away from the actual construction site).

• Environmental Substances Risk

• The risk that a site is contaminated with asbestos. Examples include attic insulation, insulation on underground or above ground tanks, piping, or equip- ment; asbestos fibers in the air or on the ground after an explosion or fire.

• The risk that a building built by the contractor, particularly a multi-family dwelling, will develop toxic mold over time. Insurance against this risk may be impossible to obtain due to extensive mold litigation in the U.S.

• The risk that dust from mines, mine areas, or heavy use of agricultural chemicals may contain arsenic and other lung damaging particulates.

• The risk that furnace insulation may contain vanadium pentoxide from fuel oil firing. When disturbed during demolition or revamp, the dust can cause severe reactions.

• Regulatory Risk

• Exposure to federal, state, regional, or municipal agency actions that impair the contractor's ability to execute its corporate strategy or successfully complete a project as planned. Examples: Buy American Act, compliance with design codes, health and safety regulations, professional/contractor license requirements, environmental permit requirements, right-of-way/condemnation procedures; building, work, or fire department permit requirements.

• Financial reporting required by regulatory agencies when incomplete, inaccurate, or untimely, it can expose the contractor to fines and penalties.

• Force Majeure Events Risk

Risk associated with events outside contractor's or client's control. Examples: extreme weather (tornadoes, hurricanes, abnormal temperatures, unusual rain, or snowfall), floods, earthquakes, fires, explosions, total power failure, major discharge of toxic substances, labor strikes, and walkouts at the project or suppliers.

• Available Work Days Risk

• The risk that religious or cultural customs prevent labor from working the typical workweek.

• Normal weather patterns in the area (rainfall, snow, wind, extreme high or low temperatures not covered by force majeure, or available daylight) limit construction activities during certain times of the year.

• Competitors Risk

• Major competitors or new entrants to the market take actions to establish or sustain competitive advantage to win a project. These actions include bidding with little or no profit/overhead/margin to keep a business afloat, increasing productivity, or reducing costs.

• Too many competitors in a particular geographic area pursuing a particular project, thus driving margins down.

3.2.2 Management Risks

• Reputation Risk

• The risk that the company may lose clients, key employees, its ability to compete, not get a good evaluation, does not know how to manage its business, or does not perform on its projects (safety, cost, schedule, quality).

• Business Interruption Risk

• The ability to sustain operations, provide essential products or services, or recover operating costs as a result of a major disaster (accident, sabotage, work stoppages, and acts of God). The inability to recover from such events could damage the reputation of the company, ability to obtain capital, or investor relations.

• Business Portfolio Risk

• The risk that the firm will not maximize business performance by effectively prioritizing its products or balancing its business in a strategic context. Examples: selling projects outside of the company's risk tolerance, low-margin projects, or projects for which there is no available expertise or resources, while at the same time not preparing and planning for high-value, profitable opportunities that maximize return.

• Management Incentives Risk

• This risk occurs when management is incentivized to act in a manner inconsistent with the company's business objectives, strategies, ethical standards, and prudent business practice. In these cases, managers and employees do not buy into the performance measures because they are not realistic, understandable, objectively determinable, or actionable. The risk also occurs when performance indicators do not accurately measure the skills or characteristics that are predictive of success in a given position. Such performance measures ultimately prove to be irrelevant.

• Market Sensitivity Risk

• Market sensitivity risk results when management commits the company's resources and expected cash flows from future operations to such an extent that it reduces the company's tolerance for changes in the business environment that are totally beyond its control. Sensitivity risk also results when an organization is too inflexible to adapt in response to change. Example: a strategy to grow rapidly, expand geographically, or invest in significant high-risk ventures can increase the company's sensitivity exposure to economic, regulatory, or market developments.

• Outsourcing/Consultants Risk

• The risk that outside service providers, such as third-party administrators, local or foreign partners, consultants or agents, will not act within their defined limits of authority and will not perform in a manner consistent with the values, strategies, and objectives of the company.

The risk that strategic business processes' outsources will ultimately create competition for the outsourcing organization because the know-how shared with the consultant will be later exploited by the consultant or given to a competitor.

The risk of not outsourcing non-core activities when financially advantageous to the company when higher value can be obtained by involving outside consultants.

• Strategic Information Risk

Risk that:

• Financial accounting information used to manage business processes is not properly integrated with non-financial information, such as customer satisfaction, quality, and increased efficiency. The result is a myopic, short-term fixation on manipulating outputs to achieve financial targets, rather than fulfilling customer expectations by controlling and improving processes. Key decision makers are unable to reliably measure the value of a specific business or any of its significant segments in a strategic context. This risk affects the evaluation of both owned businesses (e.g. to decide whether to invest/grow, maintain/harvest, or divest/liquidate) and prospective businesses (e.g. acquire, joint venture, or strategically align). Example: unknown project commitments still outstanding at any point in time.

• Key assumptions about the external environment are inconsistent with reality or are not being monitored by the company, resulting in obsolete business strategies. Example: failure to stay abreast of the business cycles of the industry the company serves.

• Business strategy is not communicated consistently and often throughout the organization or reflected in written plans of action, resulting in missed opportunities.

• Bonding/Bank Guarantees

• The risk that significant partners, subcontractors or suppliers are not sufficiently bonded to limit the company's exposure.

• The risk associated with allocating the company's bonding, guarantee, or letter of credit capacity to a long-term project that does not bring expected returns.

• Capital Availability Risk

  • The risk that the company does not have access to the capital it needs to fuel its growth, execute its strategies, and generate future financial returns. This can result in a competitive disadvantage during periods when the company is highly leveraged or its major competitors have larger cash reserves or borrowing capacity, a lower cost structure, greater market share, or access to capital through strategic alliances.

• The risk that the company's client does not have access to capital, which can result in a project award being delayed, suspended, or otherwise affected by the client's cash flow.

• Cash Flow/Liquidity

• Cash flow risk results from not having a cash flow plan when the project is bid or not aligning with the project team in the area of cash flow early in the project. Risk can also occur when paying subcontractor or supplier invoices early or not collecting from client when due; not charging interest for late payment; not resolving audit exceptions in a timely manner, and not requesting payment from suppliers or subcontractors when due; or inadequate monitoring of documentation to allow proper client billing.

• Liquidity risk is the exposure to loss because of the inability to meet cash flow obligations in a timely and cost-effective manner. It often arises because of an investment portfolio with a cash and/or maturity profile that differs from the underlying cash flows dictated by the company's operating requirements and other obligations. Operating requirements, debt service, capital expenditures, and other cash outflows can require premature liquidation of assets, which can lead to reduced profits and/or unplanned realized gains or losses. In the extreme, poor liquidity management can lead to default.

• Claims Risk

The risk that claims are filed against the company resulting in financial loss or that the company neglects to file—or aggressively pursue—claims against clients, partners, suppliers, and subcontractors when entitled to do so.

• Equity Risk

Equity risk is the exposure to fluctuations in the income stream from and/or value of equity ownership in an incorporated entity. Equity risk may arise as a result of:

• Investment in shares of publicly traded facilities, including holdings in a portfolio of equity securities or in private placements.

• Investment holdings of debt convertible into equity.

• Company share offerings and company acquisition programs that are linked to share prices.

• Investment of capital, people, or proprietary know-how with expectations of future returns.

• Financial Markets

Financial markets risk is defined as exposure to changes in the earnings capacity or economic value of the company or the company's clients or partners as a result of changes in financial market variables that affect income, expense, or balance values. Example: rising interest rates that affect the cost of money.

• Financial Reporting Risk

The risk that a firm's financial reports issued to existing and prospective business partners, investors, or lenders include material misstatements or omit material facts, making them misleading. This risk usually results from failure to obtain relevant business information from external and internal sources and assess whether adjustments are required to fairly represent the firm's financial position, results from operations, and sources and uses of cash. Examples:

• Project financial status over or under reported in project reviews or project financial status report

- Overly optimistic representation of future project profitability
- Premature profit take-up before all costs are reconciled or incentives awarded
- Project revenues entering backlog ahead of project award

• Financial Status of Partners Risk (JVs, subs, teaming partners, etc.).

- Exposure to weak banks, other financial institutions, and other companies, such as vendors, subcontractors, managing contractors, joint venture partners, and merger and acquisition parties that have potential financial obligations to the company or on behalf of the company. Due diligence must be performed early and thoroughly prior to a signed agreement. In some cases, consideration should be given to making payments to sub-suppliers or lower-tier subcontractors directly.

- Exposure to parties who would disproportionately benefit at the company's expense through use of its reputation, bonding, costing structure, or schedule performance.

• Insurance Risk

- The risk that there is no adequate coverage under the company's umbrella insurance policy of project-specific insurance or, conversely, that there is duplicate coverage, resulting in unnecessary coverage expense by the company or partner.

- The risk that prime contract requirements have not been carried into the supplier or subcontractor contracts (flow down).

• Interest Rate Risk

Risk (or opportunity) associated with fluctuating interest rates. This risk may impact the company by either directly increasing or decreasing interest rates for its debt or indirectly by impacting the borrowings of partners, vendors, or subcontractors.

• Leakage (Profit Erosion) Risk

The risk of allowing profits to be eroded on projects or company initiatives. Examples:

- Underestimated the cost of implementing software systems
- Failure to take corrective action at the right time
- Focusing on loss avoidance and not profit enhancements
- Not applying value engineering principles and having no formal value awareness program on the project
- Over designing (gold plating)
- Losing project incentives
- Incurring rework, penalties or lawsuits
- Poor safety performance, resulting in claims, additional costs, and delays
- Not managing client relations
- Poor productivity in the home office or in the field
- Doing work for free or for no fee
- Over-running the non-billable budget
- Not adding profit and extended overhead to change orders
- Underestimating lump sum costs

• Opportunity Cost Risk

Risk arising from the company's use of its resources in a manner that leads to the loss of economic value, including:

• Time value losses due to delays in invoicing, collections, claim processing, investment of funds, etc. The consequences of these delays could result in borrowing.

• Transaction costs due to inappropriate or inefficient management of cash flows. Example: the need to borrow high-cost funds or sell securities at a loss because of the failure to match the maturities of short term investment operational or financial obligations.

• Earnings exposure when funds or other resources (people, knowledge, and computers) are invested in a manner that does not generate sufficient returns to cover costs, profits, and risk, while additional opportunities are not pursued.

• Pension and Benefit Risk

Risk arising from pension funds and health benefit plans, which are not actuarially sound, meaning they are insufficient to satisfy benefit obligations defined by the plan. The consequences of this risk include reputation risk, loss of morale, work stoppages, litigation, and additional funding required by the company.

• Pricing Risk

Risk arising from inadequate pricing. Examples:

• Bidding projects at prices too high to be competitive or too low to cover costs.

• Inadequate processes exist to ensure contracts are sufficiently reviewed to substantiate whether the work the company is contracted to accomplish is reasonable for the price.

• A project converts from reimbursable to lump sum without a thorough estimate update, risk assessment, and management review.

• Subordination/Settlement Risk

This risk occurs when the company's various debt, equity, and cash flow positions are subordinated to positions held by others (client's partners, other contractors). This may result in uncollectible investments for the company. Settlement risk—also called "delivery risk"—arises when financial counterparts affect their payments to each other at different times or in different locations. The first paying party is exposed to the risk that the later paying party will fail to perform, due to delay, system failure, or default. In essence, one party performs its obligations under the contract, but has not yet received value from its counterpart.

• Taxes/Duties/Permit Fees Risk

The risk that taxes, duties, and permit fees are overlooked or not paid, resulting in fines or imprisonment, or that they are overpaid, eroding profit. Examples:

• Lack of clarity in the contract regarding who pays Value Added Tax (VAT), import duties, customs clearance fees, income or sales tax, licenses and permits.

• Cost of the above items not included in the project estimate or schedule (key permits should drive the company milestones, completion dates, LDs, etc.).

• Non-compliance with tax regulations, payments, and filing requirements.

• Significant transactions of the company, client, or partner that have adverse tax consequences and could have been avoided or reduced had they been structured differently.

• Alignment Risk

• Risk that the objectives and performance measures of the company's business processes are not aligned with its overall business objectives and strategies. The objectives and measures do not focus people on the right things and lead to conflicting, uncoordinated activities.

• Risk that the project team is not aware of the project's objectives and is not in alignment with the client and/or its own ranks. Examples: the project team is not familiar with the project business plan or lump sum estimate; engineering and procurement activities are not aligned with construction, operations, or maintenance requirements.

- Authority Limit Risk

- The risk that people either make decisions or take actions that are not within their explicit responsibility, or control or fail to take responsibility for those things for which they are accountable. Examples: not following the appropriate approval requirements; not empowering people to do their jobs; not allowing decisions to be made at the level where the knowledge and experience reside.

- The risk that the company's organizational structure does not support strategies, efficient decision making, and responsiveness to clients.

- Change Readiness Risk (Culture Change Risk)

- Management and employees are unable to implement organizational change quickly enough to keep pace with the marketplace, such as changes arising from competitor acts, regulatory requirements, consumer demands, mergers, etc.

- Management is unaware of how resistant or receptive employees are to change, how long it takes to implement change (absorption rate), and who amongst the population are the change agents and the skeptics supporting or hindering the process.

- Communication Risk

  - Communications vertically (top-down and bottom-up) or horizontally (cross-functional) within the company are ineffective and result in messages that are inconsistent with authorized responsibilities or established measures. Information does not flow in a timely manner to those who need it for decision making.

  - Project communication within the project team or with the client is incomplete, not documented in writing, not distributed to those who need it, or not timely.

    - Lack of openness in communication prevents honest feedback and free ex change of ideas, resulting in low morale, hoarding of information, and not presenting "bad news" to management as soon as possible;

  - Written or electronic communication is inappropriate or is presented in such a way that it can be later used against the company ("smoking guns").

• Employee Integrity Risk

Integrity risk is the risk of management fraud, employee fraud, and illegal and unauthorized acts, any or all of which could lead to reputation degradation in the marketplace or even financial loss. Examples:

• Employees, customers, or suppliers, individually or in collusion, perpetrate fraud against the company resulting in profit erosion.

• Physical assets are subject to unethical or unauthorized use, vandalism, sabotage, or theft.

• Management issues misleading statements with intent to deceive the investing public and the external auditor or engages in bribes, kickbacks, influence payments, and other schemes for the benefit of the company.

• Information and proprietary assets (designs, work processes, customer lists, information and knowledge, trade secrets) are compromised by industrial espionage, resulting in less of competitive advantage.

• Health and Safety Risk

• Risks resulting from unsafe practices either in the office or the field. These risks, if not controlled, expose the company to potentially significant workers' compensation liabilities. Workers' compensation laws, which vary from state to state, can result in severe financial losses. Examples: lack of good site or office housekeeping; lack of adequate and frequent safety training; exposure to asbestos, either visible or hidden (buried pipe, attic enclosures), which should have triggered immediate notification of the client; failure to enforce disciplinary rules when safety rules are violated.

• Risk that the negative publicity from highly visible human and other costs associated with health and safety issues will cause reputation loss. In addition, company managers could find themselves criminally liable for failure to provide a safe working environment for their employees.

• Key Person Risk

The risk that a key employee or manager leaves the company or a particular project or initiative, resulting in significant impact on established processes, general level of experience, and sourcing of knowledge. This risk is often a consequence of poor succession planning.

• Skilled Personnel/Leadership Risk

The risk that hiring, retention, or motivation of skilled labor is made difficult by internal company deficiencies or by the external labor market environment, which may vary across regions or business cycles. This risk may result in decreased customer satisfaction or in failure to complete projects on schedule or under budget. Examples:

• People responsible for important business processes cannot, or do not, provide the leadership, vision, and support necessary to help employees be effective and successful in their jobs.

• Lead project personnel, such as managers, lead engineers, or supervisors, are unavailable, unable, or unwilling to adequately support the project.

• Personnel responsible for supporting the company or project, such as estimators, engineers, designers, buyers, or planners, do not possess the requisite knowledge, skills, and experience to ensure that critical business objectives are achieved and significant business risks are reduced to an acceptable level.

• Training/Knowledge Analysis/Knowledge Sharing Risk

The risk that company employees, in the field or in their home office, do not receive sufficient training or that training programs are not designed to convey relevant and timely knowledge to employees, or that knowledge sharing is not encouraged or supported by a formal system accessible to those who need to participate. Examples: on-the-job and formal training in project management, contract law, and financial and business aspects of projects; safety and hazardous materials training and certification, use of tools that increase productivity, such as computers; new-hire orientation; analysis and sharing of past experience and best practices.

3.2.3 Operational Risks

• Change Orders/Scope Changes Risk

The risk that processes do not exist or are not followed to ensure change orders are either discouraged or are properly priced and the change order revenues collected. Change orders, particularly small ones, are seldom understood regarding their total impact on scope and schedule. Most importantly, they disrupt the natural, planned flow of the project and the allocation of resources, affecting other activities as well. Since most change orders do not involve additions to the scope of facilities (for example, re-prioritizing of work by the client), they are often underpriced or performed at no charge to the client, while in reality, they should carry a premium over original-scope work.

- Client-Furnished Materials

  Risk associated with equipment or materials selected and purchased by the client that are later given to the company and their timely delivery, integrity, compliance with specifications, and operating characteristics become the company's responsibility. In such cases, not only should the company make profit for taking on this responsibility—and not just on the man hours expended in the support functions—but also the risks associated with the equipment and materials need to be assessed and mitigated. Example: material received late when the company has schedule LDs.

- Client Indecision/Interference Risk

  - Client management does not reach decisions in a timely manner, which is important to completing projects or adhering to the project schedule. Client indecision risk also encompasses the risk that the client will make a decision then reverse it once the company has committed time and resources based on the original decision.

  - Client demands excessive "design studies" and special reports to justify decisions.

  - Client wants to make decisions or monitor project statuses at a level that is typically performed by the company. The client's demands reduce the company's ability to effectively manage the project.

  - Client may commission an on-the-job survey asking the company's employees for areas of project improvement. This survey data may potentially be used to harm the company later if the project comes under dispute.

- Client Obligations/Milestones Risk

  The company's client is unable or unwilling to meet obligations under the contract. Examples:

  - Not providing as built information for the project, operating data, maintenance requirements, client specifications, vendor or licensor data, inspection records, or not approving drawings and procedures in a timely manner.

- Not procuring the environmental permit on time and not supporting other permitting or reporting activities, such as building, traffic, or work permits, customs clearances.

- Not paying their bills on time.

- Client Organization Risk

Risk that the client's organization is weak, inexperienced, or not empowered to make decisions or that client management may be unstable and the job security of sponsors for the project may be low. On long-duration projects, for example, some O&M projects, there is likelihood that the decision makers will change, bringing a different operations/maintenance strategy, jeopardizing the attainment of incentives, or even deciding to self-perform some, or all, O&M functions.

- Client Profile/Culture Risk

  - The company does not understand the risks when undertaking work for specific clients. Thus, the proposal team is unable to develop an accurate and successful strategy or fail to halt the bidding process once the job is revealed to be less attractive or outside of the company's risk tolerance. Examples: requirement of a bid bond, making exiting the bidding process difficult; client's willingness to accept contract comments or tendency to throw out the bid.

  - The high likelihood that the client or client's team on the project will not approve of or be satisfied with the selection of the company as a contractor or with the outcome of the project, regardless of the effort invested. Examples: client may be "wired" to another contractor; client has a culture of contractor-bashing and adversarial stance.

- Errors in Client Information Risk

  Risk of:

  - Conflicting data in the RFP, client's scope of work, client specifications

  - Obsolete, inaccurate, or limited soil studies, topographic or survey information

  - As built drawings with errors, incomplete, or non-existing

- Wrong process or utility data, electrical load studies, drain capacities

- Assumptions on facility integrity jeopardized by poor inspection records and deferred or incomplete maintenance

- Contract Administration Risk

  Risk resulting from deficient prime contract administration. Examples:

  - Performing work before the contract is signed (risk increases significantly if material purchases or field activities are undertaken!) or performing work on change orders before they are signed.

  - Performing work before submittals are approved.

  - Not understanding or following the contract and not enforcing the company's rights (invoices, interest on late payments, approval of change orders, force majeure claims).

  - Not recognizing that the client is not meeting contractual requirements and notifying the client as soon as possible; not meeting the company's obligations regarding notifications, documentation, reports, approvals, budget and schedule deviations, project personnel, and overtime approvals.

  - Not aligning with the client on the prime contract early in the project or with the project team regarding roles, responsibilities, milestones, and deliverables.

  - Not communicating the contract requirements to the project team by either preparing and distributing a contract summary or having a contract reading and discussion session.

- Liquidated Damages Risk

  Risk associated with having LDs on schedule or performance in the contract (rather than with the actual schedule or performance). Examples:

  - LDs are structured in such a way that makes it attractive to the client to take advantage of them.

  - Performance LDs are not clear, leading to unnecessary discussions during project handover.

- There is no "neutral zone" between the end of the period when the project would earn an incentive on schedule and the start of LDs, making it financially advantageous for the client to push the project away from the incentives zone and into the LDs zone.

- Scope of Work (SOW) Risk

  - The risk that the SOW is not well defined, and kept current either by narratives, discussion confirmations, minutes of meeting, drawings, schematics, checklists, digital photos, responsibility matrixes, or any other means that can later be used as the control basis for price and schedule adjustments.

  - The SOW is not clear and detailed regarding the physical facilities being worked on as well as the services provided by the company. The SOW should state both what is included and excluded in the work or provided by others (vendors, subs, teaming partners, or the client).

  - The SOW includes language such as "as required," "to be verified," "etc.," "to be determined" or any other ambiguous terms.

  - The SOW includes work never done before by the company, unusual requirements from the client, and other uncertainties.

- Terms & Conditions Risk

  Risk associated with not having proper terms and conditions in the contract or from their misinterpretation. Specifically: warranties, scope changes clause, client schedule delays, indemnification, releases, budget and schedule impact, insurance and bonds, transfer and acceptance, compensation, client supplied material, consequential damages, currency fluctuation, regulatory agency changes, escalation, inflation, force majeure, taxes, hazardous waste, payment schedules, court order delays, strikes and walkouts, third-party delays, and liquidated damages.

- Warranties/Guarantees Risk

  - Risk associated with not complying with the scope of work or with faulty performance of the work, resulting in re-performance cost.

  - Risk associated with not meeting the process, mechanical, environmental, or utility consumption guarantees resulting from an inadequate margin between "as designed" and "as guaranteed" parameters.

• The risk may arise from not verifying the licensor's design basis, not monitoring the design phase to ensure implementation, not including the warranty requirements in supplier's purchase orders, and not appointing a "warranty manager" on the project.

• Cost of Cash Risk

The risk that cost of cash estimates either under or overstate the positive or negative effects of cost of cash. Cost of cash estimates must account for a variety of factors:

• Timing of the investment in the strategy to win the proposal or in the purchase of the bid bond vs. timing of project award and client payments.

• Amount and duration of any required client retention.

• Timing of expenditures to suppliers (including cancellation charges) vs. client payments (considered any payment floats if a zero-balance account is not in place).

• Timing of the award of any incentives, bonuses, and shared savings vs. timing of investments required to attain them.

• Cost of cash curve not updated during the life of the project, leading to inaccurate forecasts of project profitability, or failure to include change orders, escalation, or the impact of exchange rates in the cost of cash calculation.

• Cost of Labor Risk

Risk that the cost of labor may be too volatile or too inflationary to successfully bid a project. Unsuccessful labor cost forecasts may, in turn, squeeze margins:

• Variances in field/home office labor rates and mix; foreseeable potential variations in insurance and payroll burden costs and company overhead costs (example: the project is bid as direct-hire execution but later goes to subcontractors).

• Variations in home office, field construction, vendor shop, or subcontractor overtime or shift work requirements; drug testing and safety induction requirements, variances in field site engineering support, travel time between labor camp and site, warehouse and lay- down areas too far from site, commissioning personnel and other indirect labor work hours, timing, and costs.

- Other indirect cost variances including recruiting and training, camps, and infrastructure; home office or field cost underestimated by assuming a task is simpler than it really is or that it can be done at lower cost (example: project is bid as a work share, but it is later determined that it must be done at the site because of the revamp nature of the work).

- Cost of Materials Risk

  Risk inherent in the underestimating of tagged and bulk material quantities and unit prices, or the lack of emphasis in negotiating the lowest cost with suppliers or subcontractors when materials are in the scope of the subcontract. Also, the lack of monitoring of project cost in the disciplines, which sometimes tend to direct their energies in managing the man-hour budget while neglecting the installed-cost budget for their prime and enforcing "estimate-centric" execution.

- Escalation Risk

  The risk that prices for labor, materials, and other direct costs will rise throughout the course of the project execution, and those higher costs are not included in the estimate used in determining the project price.

- Estimate Quality Risk

  Risk arising from a substandard estimate. Examples:

  - The company does not have time or resources to produce a quality bid for a project or change order estimate. Consequences may include a bid that is too low or too high, drafting of a proposal that lacks the quality to win the project, or a change order that fails to cover all necessary costs. If possible, the contract should allow for change order adjustment.

  - Not all disciplines, including construction, are involved in the estimate.

• An inadequate review of project risks and opportunities fails to identify events that call for added costs/increased contingency.

• Productivity (Labor/Equipment) Risk

Risk of using the wrong productivity assumptions in the estimate. Examples:

• Labor productivity is not sufficient to complete the project on time or within budget. Labor productivity varies across geographic regions or economic cycles and is dependent on congestion, elevation, language skills of supervisory personnel, and many other factors, making each site unique.

• Heavy equipment productivity affects the rate of progress and the cost on infrastructure projects.

• Computer productivity is often overestimated particularly when a new system is introduced.

• Civil, Structural & Architectural Engineering and Design Items Risk Examples include:

• Lack of good information on existing facilities.

• Insufficient number of CADD model review terminals resulting in reduced efficiency.

• Adding to existing structures without adequately checking, resulting in possible failure of structure and/or possible substantial liability.

• Decision to eliminate or reduce engineering deliverables without proper consultation with construction manager, resulting in possible increased level of effort required in field.

• Reduced level of checking of drawings, resulting in possible field rework, with resulting schedule delays, cost overruns, and increased field supervision cost.

• Work sharing with inexperienced offices, resulting in both increased possibility of not meeting schedule and quality problems.

• Use of non-sophisticated steel fabricators, resulting in being unable to either use electronic transfer of CADD model or request connection design.

- Control Systems Engineering Items Risk

    Examples include:

    - Local code requirements, such as city or government codes or manuals, etc., resulting in startup or installation approval delays, extra cost for purchase of replacement material.

    - Use of new, unproven control systems to reduce cost may result in increased labor and schedule delay in field if the system does not operate as expected.

    - Complex controls furnished by mechanical package vendor may result in field and office rework revision if the instrumentation does not meet project requirements.

- Electrical Engineering Items Risk

    Examples include:

    - Out of specification vendor electrical installation on mechanical packages, resulting in cost increases for rework at schedule delay.

    - Late definition of control circuits, motors, and other equipment, resulting in:

        - Late release of materials

        - Late release and/or rework of drawings and material takeoffs

    - Missed equipment that requires electrical supply, resulting in:

        - Late changes to motor control centers

        - Late ordering of materials

        - Loss of control over equipment costs

    - Delivery of vendor data after issue of construction drawings, resulting in:

        - Rework

        - Cost increase due to increased man hours for drawings

- Scope growth of electrical, resulting in rework, late design, and delay of engineering and construction schedule.

- Reduced deliverables to construction to reduce home office costs, resulting in increased field supervision cost.

- Mechanical Engineering Items Risk

  Risk associated with mechanical engineering and design activities and responsibilities. Examples include:

  - Using a design code that the home office is not familiar with, resulting in:

    - Excessive man hours to familiarize all users with code

    - Equipment vendor not properly applying code

  - Overrun of equipment count and cost, resulting in:

    - Likely overrun in equipment count due to process changes or sparing

    - Philosophy change

    - More man hours for additional items

    - Delay in schedule

    - More RFQ packages than planned

    - Overrun of capital cost budget

    - Impact on plot plan/detailed design

  - Improper rejection of technical design, resulting in cost and schedule delay and lack of client confidence, resulting in excessive review and approval time. Late changes to equipment while in fabrication caused by late Hazwoper review, resulting in increased price and late delivery.

  - Reduced deliverables to construction to reduce home office costs, resulting in increased field supervision cost.

• Change Management Risk

While change order risk pertains to the likelihood of the client introducing changes to scope, schedule, sequence of work, deliverables, etc., change management risk comes from project teams who fail to comply with, or implement on day one, the change management process. Examples:

• Project manager wants to have the "client on his side" and continually fails to invoke the company's contractual right to recover base cost, overheads, and profit from changes or even recognize and document these changes as soon as they occur.

• Many "minor changes" are accepted and believed to have no impact on cost/ schedule while in reality their aggregate has a major effect on both cost and schedule.

• Resource levels are not adjusted to accommodate for changes.

• The project team uses client changes as a reason to introduce their own changes or cover inefficiencies and to delay project milestones and deliverables.

• Change is not aggressively discouraged amongst the project team and/or with the client.

• Claims against suppliers, subcontractors, or client are not filed as soon as possible.

• Compliance with Specs/Procedures Risk

As a result of a flaw in design or operation or due to human error, oversight, or indifference, the company's processes do not meet customer requirements the first time or do not comply with prescribed codes, procedures, and policies required by the government. Non-compliance introduces the risk of lower quality, unrecoverable rework cost, and unnecessary delays.

• Construction/Constructability Risk

Risks and opportunities associated with constructability and construction activities and responsibilities in the home office and field. Examples:

• Not addressing constructability issues early in the design.

• Not considering labor density vs. productivity, construction in winter or during high wind or rain, import of construction equipment, and efforts related to enforcing a drug-free workplace.

- No accurate assessment of local craft quality and availability resulting in escalating craft labor costs in addition to incentives required to recruit and retain craft. Lack of skilled manpower can result in lower productivity and escalating costs.

- Shortage of skilled work force due to competing projects in the area resulting in:

- Poor quality of work

- Increased reworks

- Low productivity

- Increased safety related risks

- Increased cost

- Schedule slippage

- High turnover rate

- No clear definition of requirements for mechanical completion and turnover, resulting in inability to achieve project milestones and attain incentives. No clear determination of project completion.

- Lack of an integrated schedule based on construction sequencing and system turnover, resulting in ineffective sequencing of engineering deliverables and materials. Unproductive construction execution, resulting in extended schedule and escalating direct and indirect costs.

- Engineering and procurement deliverables are not segregated or identified by work package or turnover system, resulting in ineffective and unproductive construction execution based on clear identification of deliverables and materials to support the execution sequencing mandated by the schedule.

- Weather-related circumstances such as rain, snow, or winter conditions that can prolong completion of underground activities and escalate direct and indirect costs and schedule.

- Excessive field material surplus, resulting in increased cost.

- Excessive field indirect material, resulting in increased cost.

- Lost time due to untimely issuing of daily work permits by owner, resulting in low productivity and schedule delays.

- Lost time and injuries due to plant evacuations, such as from chemical releases, resulting in low productivity and increased field labor costs.

- Working critical path activities during adverse weather conditions, resulting in missed completion dates and associated incentives, increased safety-related risks, low productivity, and increased field labor costs.

- Method of acceptance for structural connections is not clearly identified, resulting in:

    - Schedule delays

    - Rework of structural steel connections

    - Failure to provide proper equipment for testing connections

- Poor or non-existent surface water drainage system resulting in excessive lost time due to rainouts/flooding schedule delays and increased cost.

    - Deterioration and/or damage to equipment during on site storage, resulting in delay in construction schedule, project turnover, and additional cost for equipment rework/repair.

- Instruments do not get spec checked and calibrated upon receipt prior to storing, resulting in:

    - Discovery of out of spec or damaged instruments after installation, leaving little time to repurchase or repair

    - Disruption of work plans

    - Schedule delays

- Failure to implement an adequate inspection measuring and test equipment (IM&TE) program resulting in:

    - Invalid tests or measurement results requiring rework

    - Increased cost due to lost equipment

    - Lack of control of equipment

• Local contractors' lack of knowledge in OSHA, site, state, and USACE safety rules and regulations, resulting in increased number of accidents.

• Contractors lack competent safety representatives with authority to stop unsafe work, resulting in work stoppages due to safety rule violations and schedule delays.

• Environmental Compliance Risks

Environmental risks expose the company to enormous potential liabilities. The risk is highest on projects of long duration or where the company has taken responsibility for facility operation/maintenance. The exposure is twofold:

• Liability to third parties for bodily injury or property damage caused by the environmental damage

• Liability to governments or third parties for the cost of removing pollutants plus severe punitive damages. Examples: damage to natural features or existing facilities (roads, bridges); contamination of soil, water, or air; noise or odor pollution; non-compliance with environmental impact reports; negligence in applying any required best available control technology; not testing for the presence of contaminated soil or notifying client immediately when contaminated soil is discovered so client can undertake removal, if contractually obligated to do so.

• Existing Facilities/Reuse of Equipment

• Risk associated with working in an existing facility, particularly one that is, or was recently, in operation. Example: cutting into pipelines without first testing that they are liquid-free; working without a hot-permit; ignoring "Lock & Tag" procedures.

• Risk inherent in the reuse of existing plant equipment, piping, or other systems, re-rating of equipment, equipment with incomplete or lacking inspection data, equipment or systems older than their expected design life or for which replacement parts may not be available. Examples: tie-ins into pipe that may not support the internal or external stresses induced by the modifications; adding loads to structures already at their design capacity.

• Risk associated with idle time incurred waiting for hot permits or confined entry permits, evacuation drills, gas alarms, and other occurrences related to an operating plant.

• Heavy Lifts/Rigging Risk

Risk associated with unusual, heavy, or elevated lifts. Examples:

• Engineered lifts not checked by a licensed rigging engineer.

• Lateral loads on lifting lugs (wind, upending the equipment during the lift) or vertical loads over ten tons not checked by a licensed rigging engineer

• Rigging engineer not in attendance during lifts where the load exceeds 95% of the crane's capacity.

• Inter-discipline Coordination Risk

Risk inherent in inter-discipline work processes. Examples:

• The various disciplines involved in the project are not in proximity with each other or are not dedicated full time to the project, making coordination difficult.

• Team checking, peer reviews, or coordination meetings are not conducted.

• Inter-discipline procedures for the project are not published or not followed.

• Design, constructability, and joint risk reviews, value awareness programs, and all other inter-discipline feedback opportunities are untimely, do not include the required participants, or are not taking place.

• Other Contractor at Site Risk

Risk associated with another contractor moving to a site where the company is performing construction, resulting in added demands for labor, construction equipment, available materials, and local infrastructure. In extreme cases, sabotage, vandalism, and theft may result, and cost and schedule are affected from increased security measures.

• Commissioning Risk ("Turnkey" Activities Risk)

Risk resulting from the company's responsibility to either lead or support the commissioning of the completed project. Examples:

- Lack of certain systems, such as utilities, which need to be commissioned early to support startup. These systems need to be identified at the beginning of the project and design; material management and construction must be prioritized accordingly. Back-feed power must be ensured for the startup.

- Adequate resources required to support pre-commissioning, commissioning, performance testing, and operations handover of turnkey projects are not available.

- Project Incentives Risk

  The risk that the project incentive was formulated in such a way that it is un-attainable. Examples:

  - Schedule incentive is based on an unrealistic schedule; incentive payment is an "all or nothing" type, making it tempting for the client to avoid its award. Note: Multiple milestones or progressive "$ per day" incentives are easier to manage.

  - Performance incentives assume that the facility will operate optimally on the first pass or not enough margin exists between design parameters and incentive parameters

  - "Under-run of project budget" incentives are difficult to collect if the company was involved in the estimate—the budget should be verified by the client, or profit should be put at risk to counter the client's perceptions.

  - Baseline calculation on incentive-based O&M projects was not done correctly, leaving little room for improved outcomes.

- Project Schedule Risk

  The risk that key deadlines and milestones are not met. For corporate initiatives, failure to meet deadlines and milestones may lower employee support of the initiative, lengthen the time key employees are kept away from their core activities, and increase costs for the initiative. Failing to meet project deadlines and milestones may result in financial loss (liquidated damages, extra costs) or jeopardize the company's relationship with a client. Examples:

  - Not measuring actual progress vs. plan, not having a project execution plan formulated in enough detail to allow tasks to be done in the proper sequence or not using historical data to formulate a realistic schedule.

- Not reviewing execution plans and contingency/backup options on a regular basis or not giving enough emphasis to critical path activities, which require separate, dedicated monitoring.

- Not making agreements with suppliers to obtain firmed-up, key information early rather than waiting for the entire certified dimensional outline to be issued.

- Not establishing a process control philosophy and venting/ drainage requirements early.

- Receiving the building or environmental permit late (this should be a client milestone) and not adjusting the schedule accordingly.

- Project Staffing/Organization Risk

Risk that the project staff is not adequate for the size, complexity or strategic importance of the project. Examples:

- In order to cut cost, positions are eliminated or only assigned part time, or people without the necessary training and experience are placed in leading positions.

- The project manager is not aggressive enough to stand up to a demanding client and protect the profitability, schedule, or technical integrity of the project. The project manager lets the client lead the project team rather than leading it on behalf of the client toward the jointly established objective.

- The project team is not business focused, allowing profit erosion to occur.

- Quality Control/Validation Risk

Checks and balances intended to ensure quality (compliance with require- ments) are not in place or are ignored, resulting in quality risk. The CQC plan is not followed, resulting in deficiencies and client dissatisfaction. Examples: constructability, peer reviews, team checks, timely interference detection, design reviews and material engineering reviews, field surveys, shop inspection, supplier evaluations, soil tests, welder certification, etc.

• Work-sharing/Joint Execution Risk

Risk associated with project work being done in multiple offices through work sharing or with other contractors. The more offices involved, the higher the risk. Examples:

• Not defining technical requirements and interface/coordination procedures, not monitoring the performance of the teams in the global execution office by assigning appropriate lead engineers in the lead office.

• When working with other companies, not ascertaining that their execution methods parallel as closely as possible the company's in terms of use of task forces, compatible software, and methods of checking/levels of quality, document control, etc.

• Organized Labor Risk

The risks associated with dealing with organized labor management and retaining union employees for projects. Examples:

• Strikes

• Work slowdowns

• Demands for work hour reductions

• Wage increases or changes in working conditions

• Contract re-negotiations

• Non-union work in areas of union labor dominance

• Difficulties in dealing with union management

• Critical Deliveries Risk

Risk associated with late delivery of critical equipment or with faulty or damaged equipment, as well as risk resulting from poor planning and coordination of large/heavy deliveries. Key deliveries often determine the schedule critical path. The risk can be mitigated by selecting a reliable equipment supplier and a reputable logistics and freight forwarding customs clearance company. The project manager should be closely involved in the planning and monitoring of key deliveries, particularly those that are large or heavy, as non-standard routes, times, and delivery methods may be required.

- Key Suppliers/Subcontractors Risk

  Examples:

  - Supplier or subcontractor is known to perform below expectations in terms of missing schedules, not providing adequate or timely project documents, filing nuisance claims, not having enough resources in the field or in the shop, poor quality control, etc. However, due to lack of competition or client preference, this substandard performance plays a significant role on the project and must be closely managed to attain acceptable results.

  - Supplier or subcontractor has control over a disproportionate portion of the project or corporate initiative and its ability to manage risk affects the risk profile of the project or initiative. Where possible, multiple subcontractors should be splitting the work.

- Material Management/Procurement Risk

  Examples:

  - Scope of purchase order is poorly written, leading to uncertainties in cost and schedule performance, excessive change orders, and eventually claims.

  - Supplier is not adequately managed through the enforcement of the purchase order, use of the company's standard terms and conditions, timely technical and commercial approval by the project team and the client, buy-down plan, shop and field inspection program, collection of back-charges for faulty work, and proper close-out of purchase orders and subcontracts.

  - Material management is not integrated into the project schedule, resulting in shortages, surplus, emergency purchases at a premium, and out of sequence deliveries.

  - Materials or equipment owned by the company or third parties, such as vendors or subcontractors, is not adequately protected from weather damage, mishandling, misuse, or theft.

- Warehouse/lay-down areas are remote from the construction site area and double handling of materials is affecting cost and schedule.

- Flow-down requirements resulting in supplier or contractor schedule impact and supplier or contractor cost increase.

- Not using material manager, resulting in inaccurate reporting, forecasting, inefficiency, and inadequate corporate roll-up.

- Material escalation, resulting in budget overruns and delivery delays.

- RFQ/RFP cycle too short, resulting in increased contingency, incomplete milestone schedules, and untimely vendor data/information.

- Late issuance of long lead equipment purchase orders, resulting in construction delays, increased execution costs, and potential liquidated damages.

- Lack of involvement of logistics in material/equipment delivery, resulting in construction delays, exposure to liquidated damages when deliveries slip due to inadequate logistics effort by the suppliers and inaccurate information, import duties, duty exemptions, freight forwarding challenges, etc.

- Material Sourcing/Selection/Certification Risk

  - Risk associated with certain commodities that historically have wide price fluctuations or are typically in short supply—for example chrome or titanium—or require specialized fabrications.

  - Risk that the material selected for a particular application is unsuitable or impractical, resulting in decreased operator or public safety, potential environmental contamination, or increased lifecycle cost for the facility.

  - Risk that materials purchased do not comply with codes and specifications, may not be fit for service, or have been acquired illegally, such as counterfeit materials, faked certificates, metallurgy not as shown on the certificate but discovered later.

- Small Business/Buy American Compliance Risk

  - The company does not contract sufficient minority or previously disadvantaged businesses to comply with federal requirements.

• Contractual provisions to source materials and equipment or issue subcontracts to a SDB are not followed, resulting in fines.

• Subcontract Administration Risk

Risk resulting from home-office or field subcontract administration. Examples:

• Authorizing subcontractors to perform work before the scope is clearly defined. kept current, documented and price is agreed to by both parties and not aligning the project team about the scope of the subcontract early in the project.

• Not conducting weekly subcontractor meetings and asking the question "are there any claims?" and then not documenting the answer (or no answer) in the minutes of the meeting.

• Not filing back-charges against subcontractors in a timely manner and with proper documentation or not meeting the company's contractual requirements such as notifications.

• Failing to request subcontractor bonding, insurance, and other certificates, making sure that they are valid for the duration and type of work performed, and keeping them on file.

• Not reviewing subcontractor plans vs. actual performance to make sure they are meeting their commitments or allowing change orders to become claims.

• Late assignment/involvement of project contracts manager, resulting in ineffective or no contracting plan, inadequate pre-qualification of potential bidders, and assuming unnecessary risks.

• Insufficient discipline reviews of work processes, usually from too much working in isolation, resulting in conflict and/or duplication of effort, poorly defined scopes of work, inadequate contract language, inadequate instruments of surety, such as bonds, etc.

• Insufficient emphasis given to the prevention of contractor claims resulting in excess claims and "leakage" and current approach being reactive rather than proactive.

• High rate of contract growth resulting in unnecessary "leakage" and end of project surprises in unanticipated growth.

- Too much commercial authority either given to or assumed by project manager, resulting in unqualified commercial decisions equaling "leakage."

- Unsafe/Inexperienced Subcontractor Risk

  Risk associated with a subcontractor who does not have the same high safety performance goals as the company or who is not familiar with the client's requirements or with local regulations and standards. To mitigate this risk, subcontractors should be informed, educated, trained, and audited at regular intervals.

- Inventory/Spares Risk

  - Risk of spare parts or specialized equipment not being available when needed or not meeting requirements.

  - Risk that the procurement or replacement of spare parts is not clearly defined in the contract, or that taxes, financing cost, inflation, storage costs, or other time- dependent costs have not been accounted for in the proposal.

- Information Technology (IT) Risk

  Risk that information technologies do not efficiently and effectively support the current and future needs of the business, are not operating as intended, are compromising the integrity and reliability of data and information, are exposing significant assets to potential loss or misuse, or threaten the company's ability to sustain the operation, its critical business processes, or its projects. Examples:

  - New software or software release is implemented without first being tested or at the wrong time during a project, causing disruption, delays, and errors from program "bugs."

  - Transactions are not authorized, complete, accurate, or timely as they are entered into or reported by the various application systems at the company.

  - Access to information, such as data or programs, is inappropriately granted or refused, meaning unauthorized people can access confidential information while those who need to access it do not have the right kind of access. As an example: read, copy, and write.

- Information is not available when needed or there is loss of communication— for example, from cut cables, telephone or electrical system outage, or network downtime—or a loss of basic processing capability and operational difficulties, such as a disk drive breakdown, operator errors, computer viruses, and industrial espionage.

- Licenses/Patents/Confidentiality Risk

The risk that patents, confidentiality agreements, licensor data, attorney- client- privileged information and other intellectual property commitments are not honored, resulting in legal action against the company. Conversely, the risk that the company's confidential information is intentionally or unintentionally given to others. Examples: giving access to clients to ftp site; licensor information granted on a particular project is used on other projects; unauthorized use of the company's developed software on client computers.

- Technology Change Risks

  - The risk that the technology or process selected is superseded by a cheaper, better one, thus rendering the original selection obsolete, with replacement parts no longer available.

  - The risk that a licensor package or proven technology is modified extensively to accommodate client requirements, potentially invalidating the license. Note: Licensor requirements should be challenged if excessive, but approval must be obtained for deviations.

  - The risk that HAZWOP reviews are performed late on the project, introducing untimely yet mandatory changes into the design.

- Technology Implementation Risk

  - The risk that the process or technology selected will not attain the clients' objectives in terms of capacity, economics, product slate, operability, availability, utility consumption, effluents, environmental or safety constraints, or consistent operation.

  - Risk associated with a new technology, particularly one for which there are no existing full-scale running operations. Note: Prototype operations or equipment should be left out of the lump sum, if possible. Examples: the company having to rely on technology by others or being responsible to verify and guarantee technology by others; no clarity as to who has material selection responsibility.

4.0 RFP Requirements/Proposal Preparation

Now that you have found the project that may meet your strategic goals, it is time to decide whether to prepare a proposal and submit your bid. Some solicitations will require simple "go/no-go" proposals and some will require very costly, time consuming, and very complex proposals, so the bidder must make some timely and in- depth decisions prior to starting the process. Are you eligible to bid the project? Is it feasible to bid the project? Have you done a self-assessment to decide if you have the resources to perform the work as required and to a high quality? Have you analyzed the competition to determine if you have a good chance of winning the bid? Have you analyzed the solicitation and understand what it requires? Are you willing to spend the time and money, and can you devote the resources necessary to prepare a "winning" proposal?

These are all questions that you must ask yourself prior to preparing a bid and submitting the proposal. Remember, the process can take quite a bit of time, so these questions must be asked early on so that the decision to go forward allows you enough time to make a thorough and well thought out proposal. You are doing all this work to "win" the bid, so don't waste your time on a bid that is sloppily put together.

4.1 Bidder Eligibility:

You must decide whether you are eligible to bid on the project. Many projects are restricted as to who can bid on them.

- Is it an "open solicitation" that anyone can bid on?
- Is it "sole source"?
- Is the contract a "set-aside"? If it is, then is it:
    - For holders of existing "master contracts" such as MATOC, MACC, etc.?
    - For small business? Applicable size standards?
    - Special socio-economic categories such as HUBZone, Small Disadvantaged Business concern, Veteran-Owned Small Business concern, Service Disabled Veteran-Owned Small Business concern, Women-Owned Small Business concern, etc.

4.2 Bid Feasibilty:

Now you need to decide if it is feasible to bid on the project. Remember, there is limited time to pull everything together and prepare a "winning" proposal.

- Can you meet the due date and still have a well-prepared and thought-out proposal?

- Do you have the resources available to:

    - Gather, read, and digest the bid documents?

    - Research the bid context?

    - Seek partners if desired or needed? Should you do a joint venture or teaming? Is there enough time to put together the bid? Remember, if you neec a partner or JV then this will take added time, so you need to start this as soon after the first solicitation notice as possible.

    - Seek technical info? Knowing the technical information is critical to preparing the bid.

    - Determine material, labor, and subcontract costs?

    - Attend pre-bid meetings, site visits, etc.?

    - Communicate with government procurement staff to ask questions and get answers in time to make decisions?

    - Assess the competition?

4.3 Self-Assessment:

Now that you have determined that you are eligible to bid on the project and it is feasible for you to bid, can you perform the work as required and provide the quality necessary for a good performance evaluation?

- Assuming that you win the bid, can you perform as required?

- Do you have all the required expertise and skills?

- Can you get all the materials?

- Is your company structure set up to handle the project?

- Can you obtain the required bonding and insurance? Is there any special insurance such as environmental insurance?

- Do you need any special licenses or other credentials?

- Do you understand what quality control systems will be required?

- Will cash flow be an issue?

- Is the project the right size for you?

- Have you performed your risk analysis, and are the risks worth it?

- Are the rewards worth doing the project? Can you keep your profit margin high enough to make it worthwhile doing the project? Remember, you are not doing this because you need the practice.

- Does this contract fit with your short, intermediate, and long-term goals?

- Is this project consistent with your business plan?

- Are you prepared for any special requirements such as ITAR (International Traffic in Arms Regulations), security clearances, financial audits, etc.?

4.4 Competition:

You have now decided that bidding on this project is feasible, you are eligible to bid, and you have the resources to bid and perform the work, so it is time to assess the competition. This can sometimes be very difficult because some firms will not be involved yet when you must make your decision to bid on the project; however, assessing the competition is paramount to developing your bid strategy. You need to consider:

- Who are your competitors?

- What do you know about them?

- What more can you learn about them?

- Do you have competitive advantage?

- How can you best communicate your advantage?

• If you can't win, you shouldn't bid the project unless you want the experience and the exposure, or if it costs you nothing.

4.5 Preparing the Proposal:

Now that you have decided you want to bid on the project, the work really begins—PREPARING THE PROPOSAL! The bid/proposal must be responsive, attention-getting, and competitive. You must understand all the solicitation requirements, including evaluation factors, and your proposal must be complete and delivered exactly as required.

RESPONSIVENESS:

- You must provide everything that is asked for.
    - Provide all that is required by the solicitation including all associated documents.
    - Include the SF1442, "Solicitation, Offer, and Award" page signed.
    - Include the acknowledgement of all amendments. Check to make sure you have all the amendments.
    - Include any representations and certifications that may be in addition to what is included in SAM.
    - The burden to be responsive is on you.
- You must give it to them the way they want it.
    - Read and re-read the solicitation.
    - Take notes, highlight important requirements, use post-its or clips.
    - Make lists for what is required.
    - Get some clues as to their perspective. Review "Evaluation Factors for Award."
    - Make sure you are clear in satisfying all their evaluation criteria.
    - When in doubt, default to their structure.
- You must check for other requirements such as:

- Is your SAM registration current, correct, and complete?
- Are any security clearances required? If so, can you get them in time?
- Is an ITAR license required?
- Are any state or local licenses required?
- Are your taxes paid?
- Are you debarred or on the "Excluded Parties List"?
- You must pay attention to the bid/proposal delivery.
- It must be delivered on or before the time and date due.
- It must be delivered to the correct person and at the correct address.
- The package must be complete and marked as required by the solicitation.
- Hard copies, electronic submittals, and number of copies must be delivered as specified.
- Fax or email proposals only as expressly permitted.
- Get confirmation of delivery date and time from the carrier and recipient.

ATTENTION GETTING:

- Up-front communication.
    - Get on the "Interested Parties List."
    - Ask intelligent questions.
    - If possible, ask the questions in person or by telephone.
- Attend pre-bid meetings or site visits.
- Try to understand the bigger picture, such as the history, the present, and the future.
- Be on their team! Be a part of their solution!
- Don't be fancy, flashy, or trashy. Keep it simple. You want to be noticed, but you don't want to be looked down on.

- Avoid irrelevant references.

WIN THE COMPETITION:

- Read the evaluation factors for award.
- The strengths of your proposal must match their most important evaluation factors.
- The factors are sometimes scored; if not, they are probably presented in order of strength.
- You must convincingly address all the evaluation factors.
- You may not propose something other than what is asked for—even if it is better. The only exception would be if the solicitation asks for "Betterments." Betterments can sometimes put you "Over the Top." If you propose betterments, then be prepared to implement them.

WINNING PROPOSALS ARE:

- Responsive
    - Complete—contains everything required
    - Delivered on time
    - Meet all format requirements
    - Don't include extraneous "junk"
- Clear and simple
- Easy to evaluate

Remember, proposals reflect the competence of their authors, and they should inspire confidence in your firm. You are trying to show the government that you are the most qualified firm to do their work. You should not get discouraged if you do not win some bids right off the bat. Preparing proposals takes practice and great skill and can be learned only after doing them numerous times. Consideration should be given to using a professional proposal writer with a proven record of winning proposals.

I recommend that you prepare a project summary of each project that you either built or worked on that includes all the relevant data, such as owner, original cost, final cost including all change orders, the project team, subcontractors, complexity, project duration including original scheduled completion date, and actual completion date, etc. Keep these project summaries up to date and it will make providing this information to the government for each project much easier.

You should request a debriefing after every award even if you win the award, because it will show you what you did wrong and what you did right. It will help you to strengthen your future proposal.

5.0 Protest after Award

A challenge to the government's conduct of a procurement action is known as a "bid protest." Protests can be made either prior to award of a contract or afterward. However, most protests for construction contracts are protested after award because the protesting contractor will generally base the protest on the successful offeror's proposal to meet one or more of the solicitation requirements, such as lowest bid, responsibility of the contractor, responsiveness to the solicitation, or the agency's failure to evaluate the successful offeror's proposal consistent with the evaluation criteria as listed in the solicitation.

The contractor can file a protest with:

- The contracting agency responsible for the procurement
- The Comptroller General of the Government Accountability Office
- The United States Court of Federal Claims

Time limits and procedures are contained in FAR Clauses 33.101 and 33.103; however, the contractor must be aware of when the time for filing the protest starts (generally ten days) after the basis for the protest is known or should have been known, whichever is earlier. If a debriefing is requested by the protester and the protest is based upon what was learned at the debriefing, then the GAO has held that the protest must be filed within ten calendar days after the debriefing. Agency and GAO regulations must be followed closely, as any procedural or untimely filing cause the GAO or the procuring agency to disallow the protest. I highly recommend that the contractor obtain the services of a competent attorney immediately if a protest is contemplated.

FAR Clause 52.233-2 Service of Protest

As prescribed in 33.106, insert the following provision:

Service of Protest (Sept 2006)

Protests, as defined in section 31.101 of the Federal Acquisition Regulation, that are filed directly with an agency, and copies of any protests that are filed with the Government Accountability Office (GAO), shall be served on the Contracting Officer (addressed as follows) by obtaining written and dated acknowledgment of receipt from ______________________________.
[Contracting Officer designate the official or location where a protest may be served on the Contracting Officer.]

The copy of any protest shall be received in the office designated above within one day of filing a protest with the GAO.

(End of provision)

FAR Clause 52.233-3 Protest after Award

As prescribed in 33.106(b), insert the following clause:

Protest after award (Aug 1996)

- Upon receipt of a notice of protest (as defined in FAR 33.101) or a determination that a protest is likely (see FAR 33.102(d)), the Contracting Officer may, by written order to the Contractor, direct the Contractor to stop performance of the work called for by this contract. The order shall be specifically identified as a stop-work order issued under this clause. Upon receipt of the order, the Contractor shall immediately comply with its terms and take all reasonable steps to minimize the incurrence of costs allocable to the work covered by the order during the period of work stop-page. Upon receipt of the final decision in the protest, the Contracting Officer shall either —

Continues on page 78

• Cancel the stop-work order; or

• Terminate the work covered by the order as provided in the Default, or the Termination for Convenience of the Government, clause of this contract.

• If a stop-work order issued under this clause is canceled either before or after a final decision in the protest, the Contractor shall resume work. The Contracting Officer shall make an equitable adjustment in the delivery schedule or contract price, or both, and the contract shall be modified, in writing, accordingly, if—

• The stop-work order results in an increase in the time required for, or in the Contractor's cost properly allocable to, the performance of any part of this contract; and

• The Contractor asserts its right to an adjustment within 30 days after the end of the period of work stoppage; provided, that if the Contracting Officer decides the facts justify the action, the Contracting Officer may receive and act upon a proposal at any time before final payment under this contract.

• If a stop-work order is not canceled and the work covered by the order is terminated for the convenience of the Government, the Contracting Officer shall allow reasonable costs resulting from the stop-work order in arriving at the termination settlement.

• If a stop-work order is not canceled and the work covered by the order is terminated for default, the Contracting Officer shall allow, by equitable adjustment or otherwise, reasonable costs resulting from the stop-work order.

• The Government's rights to terminate this contract at any time are not affected by action taken under this clause.

• If, as the result of the Contractor's intentional or negligent misstatement, misrepresentation, or miscertification, a protest related to this contract is sustained, and the Government pays costs, as provided in FAR 33.102(b)(2) or 33.104(h)(1), the Government may require the Contractor to reimburse the Government the amount of such costs. In addition to any other remedy available, and pursuant to the requirements of Subpart 32.6, the Government may collect this debt by offsetting the amount against any payment due the Contractor under any contract between the Contractor and the Government.

(End of clause)

Continues on page 79

Alternate I (June 1985). As prescribed in 33.106(b), substitute in paragraph (a) (2) the words "the Termination clause of this contract" for the words "the Default, or the Termination for Convenience of the Government clause of this contract." In paragraph (b) substitute the words "an equitable adjustment in the delivery schedule, the estimated cost, the fee, or a combination thereof, and in any other terms of the contract that may be affected" for the words "an equitable adjustment in the delivery schedule or con- tract price, or both."

6.0 Surety Bonds

A 100% payment and 100% performance bond must be submitted within ten days after award. The bonds must be completed in accordance with their directions. No work can start until this has been submitted and approved. A bid bond may be required, and if it is, it will be shown in the solicitation. As the contractor, you should understand the definition of "original contract price" as shown in paragraph (a) below. This is very important in determining the bond amount to be supplied immediately after award for indefinite quantity contracts.

FAR Clause 52.228-15 Performance and Payment Bonds—Construction

- *Definitions.* As used in this clause:

"Original contract price" means the award price of the contract; or, for requirements contracts, the price payable for the estimated total quantity; or, for indefinite-quantity contracts, the price payable for the specified minimum quantity. Original contract price does not include the price of any options, except those options exercised at the time of contract award.

- *Amount of required bonds.* Unless the resulting contract price is $100,000 or less, the successful offeror shall furnish performance and payment bonds to the Contracting Officer as follows:
  - *Performance bonds* (Standard Form 25). The penal amount of performance bonds at the time of contract award shall be 100 percent of the original contract price.
  - *Payment Bonds* (Standard Form 25A). The penal amount of payment bonds at the time of contract award shall be 100 percent of the original contract price.

Continues on page 80

• Additional bond protection.

• The Government may require additional performance and payment bond protection if the contract price is increased. The increase in protection generally will equal 100 percent of the increase in contract price.

• The Government may secure the additional protection by directing the Contractor to increase the penal amount of the existing bond or to obtain an additional bond.

• *Furnishing executed bonds.* The Contractor shall furnish all executed bonds, including any necessary reinsurance agreements, to the Contracting Officer, within the time period specified in the Bid Guarantee provision of the solicitation, or otherwise specified by the Contracting Officer, but in any event, before starting work.

• *Surety or other security for bonds.* The bonds shall be in the form of firm commitment, supported by corporate sureties whose names appear on the list contained in Treasury Department Circular 570, individual sureties, or by other acceptable security such as postal money order, certified check, cashier's check, irrevocable letter of credit, or, in accordance with Treasury Department regulations, certain bonds or notes of the United States. Treasury Circular 570 is published in the Federal Register or may be obtained from the:

U.S. Department of the Treasury

Financial Management Service

Surety Bond Branch

3700 East West Highway, Room 6F01 Hyattsville, MD 20782.

Or via the internet at http://www.fms.treas.gov/c570/.

• *Notice of subcontractor waiver of protection (40 U.S.C. 3133(c)).* Any waiver of the right to sue on the payment bond is void unless it is in writing, signed by the person whose right is waived, and executed after such person has first furnished labor or material for use in the performance of the contract.

7.0 Insurance

The contractor must provide and maintain insurance in accordance with the requirements of FAR Clause 52.228-5 Insurance—Work on a Government Installation. The required minimum limits of the insurance are found in the solicitation and generally in Section 00 73 00. The contractor must also ensure that all subcontractors maintain the same minimum level of insurance and include the substance of this clause in all subcontracts. The contractor also must provide proof of subcontractor required and maintained insurance to the contracting officer upon request. This insurance is generally liability insurance and is designed to protect the government and not the contractor.

You should be aware that even though the contract may only require a minimum level of insurance, there are other insurances that should be considered. If you will be working over water as defined by the "United States Longshoremen and Harbor Workers Act" then this insurance will be mandatory by law but may not be required by the solicitation. The government does not require "Builders Risk" insurance because this insurance does not cover the government but instead covers the contractor. "Builders Risk" insurance is normally paid for by the owner for commercial projects and may be missed by the contractor, but if there is a fire or other disaster on the project being constructed, then this insurance will be needed. Worker's compensation insurance will also have to be maintained even though the government may not require it. There are also other types of insurance, such as environmental insurance that may need to be considered depending upon the type and scope of the contract.

You should explore the various types of insurance required and add other insurance that will protect your firm.

FAR Clause 52.228-5 Insurance—Work on a Government Installation

As prescribed in 28.310, insert the following clause:

Insurance—Work on a Government Installation (Jan 1997)

- The Contractor shall, at its own expense, provide and maintain during the entire performance of this contract, at least the kinds and minimum amounts of insurance required in the Schedule or elsewhere in the contract.

- Before commencing work under this contract, the Contractor shall notify the Contracting Officer in writing that the required insurance has been obtained. The policies evidencing required insurance shall contain an endorsement to the effect that any cancellation or any material change adversely affecting the Government's interest shall not be effective—

  - For such period as the laws of the State in which this contract is to be performed prescribe; or

  - Until 30 days after the insurer or the Contractor gives written notice to the Contracting Officer, whichever period is longer.

- The Contractor shall insert the substance of this clause, including this paragraph (c), in subcontracts under this contract that require work on a Government installation and shall require subcontractors to provide and maintain the insurance required in the Schedule or elsewhere in the contract. The Contractor shall maintain a copy of all subcontractors' proofs of required insurance and shall make copies available to the Contracting Officer upon request.

(End of clause)

8.0 Taxes

Taxes incurred by contractors vary greatly from state to state and sometimes from county to county. Business, sales, and use taxes, etc. can make a big difference in the profitability of a project. Some states will allow all costs for work on a federal installation to be tax free. Some states may charge sales tax on materials only but not on labor and vice versa. Contact the state department of revenue in the state where the project is to be built to determine exactly what taxes must be paid.

There are no special federal taxes levied upon a contractor for performing work on a government installation.

9.0 Utilization of Small Business Concerns

The F**AR Clause 52.219-8 Utilization of Small Business Concerns** is normally added to contracts when the award is made to a large business and requires that the contractor make a "good faith effort" to utilize small businesses as defined below. The contract will normally have small business and small disadvantaged business goals that must be met. As the contractor, you need to determine how to meet these goals and make every effort to meet them. You will also have to make a subcontracting plan and file the SF294 and SF295 forms as required by **FAR Clause 52.219-9 Small Business Subcontracting Plan.** You will not have to get certifications from these firms and may rely on the subcontractor's written representation unless the **FAR Clause 52.219-25 Small Disadvantaged Business Participation Program— Disadvantaged Status and Reporting** is included in the contract. In this case, you must get certification through the SAM database or the SBA's Office of Small Disadvantaged Business Certification and Eligibility for a joint venture partner, team member, or subcontractor representing itself as a small, disadvantaged business concern.

Currently only Small Disadvantaged businesses, Women Owned businesses, HUBZone businesses, and Service- Disabled Veteran-Owned businesses must be certified by the SBA.

FAR Clause 52.219-8 Utilization of Small Business Concerns

As prescribed in 19.708(a), insert the following clause:

Utilization of Small Business Concerns (May 2004)

• It is the policy of the United States that small business concerns, veteran-owned small business concerns, service-disabled veteran-owned small business concerns, HUBZone small business concerns, small disadvantaged business concerns, and women-owned small business concerns shall have the maximum practicable opportunity to participate in performing contracts let by any Federal agency, including contracts and subcontracts for subsystems, assemblies, components, and related services for major systems. It is further the policy of the United States that its prime contractors establish procedures to ensure the timely payment of amounts due pursuant to the terms of their subcontracts with small business concerns, veteran-owned small business concerns, service-disabled veteran-owned small business concerns, HUBZone small business concerns, small disadvantaged business concerns, and women-owned small business concerns.

• The Contractor hereby agrees to carry out this policy in the awarding of subcontracts to the fullest extent consistent with efficient contract performance. The Contractor further agrees to cooperate in any studies or surveys as may be conducted by the United States Small Business Administration or the awarding agency of the United States as may be necessary to determine the extent of the Contractor's compliance with this clause.

• *Definitions.* As used in this contract—

"HUBZone small business concern" means a small business concern that appears on the List of Qualified HUBZone Small Business Concerns maintained by the Small Business Administration.

"Service-disabled veteran-owned small business concern"—

• Means a small business concern—

• Not less than 51 percent of which is owned by one or more service-disabled veterans or, in the case of any publicly owned business, not less than 51 percent of the stock of which is owned by one or more service- disabled veterans; and

Continues on page 85

• The management and daily business operations of which are controlled by one or more service-disabled veterans or, in the case of a service- disabled veteran with permanent and severe disability, the spouse or permanent caregiver of such veteran.

• Service-disabled veteran means a veteran, as defined in 38 U.S.C. 101(2), with a disability that is service-connected, as defined in 38 U.S.C. 101(16).

"Small business concern" means a small business as defined pursuant to Section 3 of the Small Business Act and relevant regulations promulgated pursuant thereto.

"Small disadvantaged business concern" means a small business concern that represents, as part of its offer that—

• It has received certification as a small disadvantaged business concern consistent with 13 CFR part 124, Subpart B;

• No material change in disadvantaged ownership and control has occurred since its certification;

• Where the concern is owned by one or more individuals, the net worth of each individual upon whom the certification is based does not exceed $750,000 after taking into account the applicable exclusions set forth at 13 CFR 124.104(c) (2); and

• It is identified, on the date of its representation, as a certified small disadvantaged business in the database maintained by the Small Business Administration (PRO-Net).

"Veteran-owned small business concern" means a small business concern—

• Not less than 51 percent of which is owned by one or more veterans (as defined at 38 U.S.C. 101(2)) or, in the case of any publicly owned business, not less than 51 percent of the stock of which is owned by one or more veterans; and the management and daily business operations of which are controlled by one or more veterans.

"Women-owned small business concern" means a small business concern—

• That is at least 51 percent owned by one or more women, or, in the case of any publicly owned business, at least 51 percent of the stock of which is owned by one or more women; and

Continues on page 86

• Whose management and daily business operations are controlled by one or more women.

• Contractors acting in good faith may rely on written representations by their subcontractors regarding their status as a small business concern, a veteran-owned small business concern, a service-disabled veteran-owned small business concern, a HUBZone small business concern, a small disadvantaged business concern, or a women-owned small business concern.

(End of clause)

FAR Clause 52.219-25 Small Disadvantaged Business Participation Program—Disadvantaged Status and Reporting

As prescribed in 19.1204(b), insert the following clause:

Small Disadvantaged Business Participation Program—Disadvantaged Status and Reporting (Apr 2008)

• *Disadvantaged status for joint venture partners, team members, and subcontractors*. This clause addresses disadvantaged status for joint venture partners, teaming arrangement members, and subcontractors and is applicable if this contract contains small disadvantaged business (SDB) participation targets. The Contractor shall obtain representations of small disadvantaged status from joint venture partners, teaming arrangement members, and subcontractors through use of a provision substantially the same as paragraph (b)(1)(i) of the provision at FAR 52.219-22, Small Disadvantaged Business Status. The Contractor shall confirm that a joint venture partner, team member, or subcontractor representing itself as a small disadvantaged business concern is a small disadvantaged business concern certified by the Small Business Administration by using the SAM database or by contacting the SBA's Office of Small Disadvantaged Business Certification and Eligibility.

• *Reporting requirement.* If this contract contains SDB participation targets, the Contractor shall report on the participation of SDB concerns at contract completion, or as otherwise provided in this contract. Reporting may be on Optional Form 312, Small Disadvantaged Business Participation Report, in the Contractor's own format providing the same information, or accomplished through using the Electronic Subcontracting Reporting System's Small Disadvantaged Business Participation Report. This report is required for

Continues on page 87

each contract containing SDB participation targets. If this contract contains an individual Small Business Subcontracting Plan, reports shall be submitted with the final Individual Subcontract Report at the completion of the contract.

(End of clause)

Chapter 3
Contracts

1.0 Chapter Description and Use

2.0 Types of Contracts

2.1 Fixed-Price Contracts

2.2 Cost-Reimbursement Contracts

2.3 Incentive Contracts

2.4 Indefinite – Delivery Contracts

2.5 Time and Materials, Labor Hours, and Letter Contracts

3.0 Types of Contracting Officers

4.0 Contracting Officer's Representative

1.0 Chapter Description and Use

The objective of this chapter is to show you all the contract types that the federal government can use and what they are used for. You will understand what the federal government's intent is by knowing what the contract type is. This section also talks about the various contracting officers and their authority, along with what the contracting officer's representative is and what authority he or she has. Understanding these authorities is critical to avoiding claims because only a duly authorized contracting officer can direct a contractor to make a change.

2.0 Types of Contracts

A wide selection of contract types is available to the government to provide needed flexibility in acquiring the large variety and volume of supplies and services required by agencies. Contract types vary according to:

- The degree and timing of the responsibility assumed by the contractor for the costs of performance;
- The amount and nature of the profit incentive offered to the contractor for achieving or exceeding specified standards or goals.

The contract types are grouped into two broad categories: fixed-price contracts and cost-reimbursement contracts. The specific contract types range from firm-fixed-price, in which the contractor has full responsibility for the performance costs and resulting profit (or loss), to cost-plus-fixed-fee, in which the contractor has minimal responsibility for the performance costs and the negotiated fee (profit) is fixed. In between are the various incentive contracts, in which the contractor's responsibility for the performance costs and the profit or fee incentives offered are tailored to the uncertainties involved in contract performance. Indefinite-delivery contracts and time- and-materials, labor-hour, and letter contracts can be either fixed-price contracts or cost-reimbursement type. All these types of contracts can be used for construction-type activities; however, many of the contracts will either be firm-fixed-price or indefinite-delivery, indefinite quantity (IDIQ) contracts.

The most commonly used types of contracts for construction are stand-alone projects that will be firm-fixed-price; multiple award task order contracts (MATOC) that are indefinite-delivery, indefinite-quantity contracts; multiple award construction contracts (MACC) that are indefinite-delivery, indefinite-quantity contracts; job order contracts (JOC) that are indefinite-delivery, indefinite-quantity contracts; single award task order contracts (SATOC) that are indefinite-delivery, indefinite-quantity contracts; and simplified acquisition of base engineering resources (SABER) contracts, which are indefinite-delivery, indefinite-quantity contracts.

Any type of contract can be either design-bid-build or design-build. The indefinite- delivery, indefinite-quantity contracts normally have a base year(s) with option years that can extend the contract up to two to ten years. IDIQ contracts are excellent contracts for contractors because they generally provide business for many years and can be very lucrative. These contracts can also have incentives built into them depending upon the customer's needs.

The determination for what type of contract to be used is made by the contracting officer assigned to the project. The decision is based on the requirements of the project, customer requirements, and other factors as determined by the Federal Acquisition Regulations (FAR). The Small Business Administration (SBA) also may be a part of the decision-making process as it must determine the extent that small businesses will participate in the project.

The following is a list of contracts showing when they are generally used.

2.1 Fixed-Price Contracts

These contracts provide for a firm price or, inappropriate cases, an adjustable price. Fixed-price contracts providing for an adjustable price may include a ceiling price, a target price (including target cost), or both. Unless otherwise specified in the contract, the ceiling price or target price is subject to adjustment only by operation of contract clauses providing for equitable adjustment or other revision of the contract price under stated circumstances.

1.) **Firm-Fixed-Price Contracts.** This contract provides for a price that is not subject to any adjustment based on the contractor's cost experience in performing the contract, and it places upon the contractor maximum risk and full responsibility for all costs and resulting profit or loss. It provides maximum incentive for the contractor to control costs and perform effectively and imposes a minimum administrative burden upon the contracting parties. The government may use a firm-fixed-price contract in conjunction with an award-fee incentive and performance or delivery incentives based solely on factors other than cost. The contract type remains firm-fixed-price when used with these incentives.

2.) **Fixed-Price with Economic Price Adjustment Contracts.** A fixed-price contract with economic price adjustment provides for upward and downward revision of the stated contract price upon the occurrence of specified contingencies. The government may use a fixed-price contract with economic price adjustment in conjunction with an award- fee incentive and performance or delivery incentives based solely on factors other than cost. The contract type remains fixed price with economic price adjustment when used with these incentives.

3.) **Fixed-Price Incentive Contracts.** This is a fixed-price contract that provides for adjusting profit and establishing the final contract price by a formula based on the relationship of final negotiated total cost to total target cost.

4.) **Fixed-Price Contracts with Prospective Price Redetermination.** This contract may be used in acquisitions of quantity production or services for which it is possible to negotiate a fair and reasonable firm fixed price for an initial period, but not for subsequent periods of contract performance.

5.) **Fixed-Ceiling-Price Contracts with Retroactive Price Redetermination.** This contract is used for research and development contracts estimated at $100,000 or less when it is established at the outset that a fair and reasonable firm fixed price cannot be negotiated and that the amount involved, and short performance period make the use of any other fixed-price contract type impracticable.

6.) **Firm-Fixed-Price, Level-Of-Effort Term Contracts.** This contract is used for investigation or study in a specific research and development area. The product of the contract is usually a report showing the results achieved through application of the required level of effort. However, payment is based on the effort expended rather than on the results achieved.

2.2 Cost-Reimbursement Contracts

These contracts provide for payment of allowable incurred costs, to the extent prescribed in the contract. These contracts establish an estimate of total cost for the purpose of obligating funds and establishing a ceiling that the contractor may not exceed without the approval of the CO. Cost-reimbursement contracts are suitable for use only when uncertainties involved in contract performance do not permit costs to be estimated with sufficient accuracy to use any type of fixed-price contract.

1.) **Cost Contract.** This is a cost-reimbursement contract in which the contractor receives no fee. It may be used for research and development work, particularly with nonprofit educational institutions or other nonprofit organizations.

2.) **Cost-Sharing Contracts.** This is a cost-reimbursement contract in which the contractor receives no fee and is reimbursed only for an agreed-upon portion of its allowable costs. A cost-sharing contract may be used when the contractor agrees to absorb a portion of the costs in the expectation of substantial compensation benefits.

3.) **Cost-Plus-Incentive-Fee Contract.** This cost-reimbursement contract provides for an initially negotiated fee to be adjusted later by a formula based on the relationship of total allowable costs to total target costs.

4.) **Cost-Plus-Award-Fee Contract.** This cost-reimbursement contract provides for a fee consisting of (a) a base amount (which may be zero) fixed at inception of the contract and (b) an award amount based upon a judgmental evaluation by the government, sufficient to provide motivation for excellence in contract performance.

5.) **Cost-Plus-Fixed Fee Contract.** This cost-reimbursement contract provides for payment to the contractor of a negotiated fee that is fixed at the inception of the contract. The fixed fee does not vary with the actual cost but may be adjusted because of changes in the work to be performed under the contract. This contract type permits contracting for efforts that might otherwise present too great a risk to contractors but provides the contractor only a minimum incentive to control costs.

2.3 Incentive Contracts

Incentive contracts are used when a firm-fixed-price contract is not appropriate and the required supplies or services can be acquired at lower costs and, in certain instances, with improved delivery or technical performance, by relating the amount of profit or fee payable under the contract to the contractor's performance. Incentive contracts are designed to obtain specific acquisition objectives.

1.) Fixed-Price Incentive Contracts. This is a fixed-price contract that provides for adjusting profit and establishing the final contract price by application of a formula based on the relationship of total final negotiated cost to total target cost. The final price is subject to a price ceiling, negotiated at the outset.

2.) Fixed-Price Incentive (Firm Target) Contracts. This contract specifies a target cost, a target profit, a price ceiling (but not a profit ceiling or floor), and a profit adjustment formula. These elements are all negotiated at the outset. The price ceiling is the maximum that may be paid to the contractor, except for any adjustment under other contract clauses. When the contractor completes performance, the parties negotiate the final cost, and the final price is established by applying the formula. Note: When the final cost is less than the target cost, application of the formula results in a final profit greater than the target profit; conversely, when final cost is more than target cost, application of the formula results in a final profit less than the target profit or even a net loss. If the final negotiated cost exceeds the price ceiling, the contractor absorbs the difference as a loss. Because the profit varies inversely with the cost, this contract type provides a positive, calculable profit incentive for the contractor to control costs.

3.) Fixed-Price Incentive (Successive Targets) Contracts. This type of contract specifies an initial target cost, target profit, and initial profit adjustment formula to be used for establishing the firm's target profit, including a ceiling and floor for the firm's target profit. Note: This formula normally provides for a lesser degree of contractor cost responsibility than a formula for establishing final profit and price; the production point at which the firm target cost and target profit will be negotiated (usually before delivery or shop completion of the first item); a ceiling price that is the maximum that may be paid to the contractor. When the production point specified in the contract is reached, the parties negotiate the firm's target cost, considering cost, experience under the contract, and other pertinent factors. The firm's target profit is established by the formula. At this point, the parties have two alternatives:

- They may negotiate a firm fixed price, using the firm target cost plus target profit as a guide.

- If negotiation of a firm fixed price is inappropriate, they may negotiate a formula for establishing the final price using the firm target cost and target profit. The final cost is then negotiated at completion, and the final profit is established by formula, as under the fixed-price incentive (firm target) contract.

4.) Fixed-Price Contracts with Award Fees. Award-fee provisions may be used in fixed-price contracts when the government wishes to motivate a contractor and other incentives cannot be used because contractor performance cannot be measured objectively. Such contracts will establish a fixed price (including normal profit) for the effort. This price will be paid for satisfactory contract performance. The award fee earned (if any) will be paid in addition to that fixed price.

5.) Cost-Plus-Incentive-Fee Contracts. This cost-reimbursement contract provides for the initially negotiated fee to be adjusted later by a formula based on the relationship of total allowable costs to total target costs. This contract type specifies a target cost, target fee, minimum and maximum fees, and a fee adjustment formula. After contract performance, the fee payable to the contractor is determined in accordance with the formula. The formula provides, within limits, for increases in fee above target fee when total allowable costs are less than target costs and decreases in fee below target fee when total allowable costs exceed target costs. This increase or decrease is intended to provide an incentive for the contractor. This type of contract is generally used for services or development and test programs.

6.) Cost-Plus-Award-Fee Contracts. This cost-reimbursement contract provides for a fee consisting of (1) a base amount fixed at inception of the contract, if applicable and at the discretion of the CO, and (2) an award amount that the contractor may earn in whole or part during performance that is sufficient to provide motivation for excellence in the areas of cost, schedule, and technical performance.

2.4 Indefinite-Delivery Contracts

There are three types of indefinite-delivery contracts: definite-quantity contracts, requirements contracts, and indefinite-quantity contracts. The appropriate type of indefinite-delivery contract is used to acquire supplies and/or services when the exact times and/or quantities of future deliveries are not known at the time of the contract award. Requirements contracts and indefinite-quantity contracts are also known as delivery order contracts or task order contracts.

1.) Definite-Quantity Contracts. This contract provides for delivery of a definite quantity of specific supplies or services for a fixed period, with deliveries or performance to be scheduled at designated locations once ordered.

2.) Requirements Contracts. This contract provides for filling all actual purchase requirements of designated government activities for supplies or services during a specified contract period, with deliveries or performance scheduled by placing orders with the contractor. It is generally used for acquiring any supplies or services when the government anticipates recurring requirements but cannot predetermine the precise quantities that will be needed during a definite period.

3.) Indefinite-Quantity Contracts. This contract provides for an indefinite quantity, within stated limits, of supplies or services during a fixed period. The government places orders for individual requirements, and quantity limits may be stated as number of units or dollar values. This type of contract is used when the government cannot predetermine, above a specified minimum, the precise quantities of supplies or services it will require during the contract period, and it is inadvisable to commit itself for more than a minimum quantity. A job order contract (JOC) is this type of contract.

2.5 Time-and-Materials, Labor-Hours, and Letter Contracts

1.) Time-and-Materials Contracts. This contract provides for acquiring supplies or services based on direct labor hours at specified fixed hourly rates that include wages, overhead, general and administrative expenses and profit, and actual cost for materials. This contract may be used only when it is not possible at the time of placing the contract to estimate accurately the extent or duration of the work or to anticipate costs with any reasonable degree of confidence.

2.) Labor-Hour Contracts. This contract is a variation of the time-and-materials contract, differing only in that materials are not supplied by the contractor.

3.) Letter Contracts. This is a written preliminary contractual instrument that authorizes the contractor to begin manufacturing supplies or performing services immediately. A letter contract may be used when the government's interests demand that the contractor be given a binding commitment so that work can start immediately and when negotiating a definitive contract is not possible in sufficient time to meet the requirement.

3.0 Types of Contracting Officers

The three types of contracting officers are:

1.) Procuring Contracting Officer (PCO). The PCO does the procurement for a very large contract. This type of CO is usually used only on projects where there is a need to manage parts of the contract separately and is generally needed when a contract affects multiple bases that would be much better handled by a CO at each base. Typical examples would be a regional JOC or MATOC contract. The PCO usually has the final determination on a contract because he or she is over the total contract and not just a task order.

2.) Contracting Officer (CO). This person has total contractual authority over the contract. The CO is assigned either by the regional director of contracting for standalone projects or can be assigned by the PCO. If assigned by the PCO, then upon award of a contract/task order, the CO will be assigned by a "Letter of Delegation." This person has full authority to act on behalf of the U.S. government in all contractual matters. When given formal direction from the CO, the contractor, by federal law, must do what is directed and then file a claim if in dispute. The final decision by a CO is binding until overturned by a court. A CO is granted a warrant by the U.S. government to issue and oversee contracts that obligate the government financially and otherwise in all matters relating to a contract for services or goods.

The level of authority of the CO is determined by the level of the warrant, which ranges from $2,000 to unlimited. There are many levels of warrants, but a CO cannot sign a contract or change order without a warrant at least equal to the contract or change order amount. To be granted a warrant, a CO must have certain levels and types of education, government-sponsored courses, and have passed certain tests. A CO can give direction that commits the government both verbally and in writing; however, the CO must either have money in hand or a "promise" that funds are available or will be made available.

3.) Administrative Contracting Officer (ACO). This person is designated by the CO to handle the day-to-day contract actions for a project. The ACO has the authority to make commitments or changes that affect price, quality, quantity, delivery, or any other terms or conditions of the contract that may have been authorized by the CO. The changes that the ACO can make are limited by this authority and by the level of warrant this person has. Generally the ACO will be making construction change orders.

FAR Clause 33.210 Contracting Officer's Authority

Except as provided in this section, contracting officers are authorized, within any specific limitations of their warrants, to decide or resolve all claims arising under or relating to a contract subject to the Act. In accordance with agency policies and 33.214, contracting officers are authorized to use ADR procedures to resolve claims. The authority to decide or resolve claims does not extend to—

- A claim or dispute for penalties or forfeitures prescribed by statute or regulation that another Federal agency is specifically authorized to administer, settle, or determine; or

- The settlement, compromise, payment, or adjustment of any claim involving fraud.

4.0 Contracting Officer's Representative

The Contracting Officer's Representative (COR) is defined as an individual designated in accordance with subsection 201.602-2 of the Defense Federal Acquisition Regulation Supplement and authorized in writing by the CO to perform specific technical or administrative functions. If the CO designates a COR, the contractor will receive a written copy of the designation. It will specify the extent of the COR's authority to act on behalf of the CO.

The COR is not authorized to make any commitments or changes that will affect price, quality, quantity, delivery, or any other term or condition of the contract. Only the CO or the ACO can make commitments or changes of any kind that affect price, quality, quantity, delivery, or any other term or condition of the contract. The COR will usually be designated in the "Notice of Award" letter signed by the CO but can also be designated later. The COR is the CO's "eyes and ears" and is the first person that the CO will go to in a contract dispute.

Chapter 4
Design

1.0 Chapter Description and Use

2.0 Requirements for Registration of Designers

3.0 Correlating Design to RFP and proposal

4.0 Shop Drawings

5.0 Specifications and Drawings

5.1 Partnering and Project Progress Processors

5.2 Stages of Design Submittal

5.3 Specifications

5.4 Drawings

5.5 Design Analysis

6.0 Design Quality Control

6.1 Acceptance of Plan

6.2 Notification of Changes

6.3 DQC Plan

7.0 DrChecks Design Review and Checking System

7.1 Procedures

7.2 Tracking Design Review Comments

8.0 Preliminary Construction/Design Progress Schedule

9.0 Fast – Tracking

9.1 Why the Government Uses Design – Build

9.2 Fast – Track Construction

10.0 Understanding Government Specific Codes

11.0 Anti – Terrorism/Force Protection (AT/FP) Requirements

12.0 LEED

13.0 Procedure for Obtaining Variances after Design is Complete

1.0 Chapter Description and Use:

The objective of this chapter is to show the contractor, architect, and engineers the requirements for design of federal government projects and, more specifically, design-build projects. The design-build process was chosen for analysis as this is generally the most complicated and different process for the designer. The design-build method of construction as used by the federal government is significantly different from the commercial sector as it is designed to shift liability from the government to the contractor, whereas in the commercial sector, the design-build process is designed to save time and get the most "bang for the buck." This process has also become the federal government's project delivery method of choice.

This chapter will show you what design submittals will normally be required; how to incorporate the RFP and proposal into the design; know when the designer must be registered; know what the specifications and drawings must contain and what format to use; know how to develop a design quality control plan; acquaint you with the federal government's design review process (DrChecks); requirements for design schedules; the federal government's fast tracking requirements; how to make the designer aware that the federal government codes and technical manuals may be significantly different from the commercial codes and to become familiar with them; how to make the designer aware that federal government construction requires the use of anti-terrorism/force protection design guidelines and where to find them; the federal government's requirement for "green design" through the LEED process; and shows the process for obtaining a variance after design is complete.

2.0 Requirements for Registration of Designers

This clause requires that all projects be designed by registered architects and engineers. The federal government requires that the architects and engineers be registered in the state where the work is being performed. The intent of this clause was clarified in 2009 by the Council on Federal Procurement of Architectural and Engineering Services stating that "individuals performing architecture, engineering, landscape architecture, or surveying and mapping on federal contracts must be licensed in the state/ jurisdiction where the work is being performed, if the state has such a licensing law." All architects and engineers are subject to liability for defects in design in accordance with the statute of limitations and statute of repose for the states that they are registered in.

FAR Clause 52.236-25, Requirements for Registration of Designers

As prescribed in 36.609-4, insert the following clause:

Requirement for Registration of Designers (June 2003)

Architects or engineers registered to practice in the particular professional field involved in a State, the District of Columbia, or an outlying area of the United States shall prepare or review and approve the design of architectural, structural, mechanical, electrical, civil, or other engineering features of the work.

(End of clause)

3.0 Correlating Design to RFP and Proposal:

The architect and engineers are key players during the proposal preparation for design-build projects. The architect may have to prepare preliminary drawings including floor plans, elevations, and sections that show the government what you and your team propose to meet the RFP requirements. Your team will have to propose materials and systems, i.e. HVAC, electrical, security, etc., for incorporation into the project. This process should be in conjunction with teaming subcontractors, and their recommendations as to materials and systems should be solicited and used wherever possible if they meet the RFP requirements. The proposal will usually have to be prepared in a short period of time (thirty to sixty days is normal), and because the various trades will have to perform a cost estimate, the architect will have to prepare the preliminary drawings first before the rest of the proposal can be prepared.

4.0 Shop Drawings:

Shop drawings as required by **DFAR clause 252.227-7033 Rights in Shop Drawings,** and possibly by **Section 00 73 00 Special Contract Requirements**, are considered by the contract to be an extension of design and as such the DOR must approve them. You also have the responsibility to make sure that the shop drawings are in full compliance with the design drawings, as the design drawings will supersede the shop drawings for legal import.

Shop drawings for a government design-build project very seldom require government approval and generally will be provided to the government as a "For Information Only" submittal. Government design-bid-build contracts generally require numerous superfluous shop drawings; however, through the design-build process you can limit this to only those deemed necessary for construction, quality, or liability reasons.

Limit the number of shop drawings and tests required to only those dictated by the RFP and limit the liability of the contractor and designer. Requiring more than is needed will only cost you more money and opens the door for more government review.

DFAR Clause 252.227-7033 Rights in Shop Drawings

As prescribed at 227.7107-1(c), use the following clause:

Rights in Shop Drawings (Apr 1966)

Shop drawings for construction means drawings, submitted to the Government by the Construction Contractor, subcontractor or any lower-tier subcontractor pursuant to a construction contract, showing in detail (i) the proposed fabrication and assembly of structural elements and (ii) the installation (i.e., form, fit, and attachment details) of materials or equipment. The Government may duplicate, use, and disclose in any manner and for any purpose shop drawings delivered under this contract.

This clause, including this paragraph (b), shall be included in all subcontracts hereunder at any tier.

5.0 Specifications and Drawings:

The specifications and drawings required by the design-build contract are considered "deliverables" as per Section 01 33 16 and are not "approved" by the government but rather "accepted" by the government. The government reviews the design documents only for contract "conformance." All extensions of design, i.e. shop drawings will be approved by the DOR. **FAR Clause 52.236-21 Specifications and Drawings for Construction** and **DFAR Clause 252.236-7001 Contract Drawings and Specifications** implement this requirement.

The basic process and design requirements for each design submitted are as follows: *The Government will delineate all the design requirements and the process here.*

5.1 Partnering and Project Progress Processes:

The "Initial Partnering Conference" may be scheduled and conducted at any time with or following the post-award conference. The government proposes to form a partnership with you to develop a cohesive building team. This partnership will involve the COE project delivery team members, facility users, facility command representatives, installation representatives, DOR, major subcontractors, and your quality control and construction management staff. This partnership will strive to develop a cooperative management team drawing on the strengths of each team member to achieve a quality project within budget and on schedule. This partnership will be bilateral in membership and participation will be totally voluntary.

As part of the partnering process, you and the government will develop, establish, and agree to comprehensive design development processes, including conduct of conferences, expectations of design development at conferences, fast tracking, design acceptance, structural interior design (SID)/furniture, fixtures and equipment (FF&E) design approval, project closeout, etc. The government will explain contract requirements and you, as the design-build contractor, should review their proposed project schedule and suggest ways to streamline processes.

The **Initial Design Conference** may be scheduled and conducted at the project installation any time after the post-award conference, although it is recommended that the partnering process be initiated with or before the initial design conference. Any design work conducted after the award and prior to this conference should be limited to site work and is discouraged for other items. All DORs shall participate in the conference. The purpose of the meeting is to introduce everyone and to make sure any needs you have are assigned and due dates established as well as who will get the information. You, as the contractor, will conduct the initial design conference.

5.2 Stages of Designs Submittals:

The stages of design submittals described below define government expectations with respect to process and content. As the contractor, you must determine how to best plan and execute the design and review process for this project within the parameters listed below. As a minimum, the government expects to see at least one interim and one final design submittal before construction of a design package may proceed and at least one "Design Complete" submittal that documents the accepted design. You may subdivide the design into separate packages for each stage of design and may proceed with construction of a package after the government accepts the final design for that package. (See also discussion on waivers to submission of intermediate design packages where the parties' partner during the design process.)

Site/Utilities: To facilitate fast track design-construction activities you may submit a final (100%) site and utility design as the first design submittal or elect to submit interim and final site and utility design submittals as explained below. Following review, resolution, and incorporation of all government comments and submittal of a satisfactory set of site-utility design documents, after completing all other pre-construction requirements in the contract and after the preconstruction meeting, the government will allow you to proceed with site development activities, including demolition where applicable, within the parameters set forth in the accepted design submittal. For the first site and utility design submission, whether interim or final, the submittal review, comment, and resolution times from this specification apply, except that the government will require a maximum fourteen-calendar day review period, exclusive of mailing time. No on-site construction activities shall begin prior to written government clearance to proceed.

Interim Design Submittals: You may submit either a single interim design for review, representing a complete package with all design disciplines, or split the interim design into smaller, individual design packages as deemed necessary for fast-track construction purposes. As required in Section 01 32 01.00 Project Schedule, you must schedule the design and construction packaging plan to meet the contract completion period. This submission is the government's primary opportunity to review the design for conformance to the solicitation, the accepted contract proposal, and the building codes and reference documents at a point where required revisions may be still made, while minimizing lost design effort to keep the design on track with the contract requirements.

You should designate the interim design submittal(s) as a snapshot and proceed with design development at your own risk. This will cut down the required design time with little risk of having to redo the documents. Remember, the drawings and specifications are yours, and the government can only review them for conformance to the RFP and proposal.

Note: See below for a waiver where the parties establish an effective over-the-shoulder process review procedure through the partnering process, eliminating the need for a formal intermediate design review.

Over-the-Shoulder Process Reviews: To facilitate a streamlined design-build process, you and the government may agree on one-on-one review or small group reviews, electronically, online (if available within your standard design practices), or at your design offices or other agreed location, when practicable to the parties. You and the government will coordinate such reviews to minimize or eliminate disruptions to the design process. Any data required for these reviews will normally be provided in electronic format rather than in hard copy.

If you and the government establish and implement an effective, mutually agreeable partnering procedure for regular (e.g. weekly) over-the-shoulder review procedures that keep the government reviewers fully informed of the progress, contents, design intent, design documentation, etc., of the design package, the government will agree to waive the formal intermediate design review period for that package. You will still need to submit the required intermediate design documentation; however, you and the reviewers may agree on how that material will be provided in lieu of a formal consolidated submission of the package. It should be noted that government funding is extremely limited for non-local travel by design reviewers, so the maximum use of virtual teaming methods must be used. Some possible examples include electronic file sharing, interactive software with online or telephonic conferencing, video conferencing, etc.

The government must still perform its code and contract conformance reviews, so you are encouraged to partner with the reviewers to find ways to facilitate this process as well as meeting or bettering the design-build schedule. You must maintain a fully functional configuration management system to track design revisions, regardless of whether there is a need for a formal intermediate design review. The formal intermediate review procedures form the contractual basis for the official schedule, if the partnering process determines that this review process is best suited for efficient project execution. However, the government pledges to support and promote the partnering process to work with you to find ways to better the design schedule. You and/or your designer will need to keep very accurate meeting minutes as this will take the place of a DrChecks review.

Final Design Submissions: This submittal is required for each design package prior to government acceptance of said package for construction.

Design Complete Submittals: After the final design submission and review conference for a design package, you must revise the design package to incorporate any comments generated and resolved in the final review conferences, perform and document a back-check review, and submit the final, design complete documents, which represent released for construction documents.

Holiday Periods for Government Review or Actions: You should not schedule meetings, government reviews, or responses during the last two weeks of December or other designated government holidays, including the Friday after Thanks- giving, and exclude these same dates and periods for any government actions.

It is important that you and the designer schedule and meet dates for design reviews and any other critical submittals as the lack of a government review can cause serious delays in both the design and construction.

Late Submittals and Reviews: If you can't meet your scheduled submittal date for a design package, you must revise the proposed submittal date and notify the government in writing, at least one week prior to the submittal, to accommodate the government reviewers' other scheduled activities. If a design submittal is over one day late in accordance with the latest revised design schedule, or if notification of a proposed design schedule change is less than seven days from the anticipated design submission receipt date, the government review period may be extended up to seven days due to reviewers' schedule conflicts. If the government is late in meeting its review commitment and the delay increases your cost or delays completion of the project, the **FAR Clauses 52.242-14 Suspension of Work** and **52.249-10 Default** provide the respective remedy or relief for the delay. You should pay special attention to the notification of times under these clauses.

5.3 Specifications:

These may be any one of the major, well-known master guide specification sources (use only one source) such as MASTERSPEC from the American Institute of Architects, SPECTEXT from Construction Specification Institute, or Unified Facility Guide Specifications (UFGS), etc., including specifications from these sources. The DORs must edit and expand the appropriate specifications to ensure that all project design, current code, and regulatory requirements are met. Specifications must clearly identify the appropriate, specific products chosen to meet the contract requirements (i.e. manufacturers' brand names and model numbers or similar product information)

5.4 Drawings:

Drawings must include comments from any previous design conferences incorporated into the documents to provide an interim design for the "package" submitted.

5.5 Design Analysis:

The designers of record will prepare and present design analyses with calculations necessary to substantiate and support all design documents submitted. Address design substantiation as required by the applicable codes and references.

FAR Clause 52.236-21 Specifications and Drawings for Construction

As prescribed in 36.521, insert the following clause:

Specifications and Drawings for Construction (Feb 1997)

The Contractor shall keep on the work site a copy of the drawings and specifications and shall always give the Contracting Officer access thereto. Anything mentioned in the specifications and not shown on the drawings or shown on the drawings and not mentioned in the specifications, shall be of like effect as if shown or mentioned in both. In case of difference between drawings and specifications, the specifications shall govern. In case of discrepancy in the figures, in the drawings, or in the specifications, the matter shall be promptly submitted to the Contracting Officer, who shall promptly make a decision in writing. Any adjustment by the Contractor without such a determination shall be at its own risk and expense. The Contracting Officer shall furnish from time to time such detailed drawings and other information as considered necessary, unless otherwise provided.

Wherever in the specifications or upon the drawings the words "directed," "required," "ordered," "designated," "prescribed," or words of like import are used, it shall be understood that the "direction," "requirement," "order," "designation," or "prescription," of the Contracting Officer is intended and similarly the words "approved," "acceptable," "satisfactory," or words of like import shall mean "approved by," or "acceptable to," or "satisfactory to" the Contracting Officer, unless otherwise expressly stated.

Where "as shown," "as indicated," "as detailed," or words of similar import are used, it shall be understood that the reference is made to the drawings accompanying this contract unless stated otherwise. The word "provided" as used herein shall be understood to mean "provide complete in place," that is "furnished and installed."

Shop drawings means drawings, submitted to the Government by the Contractor, subcontractor, or any lower tier subcontractor pursuant to a construction contract, showing in detail (1) the proposed fabrication and assembly of structural elements, and (2) the installation (i.e., fit, and attachment details) of materials or equipment.

It includes drawings, diagrams, layouts, schematics, descriptive literature. illustrations, schedules, performance and test data, and similar materials furnished by the contractor to explain in detail specific portions of the work required by the contract. The Government may duplicate, use, and disclose in any manner and for any purpose shop drawings delivered under this contract.

If this contract requires shop drawings, the Contractor shall coordinate all such drawings, and review them for accuracy, completeness, and compliance with contract requirements and shall

Continues on page 106

indicate its approval thereon as evidence of such coordination and review. Shop drawings submitted to the Contracting Officer without evidence of the Contractor's approval may be returned for resubmission. The Contracting Officer will indicate an approval or disapproval of the shop drawings and if not approved as submitted shall indicate the Government's reasons therefore. Any work done before such approval shall be at the Contractor's risk. Approval by the Contracting Officer shall not relieve the Contractor from responsibility for any errors or omissions in such drawings, nor from responsibility for complying with the requirements of this contract, except with respect to variations described and approved in accordance with (f) of this clause.

If shop drawings show variations from the contract requirements, the Contractor shall describe such variations in writing, separate from the drawings, at the time of submission. If the Contracting Officer approves any such variation, the Contracting Officer shall issue an appropriate contract modification, except that, if the variation is minor or does not involve a change in price or in time of performance, a modification need not be issued.

The Contractor shall submit to the Contracting Officer for approval four copies (unless otherwise indicated) of all shop drawings as called for under the various headings of these specifications. Three sets (unless otherwise indicated) of all shop drawings, will be retained by the Contracting Officer and one set will be returned to the Contractor.

(End of clause)

Alternate I (Apr 1984). When record shop drawings are required and reproducible shop drawings are needed, add the following sentences to paragraph (g) of the basic clause:

Upon completing the work under this contract, the Contractor shall furnish a complete set of all shop drawings as finally approved. These drawings shall show all changes and revisions made up to the time the equipment is completed and accepted.

Alternate II (Apr 1984). When record shop drawings are required and reproducible shop drawings are not needed, the following sentences shall be added to paragraph (g) of the basic clause:

Upon completing the work under this contract, the Contractor shall furnish _________ Contracting Officer complete by inserting desired amount] sets of prints of all shop drawings as finally approved. These drawings shall show changes and revisions made up to the time the equipment is completed and accepted.

Continues on page 107

DFAR Clause 252.236-7001 Contract Drawings and Specifications

As prescribed in 236.570(a), use the following clause:

Contract Drawings and Specifications (Aug 2000)

The Government will provide to the Contractor, without charge, one set of contract drawings and specifications, except publications incorporated into the technical provisions by reference, in electronic or paper media as chosen by the Contracting Officer.

The Contractor shall—

Check all drawings furnished immediately upon receipt;

Compare all drawings and verify the figures before laying out the work;

Promptly notify the Contracting Officer of any discrepancies;

Be responsible for any errors that might have been avoided by complying with this paragraph (b); and

Reproduce and print contract drawings and specifications as needed.

In general—

Large-scale drawings shall govern small-scale drawings; and

The Contractor shall follow figures marked on drawings in preference to scale measurements.

Omissions from the drawings or specifications or the misdescription of details of work that are manifestly necessary to carry out the intent of the drawings and specifications, or that are customarily performed, shall not relieve the Contractor from performing such omitted or misdescribed details of the work. The Contractor shall perform such details as if fully and correctly set forth and described in the drawings and specifications.

The work shall conform to the specifications and the contract drawings identified on the following index of drawings:

Title	File Drawing	No.

(End of clause)

6.0 Design Quality Control:

As the contractor, you must provide and maintain a design quality control (DQC) plan as an effective quality control program that will ensure that all services required by the design-build contract are performed and provided in a manner that meets professional architectural and engineering quality standards. As a minimum, all documents should be technically reviewed by competent, independent reviewers identified in the DQC plan. The same person or group that produced the product cannot perform the independent technical review (ITR). The designer will correct errors and deficiencies in the design documents prior to submitting them to the government.

You should include in the DQC plan the discipline-specific checklists to be used during the design and quality control of each submittal. These completed checklists must be submitted at each design phase as part of the project documentation. Note: Engineer Regulation 1110-1-12 provides some useful information in developing checklists.

The DQC plan must be implemented by a design quality control manager who has the responsibility of ensuring that all documents on the project have been coordinated. This individual must have verifiable engineering or architectural design experience and be a registered professional engineer or architect. As the contractor, you must notify the CO in writing of the name of the individual and the name of an alternate person assigned to the position.

The CO will notify you in writing of the acceptance of the DQC plan. After acceptance, any changes proposed by you are subject to the acceptance of the CO.

6.1 Acceptance of Plan:

Acceptance of your plan is required prior to the start of design and construction. Acceptance is conditional and is predicated on satisfactory performance during the design and construction. The government can require you to make changes in your CQC plan, including the DQC plan and operations, including removal of personnel, as necessary, to obtain the quality specified.

6.2 Notification of Changes:

After acceptance of the CQC plan, you must notify the CO in writing of any proposed change. Proposed changes are subject to acceptance by the CO.

6.3 DQC PLAN:

Each discipline should have its own DQC manager and specific DQC checklist following a similar format to the architectural DQC checklist.

The DQC manager should mark each item as follows:

DQC Initial – Item has been reviewed and corrected as needed

"NA" – Item is not applicable or is by another discipline

"INC" – Item is still in progress (for interim submittals only)

Submit this checklist to the architect at an agreed date.

The Architectural DQC Manager will verify that each discipline has completed a DQC checklist and will forward the information to the contractor.

General Scope of Review:

Completeness of Drawing Set – Are all required sheets included?

Completeness of Sheets – Is all information required on a given sheet shown?

Inter-coordination of Drawings – Do all references and callouts lead to the right reference/section/detail?

Dimension Check – Are all dimensions shown? Do the strings add up? Are the dimensions consistent between drawings?

Site Plan Coordination – Does site plan layout match civil site plan?

Floor Plan (Background) Coordination – Are all disciplines using the correct floor plan backgrounds to match the architectural floor plan?

Elevations Coordination – Do exterior and interior elevations show louvers and lights?

Roof Plan Coordination – Is mechanical and electrical equipment shown? Does structural roof plan show equipment and weights? Is roof drainage clearly shown?

Architectural/Structural Coordination – Do the architectural sections and details match the structural coordination?

Fire Sprinkler Coordination – Are all areas properly protected as required, including concealed spaces, exterior canopies, and projections? Are areas exempt from fire sprinklers clearly identified?

Language Consistency – Are the same names/callouts used throughout the documents?

Graphic Quality/Consistency – Is the set readable at half size? Does each sheet have the same font, poche, line weights, etc.? Do pochéd/shaded areas and dashed lines align the legend?

Architectural DQC Checklist

This checklist is a basic checklist that must be modified/expanded to reflect the requirements of the actual project.

Submittal Phase:

_______ 100% Civil Submittal Package

_______ Long-Lead Item Submittal Package

_______ 100% Foundation Submittal Package

_______ 60% Interim (OTS)

_______ 100% Final

Submittal Includes:

_______ Building

_______ Site/utilities

Checked By:

Name ______________________

Company ____________________

Discipline ___________________

Drawing Set:

_______ Are all the sheets and details required by this project included in the set?

Title Sheet:

_______ Project Team – Confirm information is complete and spelling correct

_______ Drawing Index – Confirm sheet names, numbers, and order matches drawing index

_______ Vicinity Map – Confirm inclusion

_______ Abbreviations List – Confirm inclusion of abbreviations used on each sheet

_______ Project General Notes – Confirm they are complete and appropriate for project

_______ Project Site Address – Confirm it is shown

_______ Sheet Dates - Confirm all sheets have the same date

_______ Confirm all sheets state "Interim Set" or "Final Set" or "For Construction" (as appropriate)

Code Summary Sheet

_______ Confirm code summary is complete

_______ Confirm fire-rated assembly location and fire rating are identified

Confirm fire-rated walls are shown correctly on floor plans

Confirm fire-rated floor and roof assemblies are shown correctly on sections

Architectural Site Plan

_______ General:

Confirm North arrow and proper orientation

Confirm scale is correct

_______ Confirm site plan layout matches civil and landscape plans layout

________ Confirm building and site improvements are properly dimensioned

Confirm dimension strings add up to total dimension

Confirm dimensions indicate they are to “face of wall,” “column centerline,” “gridline,” etc. (as appropriate)

________ Confirm different types of paving/walkways are shown as graphically distinct

________ Confirm control/construction joint layout in concrete walks/pavement is shown including details/notes

________ Confirm cast-in-place concrete curbs, extruded concrete curbs, and wheel stops are shown and are graphically distinct

________ Confirm painted striping and traffic marks on pavement are shown and dimensioned

________ Confirm traffic and site signage is shown

________ Confirm concrete retaining walls and other site structures are detailed on structural drawings

________ Confirm retaining walls over four feet high are designed/detailed/stamped by engineer

________ Confirm fire hydrants, fire department connection, post indicator valve, bollards, etc. are shown and match those shown on civil drawings

Floor Plan

________ General

Confirm North arrow and proper orientation

Confirm scale is correct

Confirm floor plan layout and grid lines match layout and grid lines shown on structural, mechanical, and electrical sheets

________ General Notes Review

Confirm inclusion of note indicating what point dimensions are taken

_______ Legend Review

Confirm each item is graphically distinct, readable, and descriptions are complete

_______ Dimension Review

Confirm all exterior walls are dimensioned

Confirm all interior walls and columns are dimensioned

Confirm windows and doors are dimensioned

Confirm dimension strings add up to total dimensions shown

_______ Wall Type Review

Confirm fire-rated wall types match layout and rating of rated walls on code summary sheet

Confirm mechanical drawings show corresponding smoke/fire dampers in the correct walls

Confirm half-high walls are designed/detailed to resist lateral loads (may need detail for vertical steel tube braces especially at dead-end walls)

_______ Building and Wall Section Cuts

Confirm each cut has a corresponding section on the sheet noted

Confirm sections are cut at each different major building condition/element

_______ Detail Bubbles

Confirm each bubble has a corresponding detail on the sheet noted

_______ Masonry Exterior Walls

Confirm overall dimensions and rough openings are to brick module

Reflected Ceiling Plan

_______ General

Confirm North arrow and proper orientation

Confirm scale is correct

________ Legend

Confirm poché in legend matches poché on plan in scale and appearance

Confirm similar type ceilings are scheduled (ACT-1, ACT-2, etc.)

Confirm hard ceilings detail or note type of framing support system

________ Confirm ceiling heights are shown in all rooms/areas

________ Confirm exterior soffits are shown

________ Confirm light layout matches layout shown on electrical drawings

________ Confirm HVAC grill layout matches layout shown on mechanical drawings

Roof Plan

________ General

Confirm North arrow and proper orientation

Confirm scale is correct

________ Roofs With Batt Insulation

Confirm ventilation path above insulation (under deck) between eaves and ridge conform to code

Confirm eave and ridge vents are shown/detailed on sections and plans

Confirm ventilation space and paths are shown on sections

Confirm roof structural members are deep enough to accommodate insulation depth plus two inches for ventilation space

Confirm structural drawings do not conflict with or block ventilation path

________ Roof Notes

Confirm roofing system is noted

Confirm rigid roof insulation R-value is noted

Confirm location of tapered insulation areas are noted and shown

________ Roof Drains

Confirm drains are shown and detailed

Confirm rain leader piping is shown on mechanical drawings and matches drains layout

Confirm overflow drains or through-wall scuppers are shown conforming to code

Confirm drain and piping is sized to conform to code (request copy of calculations)

________ Gutters

Confirm gutter is graphically shown and noted or included in legend

Confirm that relationship of downspouts and expansion joints is correctly shown

Confirm that downspout locations match exterior elevations and storm drains connections shown on civil drawings

________ Confirm each different roof edge condition is detailed

________ Asphalt Shingles Over Rigid Insulation – Confirm vent space and 5/8-inch T&G plywood nailer is shown along with adequate screw attachment to roof structure

________ Confirm a roof access ladder/hatch or stair is shown

________ Confirm that maintenance fall protection system or forty-two-inch-high parapet is shown (or owner has waived requirement in writing)

Roof Details

________ Confirm details are complete and constructible

________ Confirm all details shown are called out on the roof plan

Room Finish Schedule

_______ Confirm abbreviations are included on title sheet

_______ Confirm stair floor covering is noted

_______ Confirm elevator floor covering is noted

Door Schedule

_______ Confirm doors are numbered correctly

_______ Confirm all abbreviations are included on title sheet

Door & Window Details

_______ Confirm details are complete and constructible

_______ Confirm all details shown are called out on door schedule or exterior elevations

_______ Confirm details have enough separation between lines to make them easily readable

_______ Confirm details match the floor/wall conditions

_______ Confirm exterior details show primary and secondary weather barriers (sealant, sheet metal, and flexible flashing)

_______ Confirm exterior weather-resistant barrier is shown overlapping interior vapor barrier in depth of exterior wall framing

Exterior Elevations

_______ Confirm all exterior elevations are shown or noted

_______ Confirm bottom of footing line is shown

_______ Confirm existing grade is shown

_______ Confirm finish grade or top of paving is shown as a solid line and noted

_______ Confirm each floor level is shown and noted

________ Confirm roof line is shown dashed on buildings with parapet walls

________ Confirm all exterior finishes are referenced

________ Confirm window or glazing types are shown

________ Masonry Exterior Walls

Confirm brick coursing, pattern, and colors are shown

Confirm doors and windows are sized for masonry module (where appropriate)

Confirm masonry veneer is not supported on wood framing in any location

Confirm structural drawings show steel lintel at head of all openings

Confirm masonry veneer walls show weeps at bottom and vent at top

________ Below Grade Waterproofing

Confirm sections show below grade waterproofing

Building Sections

________ Confirm structure matches what is shown on the structural drawings

________ Confirm vertical dimensions are shown and consistent with dimensions shown on other drawings

________ Confirm floor and roof components are graphically shown and called out

________ Confirm inclusion of fire-rated floor and roof assemblies (where applicable)

________ Confirm building structure allows for fire sprinkler system

Wall Sections

________ Confirm structure matches what is shown on structural drawings

________ Confirm lateral support for parapet walls is shown on structural drawings

________ Confirm below grade waterproofing is shown

_______ Confirm sub-grade, capillary break, concrete slab on grade, and vapor retarder are graphically shown and called out

_______ Confirm building insulation (walls, floor overhangs, roofs) is shown and noted (including R-value)

_______ Confirm rigid foundation insulation is shown and noted (including R-value)

Stair Sections

_______ Wood Stairs (where applicable)

Confirm structural drawings show stair stringers and landing framing and detail stringer support connections at top and bottom

Confirm architectural drawings note treads and risers (should be 1⅛-inch ply wood treads and ¾-inch plywood risers glued and screwed to stringers)

Confirm square or radius nose stair treads are noted (coordinate with requirement of floor covering, if any)

Confirm drawings call out floor sheathing on landings

Confirm half-high walls between stairs runs at landings, and overlooking balconies are properly designed/detailed to resist lateral loads and movement, especially dead-end walls at bottom of stairs (usually need a steel tube to brace laterally)

_______ Pre-Engineered Steel Stairs (where applicable)

Architectural Stairs Exposed to View – Confirm size and configuration of stair stringers and connections have been detailed/noted with a note advising whether stair is required to free-span between floors or if columns are allowed. Confirm top and bottom of stringers are detailed to terminate for best appearance

Confirm square or radius nose stair treads are noted (coordinate with requirement of floor covering, if any)

Confirm stair tread type is shown (steel pan with concrete infill, steel grating, etc.)

_______ Handrails

Confirm both handrails and guardrails are drawn

Confirm radius returns are shown on ends of all handrails

Confirm handrails extend eleven inches plus depth of stair tread beyond face of bottom risers and twelve inches past top risers

Wood Handrails – Confirm each change of direction has a wall bracket shown for proper support

Handrail Support Brackets (if shown): Confirm they are shown for proper support, bottom attachment to handrail, and no more than five feet apart for 1½-inch steel pipe and four feet apart for 1½-inch diameter wood

_______ Guardrails

Confirm forty-two-inch-high guardrails are shown at all locations where drop off exceeds thirty inches

Confirm size of largest opening through guardrail will not permit passage of four-inch sphere

Confirm guardrails are designed/detailed to resist lateral loads and movement

Interior Elevations

_______ Confirm all finish components are called out

_______ Confirm finish components shown match finish schedule

_______ Confirm casework is dimensioned for both width and depth

Interior Details

_______ Confirm details are complete

_______ Confirm size and species of finish wood members are called out

Consultant Drawings

_______ Confirm each sheet has project name and date matching title sheet

_______ Confirm each sheet has been stamped and signed by engineer

_______ Confirm North arrow and proper orientation

_______ Confirm scale is correct

_______ Confirm site and floor plan layout and grid lines match layout and grid lines shown on architectural sheets

Architectural/Owner Coordination

_______ Owner-Furnished Equipment

_______ Confirm inclusion of list of owner-furnished equipment in Division 1 of specs or in equipment schedule on drawings

_______ Confirm contractor unloading, installation, connection, coordination is shown

_______Confirm floor plans show locations and proper dimensions of equipment

_______Confirm backing/support of equipment is shown/specified

_______Confirm electrical and mechanical rough-in/service/connections are provided for each piece of equipment

_______Low Voltage Equipment/Systems (Phones, Data, etc.): Confirm whether wire/ cable is required to be plenum rated and advise owner in writing

_______Owner-Furnished Materials/Finishes

_______Confirm owner-furnished materials/finishes are noted on drawings and finish schedule

_______OFOI – Owner Furnished, Owner Installed

_______OFCI – Owner Furnished, Contractor Installed

_______Confirm subfloor preparation is noted on drawings and specified

Architectural/Plumbing Coordination

Review Requirements:

_______Plumbing and architectural floor plans plotted at same scale

_______Plumbing fixture data sheets (dimensions, features, requirements, mounting options)

Best if reviewed in meeting with mechanical and structural engineers

_______ Background Plan – Confirm plumbing floor plan background matches latest architectural floor plan

_______ Plumbing In/Under Floors

Floor Cleanouts

_______ Confirm cleanout locations shown are easily accessible and do not conflict with casework, equipment, or furniture layout

Floor Drains

_______Confirm drain is located in center of area to be drained or as required to allow uniform floor slope

_______If floor slope is required, confirm slope is shown on architectural floor plan

_______Confirm each type/style of floor drain body and grate is consistent with use of the space and specified floor covering

Floor Drains in Waterproof Floor Assemblies

_______Confirm floor drain body has mechanical clamping ring and/or wide flange to allow permanent means of connecting waterproof membrane to drain for leak-free attachment (membranes under tile setting bed or topping slab require seepage holes in drain body)

_______Confirm drains do not coincide with floor joists, beams, or bearing walls

_______Confirm depth of drain and plumbing trap will fit into floor framing space

Waste, Vent & H/C Water Piping In Framed Floors

________Confirm piping is shown running parallel to framing or framing is open web to allow piping to pass through

________Confirm floor sinks are not located in fire-rated floors or are approved by building official for installation in fire-rated assemblies

Plumbing in Walls

________Confirm wall depths are adequate to receive plumbing pipes (waste, vent, and H/C water)

4" waste requires 5-1/2" stud; back-to-back fixtures require 5-1/2" stud

3" cast iron waste requires 4" stud; back-to-back fixtures require 6" stud

3" plastic waste requires 3-1/2" stud; back-to-back fixtures require 6" stud

2" waste and back-to-back fixtures require 3-1/2" stud

________Confirm wall/chase depths are adequate to receive concealed fixture carriers (wall-hung toilets, lavs, service sinks, and urinals)

________Confirm back-to-back gang toilet rooms have common chase wall between with space between studs for waste and insulated water piping to cross

________Confirm wall depths are adequate to receive rain leader piping (pipe O.D. plus 1" for insulation)

6" pipe requires 7-1/2" stud

4" pipe requires 5-1/2" stud

3" pipe requires 5-1/2" stud

2" pipe requires 3-1/2" stud

Waste Risers

________Confirm riser locations do not conflict with beams, joists, or rim joists

Wall Cleanouts

_______Confirm wall cleanouts are easily accessible and not located behind casework, equipment

Freeze-Proof Hose Bibbs

_______Confirm these are shown in wall deep enough to receive (12" minimum depth) or at intersecting wall

_______Confirm water main risers are not located in exterior walls or cold attics

Plumbing in Attic/On Roof

_______Confirm plumbing roof plan shows roof drains in same location as architectural roof plan

_______Confirm roof drains do not coincide with roof joists, beams, or bearing walls

_______Confirm roof drain leader piping is size required by roof drainage calculations/ code

_______Confirm roof overflow drains terminate at visible location and not tied into rain leaders

_______Confirm detail for support of gas piping on roof acceptable to roofing membrane manufacturer

_______Confirm plumbing vents are not located in valleys or near air intakes on HVAC equipment

_______Confirm water piping is not shown in cold attic (above insulation)

sinks

_______Confirm sinks shown on plumbing plan are in same place as shown on an architectural plan

_______Confirm counters are deep enough to accept sink size without cutting out supports

Structural/Hvac Coordination

Review Recommendations:

________BIM overlay at 100 percent

________HVAC and structural floor plans plotted at same scale

________Equipment data sheets (dimensions, weights, access requirements, mounting options)

Best if reviewed in meeting with mechanical and structural engineers

________Equipment Support (Overlay structural framing plan over HVAC plan)

________Locate each piece of HVAC equipment – Does structural show proper location and weight of equipment?

________Mounting Method – Does method shown on HVAC drawings agree with and work with structural framing shown (curb, sleeper, concrete slab, suspended, pedestal)?

________Clearance Above Ceilings (Overlay structural framing plan over HVAC plan)

________Locate structural beams/headers:

________Do duct heights that cross under these beams/headers allow for ceiling height(s) shown?

________Do any beams/headers conflict with HVAC equipment locations or required installation and access clearances?

________Locate largest sections of ductwork – Is there adequate space above ceiling to fit largest ducts below the structure?

________Does bottom of duct elevation allow room for thickness of duct insulation?

________Does bottom of duct elevation allow room for thickness of fireproofing on beams (if applicable)?

________Does bottom of duct elevation allow room for removal of ceiling tile in lay-in ceilings?

________Does bottom of duct elevation allow room for plumbing pipes?

________Does bottom of duct elevation allow room for fire sprinkler piping?

________Does bottom of duct elevation allow room for electrical conduit?

________Does bottom of duct elevation allow room for recessed lights?

________ Openings in Structure (Overlay structural plan over HVAC plan)

Exterior Walls

________Do structural and HVAC drawings agree on location of openings?

________Does structural give details and/or criteria for ducts passing through exterior walls?

________Confirm opening sizes shown on HVAC, do not exceed size limitations shown on structural.

________Confirm additional reinforcing or framing members are shown at jambs of openings

Bearing Walls

________Do structural and HVAC drawings agree on location of openings?

________Does structural give details and/or criteria for ducts passing through bearing walls?

________Do beams/headers over openings leave enough room for duct sizes shown?

________Confirm opening sizes shown on HVAC, do not exceed size limitations shown on structural

________Confirm additional reinforcing or framing members are shown at jambs of openings

Shear Walls

________Do structural and HVAC drawings agree on location of openings?

________Does structural give details and/or criteria for ducts passing through shear walls?

________Confirm opening sizes shown on HVAC, do not exceed size limitations shown on structural

________Confirm additional reinforcing or framing members are shown at jambs of openings

Floor & Roof Structure

________Do structural and HVAC drawings agree on location of openings?

________Confirm structural framing plan shows each of the required HVAC openings

________Confirm opening sizes shown on structural framing plan agree with duct sizes shown on HVAC (including duct insulation and fire/smoke damper mounting requirements)

________Does structural give details and/or criteria for reinforcing/framing around openings?

7.0 DrChecks Design Review and Checking System:

DrChecks is the government system by which all design review is managed. The system allows all contractors, designers, and government personnel to review a design, including design analysis, etc., and make comments in writing. This web-based system works very well, and its use is mandatory for all government projects.

The contractor and designer must understand how this process can help or hurt them. The contractor can post review comments about the design on DrChecks just as the government can; however, contractors very seldom do this and instead usually confer with the designer. The government reviewers seldom understand the requirements of the RFP or the proposal and often post comments that conflict with these.

Both you and your designer must be cognizant of comments that deviate from the RFP and proposal requirements because if you "concur" with the comments, then you are acknowledging that this is a contract change and that you agree to perform the additional work at no extra charge to the government. You must be thorough in reviewing the comments prior to agreeing to them. And remember that only the CO can make a change to the contract.

7.1 Procedures:

As the contractor, you must develop and maintain effective, acceptable design configuration management (DCM) procedures to control and track all revisions to the design documents after the interim design submission through submission of the as-built documents. During the design process, this will facilitate and help streamline the design and review schedule. After the final design is accepted, this process provides control of and documents revisions to the accepted design. (See Special Contract Requirement: Deviating from the Accepted Design.) The system must include appropriate authorities and concurrences to authorize revisions, including documentation as to why the revision must be made. The DCM data should be always available to the government reviewers. You may use your own internal system with interactive government concurrences where necessary or use the government "DrChecks Design Review and Checking System."

7.2 Tracking Design Review Comments:

Although you may use your own internal system for overall design configuration management, you and the government will use the DrChecks Design Review and Checking System to initiate, respond to, resolve, and track government design compliance review comments. This system may be useful for other data that needs to be interactive or otherwise available for shared use and retrieval. An attachment to the contract will detail how to establish an account and set up the DrChecks system. Note: The design review comments must all be closed out before the government will approve the "Design Complete" documents.

8.0 Preliminary Construction/Design Progress Schedule:

The Preliminary Construction /Design Progress Schedule is generally required by section 01 32 01 of the contract specifications and must include all contractor planned operations for the first ninety calendar days as well as be cost loaded to balance the contract award CLINS shown on the price schedule. The cost loading of the schedule usually satisfies the requirement for the "Schedule of Prices" and will be used for future invoices. This is important because if the CLINS are not added into the schedule properly, the QCS-RMS system will reject it and will not allow an invoice. Be aware that the cost loading will probably skew the actual work schedule. Updated schedules can be submitted at any time, but they must be approved by the CO. All required submittals and approvals should be shown in this schedule. Allow only the minimum time for the government to approve the various items as this could later prove that a compensable delay is warranted. All design packages should be included in this schedule, as well as any anticipated "Fast Track" activities. This schedule must be submitted within fifteen days after "Notice to Proceed" (NTP).

The Initial Project Schedule Submission must include the entire construction sequence, and all fast-track construction activities. It must be more detailed than the preliminary project schedule and submitted within forty-two days after the NTP.

The Design Package Schedule Submission will be a FRAGNET schedule extracted from the preliminary, initial, or updated schedule, which covers the activities associated with that design package, including construction, procurement, and permitting activities. This schedule will be included in the preliminary construction progress schedule and the initial project schedule.

The progress schedules are one of the most important documents you will have and should be treated as such. The government is highly trained in how to read and interpret them so they will be scrutinized.

9.0 Fast – Tracking:

9.1 Why the Government Uses Design – Build:

The Government uses the Design – Build construction process for the following reasons:

Part of transformation goals and objectives

Maximizes flexibility in design solution to meet cost and time goals

Reduce facility costs by 20% from that using existing acquisition methods and criteria

Performance based design criteria

Shortens time for construction—no longer than eighteen months

Fast tracking and streamlined contract execution procedures incorporated

Leverages industry standards and practices

Shifts significant liability to the contractor from the Government

Model design-build RFP can be found at ftp.usace.army.mil/pub/hqusace

9.2 Fast – Track Construction:

Fast Track Construction is encouraged for all government design-build contracts. The obvious advantage of concurrent construction and design will save time. The design of work that is fast tracked should be started first. This requires:

The fast – track design package(s) must be identified early.

The Initial schedule must clearly show the fast-track design and all associated construction activities.

Any required permits must be obtained.

All preconstruction plans must be submitted and approved.

The fast–track design period will have to be short in duration to allow for the review process. Generally, the minimum time for design including reviews is 60 to 90 days.

The design must be carefully reviewed to ensure it meets RFP, proposal, and code requirements. This is critical because government design reviewers do not have an obligation to determine whether the design meets these requirements; however, many violations are caught by the government field personnel, which can cause a lot of extra money to be spent for corrections.

10.0 Understanding Military Specific Codes:

Each RFP contains a section showing both the industry and military criteria. Most design and construction firms are familiar with the industry criteria or codes but are new to the requirements of the military criteria or codes.

Most industry criteria/codes are relatively straightforward, and if references are used, they generally refer to other parts of that code. Military criteria, however, usually refer, within a specific technical guide or manual to numerous other codes, manuals, or technical guides. An example is *Technical Guide for Installation Information Infrastructure Architecture (I3A)*. This technical guide has six pages of references.

Remember that "the devil is in the details." The designer must be totally familiar with the references and requirements and how they pertain to the project. Quite often a simple definition such as *telecommunications room* versus *telecommunications closet* can significantly alter which references will be used.

The designer should not depend on government design reviews to identify the problem areas. If you are unsure about anything in a technical manual or a reference requirement, then put the question in writing and submit it formally through the RFI process. This will make the answer an accepted part of the design and eliminate problems during construction. The government design reviewers are not the same people that will be managing the construction for the government and do not necessarily see things the same way.

Designers and the construction manager need to be aware of design review comments that may add work that is not required by either the RFP or the accepted proposal. These need to be brought to the attention of the government and delineated as to their cost and schedule impact. They should not be accepted until the CO accepts them and agrees to a contract modification. Many contractors have gotten into financial trouble because they accepted changes that went beyond what was originally proposed.

Precedence: In the event of a conflict between references and/or applicable military criteria, the most stringent requirement will apply, unless otherwise noted in the contract. The version in effect at the time of the award will be used throughout the period of the contract unless formally modified by the CO to include the latest version. The designer should make every effort to refrain from referencing military criteria on the plans and in the specifications. No one in the field will be as familiar as the designer with these criteria. It is recommended that the requirements of the military criteria be clearly shown on the plans and in the specifications.

11.0 Anti-Terrorism/Force Protection (AT/FP) Requirements:

The Anti-Terrorism/Force Protection Requirements were mandated by DoD 2000.16, DoD Antiterrorism Standards and they are mandatory for all DoD and various other agency projects. These requirements are in UFC 4-010-01 DoD Minimum Antiterrorism Standards for Buildings – With Change 2 and UFC 4-023-03 Design of Buildings to Resist Progressive Collapse. The requirements are an attempt to minimize damage to government facilities and life from a terrorist attack. These manuals include all items for anti-terrorism/force protection from standoff distances to progressive collapse to windows and airborne contamination. Various levels of protection are required depending on the facility classification.

The UFC 4-010-01 With Change 2 and UFC 4-023-03 have many reference document requirements. The designer must pay special attention to these requirements during design development and needs to be aware that they also add significantly to the cost of construction; allowances must be made for this during proposal/price preparation. Also, many of these materials, such as windows and doors/frames, may have unusually long delivery times. Even items, such as landscaping, will be affected by these requirements.

12.0 Leed:

The design-build projects currently being solicited by the government all require that a contractor meet the "silver" rating (as a minimum) as established by the USGBC. Currently LEED v4.1 is required for LEED documentation.

As the contractor, you must assign a LEED accredited professional responsible to track LEED planning, performance, and documentation for each LEED credit through construction closeout. Incorporate LEED credits in the plans, specifications, and design analyses. Develop LEED supporting documentation as a separable portion of the design analysis and provide each required design submittal. Include a separate LEED project checklist for each non-exempt facility (one checklist may be provided for multiple facilities in accordance with the *LEED-NC Application*

Guide for Multiple Buildings and On-Campus Building Projects and the LEED v4.1 Documentation Requirements and Submittals Checklist with each submittal). Final design submittal for each portion of the work must include all required design documentation relating to that portion of work (example: all site credit design documents with final site design). Submittal requirements are as indicated in LEED v4.1 Documentation Requirements.

Submit all documentation and, if applicable, USGBC Design Phase Review ruling at final design (for fast - track projects with multiple final design submittals, this will be at the last scheduled final design submittal). All project documentation related to LEED must conform to USGBC requirements for both content and format, including audit requirements, and be separate from other design analyses. You must maintain and update the LEED documentation throughout the project process. The designers of record must prepare and present LEED documentation with calculations and other data necessary to substantiate and support all design documents submitted.

The LEED requirements require that both the construction and design phase be documented. You must assign a management team member to collect all documentation for the construction from all subcontractors, vendors, and suppliers. It is highly recommended that this requirement be made a part of each individual subcontract and purchase order. The final submittal of the LEED documentation must be reviewed and approved by the DOR before it is submitted to the government. Final LEED certification may be required by the contractor, or the government as determined by the RFP. If required by the contractor then the cost must be included in the proposal as this cost can be substantial.

13.0 Procedure for Obtaining Variance after Design is Complete:

The designer of record approval is required for extensions of design, critical materials, any deviations from the solicitation, the accepted proposal, or the completed design, equipment whose compatibility with the entire system must be checked, and other items as designated by the CO. In terms of the contract clause entitled "Specifications and Drawings for Construction," these are considered "shop drawings." The DOR must ensure that submittals conform to the solicitation, accepted proposal, and completed design; however, see below for those submittals proposing a deviation to the contract or substitution of a material, system, piece of equipment identified by the manufacturer, brand name, or model description in the accepted contract proposal.

Government concurrence, as well as DOR approval, is required before you may proceed with any proposed deviation to the completed design that still complies with the solicitation and accepted proposal. The government may not concur with any deviation to the design, which could impact furniture, equipment selection, or operations decisions made because of the reviewed and concurred design.

Unless prohibited or provided for elsewhere in the contract, where the accepted proposal named products, systems, materials, or equipment by manufacturer, brand name, and/or model number or other specific identification, and you desire to substitute a manufacturer or model after award you must submit a requested substitution or deviation for government concurrence. The submittal should include substantiation, identifying information, and the DOR's approval, specifying that the substitute/deviation meets the contract requirements and is equal in function, performance quality, and salient features to that in the accepted proposal.

Government approval is also required for any deviations from the solicitation or accepted proposal that might constitute a change to the contract terms, or any item specifically designated as requiring government approval in the solicitation for internal and external color finish selection and other terms as designated by the CO.

The Designer of Record/Contractor RFI process, sometimes called a Design Clarification Request (DCR), must be initiated any time you want to deviate from the solicitation (RFP), accepted proposal, or the completed design. The DOR must approve the deviation before it may be forwarded to the government for either concurrence or approval as necessary. The requested deviation should be submitted to the government using the RFI process through QCS or other government approved processes. (QCS is the government – furnished "Construction Contractor Module of the government's RMS program used by the USACE.) It should be submitted by the CQC Manager after his or her approval, and the DOR approval must accompany the submittal. As the contractor, you may not commence any deviation work until the submittal is approved.

You should set up a system to track all DCRs because numerous DCRs will be generated as the construction progresses.

Chapter 5
Quality Control

1.0 Chapter Description and Use

2.0 Contractor Quality Control Requirements

3.0 Contractor Quality Control Plan (CQCP)

4.0 Preconstruction Submittals

5.0 Submittal Register

6.0 Three-Phase Quality Control Program

- 6.1 Preparatory Phase
- 6.2 Initial Phase
- 6.3 Follow-up Phase
- 6.4 Additional Preparatory and Initial Phases

7.0 Quality Control Manager Qualifications and Certification

8.0 Inspector's Qualifications

9.0 RMS/QCS

1.0 Chapter Description and Use

This chapter details the "Contractor Quality Control" (CQC) requirements that you can expect to have to adhere to in a federal government construction contract. The requirements for an individual solicitation can vary widely, so special attention must be given to the contract clause that contains these requirements. The requirements, processes, and personnel qualifications shown in this section are based on a large design-build project.

The objectives of this chapter are to demonstrate the requirements of the federal government's mandated CQC system; clarify the requirements for the CQC plan and submittal register;

familiarize you with the federal government's three-phase quality control process; detail the qualifications normally required for the CQC manager and specialty inspectors; and acquaint you with the requirement and use of the U.S. Army Corps of Engineers RMS/QCS system.

2.0 Contractor Quality Control Requirements

The government does not perform quality control but instead performs quality assurance. This means that government personnel monitor the contractor quality control program and not the construction. The government will monitor the project for compliance with the RFP, the proposal, and the final design documents.

Government contracts require contractor quality control with the level of quality control determined by the size and complexity of the project. The requirement may be for simple oversight for a small, non-complex project to extensive plans and inspections required for large, complex projects. FAR clause 52.246-12 Inspection of Construction (see Section 7 of this manual) will generally be included in each contract with a separate section, usually Section 01 45 04 further defining the CQC requirements.

You will be responsible for quality control and must establish and maintain an effective quality control system. The quality control system will consist of plans, procedures, and organization necessary to produce a product that complies with the contract requirements. The system will cover all construction design and construction operations, both onsite and offsite, and will be keyed to the proposed design and construction sequence. The government requires that the site project superintendent be responsible for the quality of work on the job, but there may also be a requirement for a CQC manager and/or individual specialty inspectors. Normally the contract will require that the CQC team report to the site project superintendent.

The CQC system is how the project quality is ensured and tracked and is headed by the CQC system manager. The RMS/QCS system is used by the U.S. Army Corps of Engineers for all CQC required documentation, including submittals, RFIs, reports, tests, daily reports, schedules, the three-phase inspection program, transmittals, man hour reports, deficiency tracking, payments, etc. Other agencies use other systems; however, they are very similar in requirements, which extend to the tracking of submittals, testing, inspections, punch lists, and certifications.

This system also pertains to the DQC (see Section 4 of this manual) but the design group must employ a separate independent technical review (ITR) team.

3.0 Contractor Quality Control Plan (CQCP)

As the contractor, you must prepare a quality control plan within thirty days after the "Notice to Proceed," and furnish this to the government for approval in accordance with Sections 01 45 00 and 01 33 00. This plan is critical for the government to allow operations to begin.

The CQCP is arguably the most important plan that will be developed and is the basis for all quality control actions under this contract. This plan is very detailed and must be very complete. The contract requires a DQCP as part of the CQCP and allows interim CQC plans but work outside of the features of work included in an accepted interim plan will not be permitted. The use of interim plans here is highly recommended as this will allow both design demolition and fast tracking to begin.

The government considers this plan to be of high importance and monitors its compliance very carefully.

The following is an outline of what is generally required in a CQCP:

Contents of Contractor Quality Control Plan (Section 01 45 00)

Introduction

1. CQC Organization

Organization structure narrative

Org chart

Acknowledgement of three-phase system

2. Resumes

CQC systems manager

CQC systems manager – alternate

Specialize areas

Civil

Mechanical

Electrical

Structural

Plumbing

Concrete

Testing, Adjusting, and Balancing

Fire Protection

3. Authorization Letters

Letter to the CQC systems manager delegation of duties and authorities

CQC system manager's letters of direction to specialized personnel

4. Submittal Management

System narrative

Documentation

5. Testing Procedures

System narrative

Documentation

6. Three Phases of Control

System narrative

Documentation

7. Deficiencies

System narrative

Documentation

8. Reporting

System narrative

Documentation

9. Definable Features List

4.0 Preconstruction Submittals

The following preconstruction submittals are generally required by Section 01 33 00 of the contract. The contract will state which of these must be submitted and when.

Certificate of insurance

Surety bonds

List of proposed subcontractors (may already be listed in the proposal)

List of proposed products (may already be listed in proposal)

Construction progress schedule

Submittal register

Schedule of Prices

Accident prevention plan

Work plan

Quality control plan

Environmental protection plan

5.0 Submittal Register

There are two types of submittal registers that may be used in a government contract. The first is for a fully designed project that does not require any additional design (design-bid-build type) and the other is for a design-build project that requires full design. The first type will only require that you submit all documents in accordance with the submittal items identified and at the times required. You need to be aware that these documents must be approved by the CQC manager prior to submitting them to the government for approval and that they may take an extreme amount of time (thirty days) to get approved. Submittals that are disapproved may need to go through the entire approval process again and this could take another thirty days. I recommend that you keep accurate records as to when submittals were sent to the government and when they are returned and document any impact this may cause. The courts have held that tardiness by the government in returning submittals is not justification for a claim except if the tardiness causes the contractor harm.

The initial submittal register, as required by the design-build contract and section 01 33 00, must be submitted within fifteen days after notice to proceed. It must include as a minimum the design packages and other initial submittals required elsewhere in the contract. The government requires specific plans, schedules, etc., to be submitted for their approval and as such these must be included in the submittal register. However, the remainder of what needs to be submitted is the prerogative of your design-build team. The DOR should identify required submittals in the specifications and include these in the final submittal register. To further complicate matters, the submittal register also serves as a scheduling document for submittals and will be used to control submittal actions throughout the contract period. The submit dates and need dates used in the submittal register must be coordinated with the project schedule.

The submittal requirements of the plans and specifications should be limited to only those required to ensure compliance with the RFP/proposal, mitigate your liability, and ensure the quality of the final product. Superfluous submittal requirements should be eliminated.

Submit and need dates entered into the project schedule need to be carefully thought out and then entered. Use a fifteen- day minimum time frame between the need and submit dates and stick to these dates. This is important because federal case law does not recognize specific time frames for review, i.e. seven or fifteen days, but instead recognizes whether the excessive review period caused a delay. This is common especially during the design phase as some of the reviewers have trouble closing out comments. This impact must be documented and clearly shown on the updated schedule using the Fragnet process.

The submittal register will be developed and maintained on the government's QCS/ RMS system and must be submitted both electronically and in hard copy.

6.0 Three-Phase Quality Control Program

The three-phase quality control program is required by section 01 45 00 of the contract and is used by all government agencies. It is how you will ensure that the construction, including that of subcontractors and suppliers, complies with the requirements of the contract. At least three phases of control will be conducted by the CQC system manager for each definable feature of the construction work - the preparatory phase, the initial phase, and the follow-up phase.

6.1 Preparatory Phase

This phase is performed prior to beginning work on each definable feature of work after all required plans/documents/materials are approved/accepted, and after copies are at the work site. This phase includes:

A review of each paragraph of applicable specifications, reference codes, and standards, with a copy of those sections applicable to that portion of the work to be accomplished in the field made available to you at the preparatory inspection. These copies must be maintained in the field and available for use by government personnel until final acceptance of the work.

A review of the contract drawings.

Review of provisions made to provide required control inspection and testing.

Examination of the work area to ensure all required preliminary work has been completed and is in compliance with the contract.

A physical examination of required materials, equipment, and sample work to ensure they are on hand, conform to approved shop drawings or submitted data, and are properly stored.

A review of the appropriate activity hazard analysis to ensure safety requirements are met.

Discussion of procedures for controlling quality of the work including repetitive deficiencies. Document construction tolerances and workmanship standards for that feature of work.

A check to ensure the portion of the plan for the work to be performed has been accepted by the CO

6.2 Initial Phase

This phase shall be accomplished at the beginning of a definable feature of work. The following shall be accomplished:

A check of work to ensure it is in full compliance with contract requirements. Review minutes of the preparatory meeting.

Verify adequacy of controls to ensure full contract compliance. Verify required control inspection testing.

Establish level of workmanship and verify it meets minimum acceptable workmanship standards. Compare with required sample panels as appropriate.

Resolve all differences.

Check safety to include compliance with and upgrading of accident prevention plan and activity hazard analysis. Review activity analysis with each worker.

The initial phase should be repeated any time acceptable specified quality standards are not being met.

6.3 Follow-up Phase

Daily checks should be performed to ensure control activities, including control testing, provide continued compliance with contract requirements, until completion of the feature of work. These should be made a matter of record in the CQC documentation. Final follow-up checks should be conducted, and all deficiencies corrected prior to the start of additional features of work that may be affected by the deficient work. As the contractor, you should never build on or conceal non-conforming work.

6.4 Additional Preparatory and Initial Phases

These should be conducted on the same definable features of work if the quality of on-going work is unacceptable; if there are changes in the applicable CQC staff, onsite production supervision, or work crew; if work on a definable feature is resumed after a substantial period of inactivity; or if other problems develop. A "definable feature of work" is "a task that is separate and distinguishable from other tasks."

7.0 Quality Control Manager Qualifications and Certification

The CQC system manager qualifications and certification are required by section 01 45 00 of the contract and state that he or she shall be an individual within the onsite work organization who will be responsible for overall management of CQC and have the authority to act in all CQC matters for you as the contractor. The CQC system manager usually must be a graduate engineer, graduate architect, a graduate of construction management, or an engineering technician with at least two years of college and an ICC certification as a commercial building inspector (residential building inspector certification will be required for military family housing projects), with a minimum of five years construction experience on construction similar to this contract. However, this requirement is sometimes waived if the proposed CQC system manager has a certain amount of experience.

The CQC system manager should be always on the site during construction, be employed by the prime contractor, and assigned no other duties. An alternate for the CQC system manager must be identified in the plan to serve in the event of his or her absence. The requirements for the alternate should be the same as for the designated CQC system manager but he or she may have other duties in addition to serving in a temporary capacity as the acting CQC manager.

In addition to the above experience and/or education requirements, the CQC system manager must have completed the course entitled "Construction Quality Management for Contractors." This course is required for any person who will be overseeing the CQC program. Because people get sick, go on vacation, or quit unexpectedly, you should have several people at the site with at least the "Construction Quality Management for Contractors" course. Quite often, the Associated General Contractors offers the course.

8.0 Inspector Qualifications

The contract (section 01 45 05) will quite often require specialized CQC personnel to perform QC activities, such as witnessing tests or performing inspections. The requirements and CQC personnel qualifications follow.

In addition to CQC personnel specified elsewhere in the contract, you as the contractor need to provide as part of the CQC organization specialized personnel to assist the CQC system manager in the areas of electrical, mechanical, plumbing, civil, structural, environmental, and architectural. These individuals may be employees of the prime or subcontractor; be responsible to the CQC system manager; are not intended to be full time but must be physically present at the construction site during work on their areas of responsibility; and have the necessary education and/or experience in accordance with the experience matrix listed here. These individuals may perform other duties but must be allowed sufficient time to perform their assigned quality control duties as described in the QC plan. One person may cover more than one area, provided he or she is qualified to perform QC activities for the designated areas below and has adequate time to perform these duties:

Experience Matrix

Civil – Graduate civil engineer or construction manager with four years of experience in the type of work being performed on this project or engineering technician with five years related experience.

Mechanical – Graduate mechanical engineer or construction manager with four years related experience or engineering technician with an ICC certification as a commercial mechanical inspector with five years related experience.

Electrical – Graduate electrical engineer or construction manager with four years related experience or engineering technician with an ICC certification as a commercial electrical inspector with five years related experience.

Structural – Graduate structural engineer or construction manager with four years related experience or person with an ICC certification as a reinforced concrete special inspector and structural steel and bolting special inspector (as applicable to the type of construction involved) with five years related experience.

Plumbing – Graduate mechanical engineer or construction manager with four years related experience or person with an ICC certification as a commercial plumbing inspector with five years related experience.

Concrete, Pavements, and Soils Material Technician (present while performing tests) – Two years of experience for the appropriate area.

Testing, Adjusting and Balancing (TAB) Specialist – Must be a member of American Association of Air Balance Council (AABC) or an experienced technician of the firm certified by the National Environmental Balancing Bureau (NEBB) (present while testing, adjusting, and balancing).

Design Quality Control Manager – Registered architect or professional engineer (not required on the construction site).

Registered Fire Protection Engineer – Four years related experience.

Even though the contract states that the specialized CQC personnel must be physically present at the work site during the work on their areas of responsibility, it can generally be agreed with the Government that the specialized CQC person only needs to be present for specific tests and inspections. Usually, these tests and inspections will have to be clearly shown in the schedule and in the CQCP. It is also recommended that a professional inspection company be employed to provide specialized inspection services.

9.0 RMS/QCS

The use of the RMS/QCS system for USACE contracts is required by section 01 45 02 of the contract. Other government agencies may require a similar system, but they will all have the same overall requirements. QCS is a Windows-based program that can be used on a stand-alone personal computer or on a network. It is highly recommended that the software be set up for a network with remote access. The RMS/QCS is used as a government-contractor electronic exchange of information to facilitate the management and oversight of the project. The use of this system is mandatory for all U.S. Army contracts.

QCS is the government-furnished "Construction Contractor Module" of RMS. You, as the contractor, will use QCS, to record, maintain, and submit various information throughout the contract period. The contractor module, user manuals, updates, and training information can be downloaded from the RMS website. QCS provides you with the means to input, track, and electronically share information with the government in the following areas:

Administration

Finances

Quality Control

Submittal Monitoring

Scheduling

Import/Export of Data

Request for Information

Accident Reporting

Safety Exposure Man Hours

Some USACE districts offer training on the RMS/QCS, but most do not. The user manual and video can be downloaded from the RMS website at https://rms.usace.army.mil.

Chapter 6
Safety

1.0 Chapter Description and Use

2.0 Safety Program and Safety Plans

3.0 Accident Prevention Plan

4.0 EM 385-1-1 Safety Manual

5.0 Contractor and Subcontractor Safety Training Requirements

6.0 Activity Hazard Analysis (AHA)

7.0 Environmental Protection Plan

1.0 Chapter Description and Use

This chapter discusses the requirements for the federal government's safety programs and plans and the required use of the U.S. Army Corps of Engineers safety manual EM 385-1-1 but is not meant to teach safety as it must be assumed that the contractor is well versed in OSHA requirements. Although this manual is a USACE manual, all the agencies in the federal government normally require its use. Some small projects may be the exception; however, all agencies must follow the OSHA requirements found in 29 CFR 1926 and 29 CFR 1910.

The important factor to remember is that state safety requirements do not apply on a federal reservation; however, they can apply if the facility is being built on a property being leased by the federal government for its use, i.e. by the General Services Administration. These requirements are based on the normal requirements for a large design-build project and could vary somewhat for a small project. A small project may only require minimal staffing and safety plans.

The objectives of this section are to familiarize you with the safety requirements of a federal government construction contract; comprehend what is required for the safety program, safety plans, accident prevention plan, hazardous material identification, and a drug-free work place; acquaint you with the requirements for the use of the USACE manual EM 385-1-1 and its contractor and subcontractor safety training requirements.

2.0 Safety Program and Safety Plans

Federal contracts require that the contractor, subcontractors, and vendors comply with 29 CFR 1926 and 29 CFR 1910 for safety. This means that all contractors must comply with OSHA guidelines, and in addition, FAR Clause 52.236-13 Accident Prevention requires compliance not only with OSHA regulations but also the U.S. Army Corps of Engineers Safety Manual EM 385-1-1 if the requirement is included in the contract. You will have to develop an accident prevention plan in accordance with the USACE Safety Manual EM 385-1-1. Appendix A details the "Minimum Basic Outline for Accident Prevention Plans." This plan must be a site-specific plan and must interface with the corporate health and safety program and a copy of each of these plans must be available at the site. Other appendices will need to be added to this plan as necessary in accordance with the requirements of EM 385-1-1.

The contractor will have to appoint a site safety and health officer at the beginning of each project. The requirements can vary by contract generally depending upon the size and complexity of the project, but the most prevalent is for a Level III site safety and health officer.

The site safety and health officer requirements and qualifications are as follows:

> The contractor must employ a competent person at each project to function as the site safety and health officer (SSHO) in accordance with EM 385-1-1 Section 01.A.17. The SSHO should have at least the minimum qualifications listed below.
>
> A Level III SSHO should be provided whose SSHO duties will be his or her sole, full-time responsibility. The SSHO must have, as a minimum.
>
>> Five years of safety work on a similar type of construction.
>>
>> Thirty-hour OSHA construction safety class or equivalent within the last five years.
>>
>> An average of at least 24 hours of formal safety training each year for the past five years.
>>
>> Competent person training as required based on applicability (scaffolds, cranes, fall protection, confined space, or others).
>>
>> The accident prevention plan will be the basis for all on-site safety requirements. Appendix A of EM 385-1-1 provides the requirements.

FAR Clause 52.236-13 Accident Prevention

As prescribed in 36.513, insert the following clause:

Accident Prevention (Nov 1991)

(a) The Contractor shall provide and maintain work environments and procedures which will—

> 1) Safeguard the public and Government personnel, property, materials, supplies, and equipment exposed to Contractor operations and activities;
>
> 2) Avoid interruptions of Government operations and delays in project completion dates; and
>
> (3) Control costs in the performance of this contract.

(b) For these purposes on contracts for construction or dismantling, demolition, or removal of improvements, the Contractor shall—

> 1) Provide appropriate safety barricades, signs, and signal lights;
>
> 2) Comply with the standards issued by the Secretary of Labor at 29 CFR Part 1926 and 29 CFR Part 1910; and
>
> 3) Ensure that any additional measures the Contracting Officer determines to be reasonably necessary for the purposes are taken.

(c) If this contract is for construction or dismantling, demolition or removal of improvements with any Department of Defense agency or component, the Contractor shall comply with all pertinent provisions of the latest version of U.S. Army Corps of Engineers Safety and Health Requirements Manual, EM 385-1-1, in effect on the date of the solicitation.

(d) Whenever the Contracting Officer becomes aware of any noncompliance with these requirements or any condition which poses a serious or imminent danger to the health or safety of the public or Government personnel, the Contracting Officer shall notify the Contractor orally, with written confirmation, and request immediate initiation of corrective action. This notice, when delivered to the Contractor or the Contractor's representative at the work site, shall be deemed sufficient notice of the noncompliance and that corrective action is required. After receiving the notice, the Contractor shall immediately take corrective action. If the Contractor fails or refuses to promptly take corrective action, the

Continues on page 147

Contracting Officer may issue an order stopping all or part of the work until satisfactory corrective action has been taken. The Contractor shall not be entitled to any equitable adjustment of the contract price or extension of the performance schedule on any stop work order issued under this clause.

(e) The Contractor shall insert this clause, including this paragraph (e), with appropriate changes in the designation of the parties, in subcontracts.

(End of clause)

As the contractor, you are required by FAR Clause 52.223-3 Hazardous Material Identification and Material Safety Data to list up-front with the proposal any hazardous material that is expected to be used on the project. Identification of the material and material safety data sheets must also be submitted at the same time. Generally, it is seldom done this way because very few of the hazardous materials are known prior to submitting the proposal. Even though the CO can declare that a bidder is nonresponsive if the list does not accompany the proposal, this rarely happens because it then requires the CO to determine which hazardous materials were not listed. However, you must prepare a list of all hazardous materials as soon as they become known and promptly make it available to the CO whenever updated.

FAR Clause 52.223-3 Hazardous Material Identification and Material Safety Data

As prescribed in 23.303, insert the following clause:

Hazardous Material Identification and Material Safety data (Jan 1997)

(a) Hazardous material," as used in this clause, includes any material defined as hazardous under the latest version of Federal Standard No. 313 (including revisions adopted during the term of the contract).

(b) The offeror must list any hazardous material, as defined in paragraph (a) of this clause, to be delivered under this contract. The hazardous material shall be properly identified and include any applicable identification number, such as National Stock Number or Special Item Number. This information shall also be included on the Material Safety Data Sheet submitted under this contract.

Continues on page 148

Material (If none, insert none)	Identification Number
______________________	______________________
______________________	______________________
______________________	______________________

(c) This list must be updated during performance of the contract whenever the Contractor determines that any other material to be delivered under this contract is hazardous.

(d) The apparently successful offeror agrees to submit, for each item as required prior to award, a Material Safety Data Sheet, meeting the requirements of 29 CFR 1910.1200(g) and the latest version of Federal Standard No. 313, for all hazardous material identified in paragraph (b) of this clause. Data shall be submitted in accordance with Federal Standard No. 313, whether the apparently successful offeror is the actual manufacturer of these items. Failure to submit the Material Safety Data Sheet prior to award may result in the apparently successful offeror being considered Non responsible and ineligible for award.

(e) If, after award, there is a change in the composition of the item(s) or a revision to Federal Standard No. 313, which renders incomplete or inaccurate the data submitted under paragraph (d) of this clause, the Contractor shall promptly notify the Contracting Officer and resubmit the data.

(f) Neither the requirements of this clause nor any act or failure to act by the Government shall relieve the Contractor of any responsibility or liability for the safety of Government, Contractor, or subcontractor personnel or property.

(g) Nothing contained in this clause shall relieve the Contractor from complying with applicable Federal, State, and local laws, codes, ordinances, and regulations (including the obtaining of licenses and permits) in connection with hazardous material.

(h) The Government's rights in data furnished under this contract with respect to hazardous material are as follows:

(1) To use, duplicate and disclose any data to which this clause is applicable. The purposes of this right are to—

(i) Apprise personnel of the hazards to which they may be exposed in using, handling, packaging, transporting, or disposing of hazardous materials;

Continues on page 149

(ii) Obtain medical treatment for those affected by the material; and

(iii) Have others use, duplicate, and disclose the data for the Government for these purposes.

(2) To use, duplicate, and disclose data furnished under this clause, in accordance with paragraph (h) (1) of this clause, in precedence over any other clause of this contract providing for rights in data.

(3) The Government is not precluded from using similar or identical data acquired from other sources.

(End of clause)

A drug-free workplace is a requirement of all federal contracts. FAR Clause 52.223- 6 Drug-Free Workplace mandates that the contractor develop and maintain a drug-free awareness program. This clause lists the various requirements of actions that must be taken with employees, what needs to be in the drug-free awareness program postings, and notifications. It is highly recommended that a formal drug-free awareness program be developed, and that random drug testing be implemented. This should include mandatory drug testing after any workplace accident.

FAR Clause 52.223-6 Drug-Free Workplace

As prescribed in 23.505, insert the following clause:

Drug-Free Workplace (May 2001)

(a) Definitions. As used in this clause—

"Controlled substance" means a controlled substance in schedules I through V of section 202 of the Controlled Substances Act (21 U.S.C. 812) and as further defined in regulation at 21 CFR 1308.11 - 1308.15.

"Conviction" means a finding of guilt (including a plea of nolo contendere) or imposition of sentence, or both, by any judicial body charged with the responsibility to determine violations of the Federal or State criminal drug statutes.

"Criminal drug statute" means a Federal or non-Federal criminal statute involving the manufacture, distribution, dispensing, possession, or use of any controlled substance.

Continues on page 150

"Drug-free workplace" means the site(s) for the performance of work done by the Contractor in connection with a specific contract where employees of the Contractor are prohibited from engaging in the unlawful manufacture, distribution, dispensing, possession, or use of a controlled substance.

"Employee" means an employee of a Contractor directly engaged in the performance of work under a government contract. "Directly engaged" is defined to include all direct cost employees and any other Contractor employee who has other than a minimal impact or involvement in contract performance.

"Individual" means an offeror/contractor that has no more than one employee including the offeror/contractor.

(b) The Contractor, if other than an individual, shall—within 30 days after award (unless a longer period is agreed to in writing for contracts of 30 days or more performance duration), or as soon as possible for contracts of less than 30 days performance duration—

(1) Publish a statement notifying its employees that the unlawful manufacture, distribution, dispensing, possession, or use of a controlled substance is prohibited in the Contractor's workplace and specifying the actions that will be taken against employees for violations of such prohibition;

(2) Establish an ongoing drug-free awareness program to inform such employees about—

(i) The dangers of drug abuse in the workplace;

(ii) The Contractor's policy of maintaining a drug-free workplace;

(iii) Any available drug counseling, rehabilitation, and employee assistance programs; and

(iv) The penalties that may be imposed upon employees for drug abuse violations occurring in the workplace;

(3) Provide all employees engaged in performance of the contract with a copy of the statement required by paragraph (b) (1) of this clause;

(4) Notify such employees in writing in the statement required by paragraph (b) (1) of this clause that, as a condition of continued employment on this contract, the employee will—

(i) Abide by the terms of the statement; and

Continues on page 151

(ii) Notify the employer in writing of the employee's conviction under a criminal drug statute for a violation occurring in the workplace no later than 5 days after such conviction;

(5) Notify the Contracting Officer in writing within 10 days after receiving notice under subdivision (b)(4)(ii) of this clause, from an employee or otherwise receiving actual notice of such conviction. The notice shall include the position title of the employee;

(6) Within 30 days after receiving notice under subdivision (b) (4)(ii) of this clause of a conviction, take one of the following actions with respect to any employee who is convicted of a drug abuse violation occurring in the work- place:

(i) Taking appropriate personnel action against such employee, up to and including termination; or

(ii) Require such employee to satisfactorily participate in a drug abuse assistance or rehabilitation program approved for such purposes by a Federal, State, or local health, law enforcement, or other appropriate agency; and

(7) Make a good faith effort to maintain a drug-free workplace through implementation of paragraphs (b) (1) through (b)(6) of this clause.

(c) The Contractor, if an individual, agrees by award of the contract or acceptance of a purchase order, not to engage in the unlawful manufacture, distribution, dispensing, possession, or use of a controlled substance while performing this contract.

(d) In addition to other remedies available to the Government, the Contractor's failure to comply with the requirements of paragraph (b) or (c) of this clause may, pursuant to FAR 23.506, render the Contractor subject to suspension of contract payments, termination of the contract or default, and suspension or debarment.

(End of clause)

3.0 Accident Prevention Plan

An accident prevention plan must be submitted and approved prior to any work starting in the field. Although the FAR clause 52.236-13 does not specifically require an accident prevention plan, it references the requirement to use the USACE safety manual EM 385-1-1, which requires an accident prevention plan. Use Appendix A of that manual for the basic outline of your plan.

The plan needs to be submitted as quickly as possible so that demolition and construction can begin. Section 01 33 00, Scheduling, allows the government a "minimum" of fifteen calendar days to review a submittal, with the usual time being fifteen to thirty calendar days. The USACE normally will require changes before they will approve the plan, so the time for approval can take 8 to 10 weeks from initial submittal.

This plan requirement is also a flow down requirement that ***must*** be included in all subcontracts (see FAR 52.236-13 (e). This requirement mandates that each subcontractor complies with the provisions of EM 385-1-1 but does not necessarily provide the prime contractor with an accident prevention plan.

This type of project does not fall under legal authority of any state's safety and health agency, but it does fall under the rules and regulations of OSHA, so it is highly recommended that all subcontractors provide a hazardous communications plan at a minimum. The OSHA website has templates that you can use to create your hazardous communications plan.

4.0 EM 385-1-1 Safety Manual

The USACE *Safety and Health Requirements* Manual EM 385-1-1, is the safety manual required for all government contracts. As noted earlier, the use of this manual is required by FAR Clause 52.236-13, Accident Prevention. All safety requirements for government contracts emanate from this manual. This manual dictates the requirements for all safety and health plans and accident prevention plans as well as all requirements for safe working environments.

EM 385-1-1 is supposed to follow OSHA requirements very closely; however, it should be noted that there might be some differences. Crane safety, for example, is very strict: The crane must be tested every time it comes on to a military base even though it may be up to date with all state certifications and inspections. Whenever a difference exists between the EM 385-1-1 and OSHA requirements, usually EM 385-1-1 is stricter.

The "Government Construction Agent" (i.e. USACE), other than OSHA, cannot cite a contractor on a government facility but can only stop the job. Only OSHA has police powers. In addition, the state has no authority on a federal government installation. The manual can be downloaded at www.usace.army.mil/ceso/pag HYPERLINK "http://www.usace.army.mil/ceso/pages/home.aspx"es/home.aspx.

5.0 Contractor and Subcontractor Safety Training Requirements

The prime contractor is required to conduct indoctrination and training of all new employees and employees new to the site of the work in accordance with EM 385-1-1, paragraph 01. B. Employees must be provided with safety and health indoctrination prior to the start of work as well as continuous safety and health training to enable them to perform their work in a safe manner. All training and indoctrinations must be documented in writing by date, name, content, and trainer.

Indoctrination and training should be based on the existing safety and health program as outlined in your approved safety and health plan, and it should include (but not be limited to):

Requirements and responsibilities for accident prevention and the maintenance of safe and healthful work environments

General safety and health policies and procedures and pertinent provisions of EM 385-1-1

Employee and supervisor responsibility for reporting all accidents

Provisions for medical facilities and emergency response and procedures for obtaining medical treatment or emergency assistance

Procedures for reporting and correcting unsafe conditions or practices

Job hazards and the means to control/eliminate them, including applicable activity hazard analyses (AHAs)

Specific training as required by EM 385-1-1

All workers must attend a weekly toolbox safety meeting. The meeting must be documented in writing as should the indoctrination briefing. It is highly recommended that you issue a hardhat sticker or some other visible sign to show that the worker has been indoctrinated.

6.0 Activity Hazard Analysis (AHA)

The AHA is required by EM 385-1-1, paragraph 01. A. 13 and must be prepared before beginning each work activity presenting hazards not experienced in previous project operations or where a new work crew or subcontractor is to perform the work. The contractor(s) performing that work activity must prepare an AHA. See Figure 1-2 of EM385-1-1 for an outline of an AHA. An electronic AHA can be found on the HQUSACE Safety Office website: http://www.usace.army.mil/CESO/Pages/ActivityHazardAnalyses.aspx.. The AHA defines the activities being performed and identifies the work sequences, specific anticipated hazards, site conditions, equipment, materials, and the control measures to be implemented to eliminate or reduce each hazard to an acceptable level of risk. Work cannot begin until the AHA for the work activity has been accepted by the government and discussed with all those engaged in the activity, including you as the contractor, subcontractor(s), and government on-site representatives at preparatory and initial control phase meetings.

The names of the competent/quality person(s) required for a particular activity (for example, excavations, scaffolding, fall protection, other activities as specified by OSHA and EM 385-1-1) must be identified in the AHA. Proof of their competency/qualification must be submitted to the government for acceptance prior to the start of that work activity. The AHA will be reviewed and modified as necessary to address changing site conditions, operations, or change of competent/qualified person(s).

All MSDSs for the materials included in the AHA must be attached to the AHA. The government will not allow the item of work to start until the AHA has been accepted. All employees who are to perform the work in accordance with the AHA must be made familiar with its requirements.

7.0 Environmental Protection Plan

This environmental protection plan *must* be submitted and approved before commencing any demolition or construction activities. It is required by Section 01 33 00 of the contract as a preconstruction submittal and by Section 01 57 20 defining the plan requirements. This plan should be submitted and approved prior to commencing any demolition or construction activities and should be submitted as quickly as possible. Contract section 01 33 00, Scheduling, allows the government a "minimum" of 15 calendar days to review a submittal: the usual time is 15 to 30 days. The USACE normally requires changes before approving the plan, so the time for approval can take eight to ten weeks from initial submittal.

Chapter 7
Contract Clauses

1.0 Chapter Description and Use

2.0 FAR Clauses by Reference vs. Full Text

3.0 Professional and Consultant Service Costs

4.0 Security

5.0 Liquidated Damages

6.0 Order of Precedence

7.0 Price Evaluation Preferences

8.0 Small Business Subcontracting Plan

    8.1 Clause Inclusion and Flowdown

    8.2 Recordkeeping

9.0 Davis-Bacon Act (Prevailing Wages)

    9.1 General FAR Requirements

    9.2 Who is Allowed to Work?

    9.3 Site of the Work

    9.4 Wage Determination

    9.5 Pay Determination

    9.6 Work Hours

    9.7 Payrolls and Basic Records

    9.8 Apprentices and Trainees

    9.9 Withholding of Funds

9.10 Contract Flowdown

10.0 Contract Flowdown

11.0 Buy American Act

12.0 Prompt Payment Act

12.1 Progress Payments

12.2 Final Payments

12.3 Payment Requests – U.S. Army Corps of Engineers

12.4 Interest Penalty

12.4.1 Computing Penalty Amount

12.4.2 Additional Interest Penalty

12.5 Prompt Payment for Subcontractors

13.0 Disputes

14.0 The Miller Act

14.1 Requirements

14.2 Alternatives to the Payment Bonds

14.3 Who is Covered by the Miller Act?

14.4 Who is Not Covered by the Miller Act?

14.5 Getting a Copy of the Contractor's Bond

14.6 Non-Payment Recourse under the Miller Act

14.7 Waiver of Right to Civil Action

14.8 Coverage for Taxes in the Performance Bond

15.0 Work by the Contractor

16.0 Differing Site Conditions

17.0 Site Investigations and Conditions Affecting the Work

18.0 Use and Possession Prior to Completion

19.0 Schedules

20.0 Suspension of Work

21.0 Changes

22.0 Government Furnished Property (GFP)

23.0 Inspection of Construction

24.0 Warranty of Construction

25.0 Value Engineering

26.0 Default

27.0 Indian Incentive

28.0 Government Rights

29.0 Levies on Contract Payments

1.0 Chapter Description and Use

This chapter is designed to acquaint you with the meaning and when and how to use the most generally used and important Federal Acquisition Regulations (FAR) clauses that may be found in a solicitation. This is not intended to be a complete listing as there are far too many for the scope of this book.

The objective of this chapter is to detail the meaning of each FAR clause and discuss how and when each should be used. This will empower you with the knowledge to understand your rights under federal law and thus protect yourself whenever a challenge from the federal government arises. A clear understanding of these clauses will greatly help you avoid claims situations and to file the proper documentation and give the necessary notifications to the government to protect your rights.

2.0 FAR Clauses by Reference vs. Full Text

The FAR clauses for a contract/RFP are listed as "Clauses by Reference" or "Clauses by Full Text." Some contracts/RFPs have only "Clauses by Full Text." "Clauses by Reference" are inserted into the contract/RFP by FAR number and name only and the "Clauses by Full Text" are inserts using the full written text of the clause. Most people think that just because the text is fully written that it has more meaning or takes precedence over a "Clause by Reference." This is not the case. Reference clauses and full text clauses are equal in importance except when a clause specifically allows precedence of a "Clause by Full Text" to override a "Clause by Reference."

You should be aware that many FAR and DFAR clauses have references to other clauses and that those clauses may require additional work, notifications, forms, and flowdown requirements that may not be readily apparent. Each agency has supplemental clauses that are like the DFAR clauses. It is recommended that you obtain copies of all FAR and DFAR clauses referenced in the contract/RFP. These can be downloaded at http://acquisition.gov/far and at www.acq.osd.mil.

FAR Clauses by Reference vs. Full Text

Definitions:

P.L.: Public Law, i.e. 92-500. Laws passed by Congress and signed by the president.

U.S.C.: The *United States Code* is the codification by subject matter of the general and permanent laws of the United States. It is divided by broad subjects into fifty titles and published by the Office of the Law Revision Counsel of the U.S. House of Representatives. Since 1926, the U.S.C. has been published every six years. Between editions, annual cumulative supplements are published to present the most current information, e.g. 2 U.S.C. 661.

CFR: The *Code of Federal Regulations* is the codification of the general and permanent rules published in the Federal Register by the executive departments and agencies of the federal government. It is divided into fifty titles that represent broad areas subject to federal regulation. Each volume of the CFR is updated once each calendar year and issued on a quarterly basis.

FAR: The *Federal Acquisition Regulation* is the implementation of rules for the acquisition of contract services for the federal government, e.g. 52.213-12.

DFAR: *Defense Federal Acquisition Regulation* is the DoD supplement to the FAR (e.g. 252.213-7001).

3.0 Professional and Consultant Service Costs

These costs are allowable if they meet the criteria set forth in FAR Clause 31.205-33 Professional and Consultant Service Costs. Professional and consultant services might need to be used on various construction contracts, such as IDIQ contracts, and quite often will be required if a contractor is going to file a claim. There also might be a need when a contractor must prepare a contract modification and a specialty consultant is required. I highly recommend that you keep accurate records to support the use of consultants.

FAR Clause 31.205-33 Professional and consultant service costs.

(a) *Definition.* "Professional and consultant services," as used in this subsection, means those services rendered by persons who are members of a particular profession or possess a special skill and who are not officers or employees of the contractor. Examples include those services acquired by contractors or subcontractors in order to enhance their legal, economic, financial, or technical positions. Professional and consultant services are generally acquired to obtain information, advice, opinions, alternatives, conclusions, recommendations, training, or direct assistance, such as studies, analyses, evaluations, liaison with Government officials, or other forms of representation.

(b) Costs of professional and consultant services are allowable subject to this paragraph and paragraphs (c) through (f) of this subsection when reasonable in relation to the services rendered and when not contingent upon recovery of the costs from the Government (but see 31.205-30 and 31.205-47).

(c) Costs of professional and consultant services performed under any of the following circumstances are unallowable:

(1) Services to improperly obtain, distribute, or use information or data protected by law or regulation (*e.g.,* 52.215-1(e), Restriction on Disclosure and Use of Data).

(2) Services that are intended to improperly influence the contents of solicitations, the evaluation of proposals or quotations, or the selection of sources for contract award, whether award is by the Government, or by a prime contractor or subcontractor.

(3) Any other services obtained, performed, or otherwise resulting in violation of any statute or regulation prohibiting improper business practices or conflicts of interest.

Continues on page 160

(4) Services performed which are not consistent with the purpose and scope of the services contracted for or otherwise agreed to.

(d) In determining the allowability of costs (including retainer fees) in a particular case, no single factor or any special combination of factors is necessarily determinative. However, the contracting officer shall consider the following factors, among others:

(1) The nature and scope of the service rendered in relation to the service required.

(2) The necessity of contracting for the service, considering the contractor's capability in the particular area.

(3) The past pattern of acquiring such services and their costs, particularly in the years prior to the award of Government contracts.

(4) The impact of Government contracts on the contractor's business.

(5) Whether the proportion of Government work to the contractor's total business is such as to influence the contractor in favor of incurring the cost, particularly when the services rendered are not of a continuing nature and have little relationship to work under Government contracts.

(6) Whether the service can be performed more economically by employment rather than by contracting.

(7) The qualifications of the individual or concern rendering the service and the customary fee charged, especially on non-Government contracts.

(8) Adequacy of the contractual agreement for the service (*e.g.,* description of the service, estimate of time required, rate of compensation, termination provisions).

(e) Retainer fees, to be allowable, must be supported by evidence that-

(1) The services covered by the retainer agreement are necessary and customary;

(2) The level of past services justifies the amount of the retainer fees (if no services were rendered, fees are not automatically unallowable);

(3) The retainer fee is reasonable in comparison with maintaining an in-house capability to perform the covered services, when factors such as cost and level of expertise are considered; and

Continues on page 161

(4) The actual services performed are documented in accordance with paragraph (f) of this subsection.

(f) Fees for services rendered are allowable only when supported by evidence of the nature and scope of the service furnished (see also 31.205-38(c)). However, retainer agreements generally are not based on specific statements of work. Evidence necessary to determine that work performed is proper and does not violate law or regulation shall include-

(1) Details of all agreements (*e.g.,* work requirements, rate of compensation, and nature and amount of other expenses, if any) with the individuals or organizations providing the services and details of actual services performed;

(2) Invoices or billings submitted by consultants, including sufficient detail as to the time expended and nature of the actual services provided; and

(3) Consultants' work products and related documents, such as trip reports indicating persons visited and subjects discussed, minutes of meetings, and collateral memoranda and reports.

(End of clause)

4.0 Security

This clause requires identity verification for all employees to show that they have a legal right to work in the United States. Base security performs documentation verification when a person requests a base pass; however, the prime contractor is still responsible for all employee identity verification and documentation. You must enroll in the E-Verify program within thirty calendar days after the contract award if not enrolled already. Once enrolled in the E-Verify system, you will not have to enroll again, and once the employee's background check is completed, he or she will not need to have one completed again.

FAR Clause 52.222-54 Employment Eligibility Verification.

As prescribed in 22.1803, insert the following clause:

Employment Eligibility Verification (May 2022)

(a) *Definitions*. As used in this clause-

Commercially available off-the-shelf (COTS) item—

(1) Means any item of supply that is—

(i) A commercial product (as defined in paragraph (1) of the definition of "commercial product" at Federal Acquisition Regulation (FAR) 2.101);

(ii) Sold in substantial quantities in the commercial marketplace; and

(iii) Offered to the Government, without modification, in the same form in which it is sold in the commercial marketplace; and

(2) Does not include bulk cargo, as defined in 46 U.S.C. 40102(4), such as agricultural products and petroleum products. Per 46 CFR 525.1 (c)(2), "bulk cargo" means cargo that is loaded and carried in bulk onboard ship without mark or count, in a loose unpackaged form, having homogenous characteristics. Bulk cargo loaded into intermodal equipment, except LASH or Seabee barges, is subject to mark and count and, therefore, ceases to be bulk cargo.

Employee assigned to the contract means an employee who was hired after November 6, 1986 (after November 27, 2009, in the Commonwealth of the Northern Mariana Islands), who is directly performing work, in the United States, under a contract that is required to include the clause prescribed at 22.1803. An employee is not considered to be directly performing work under a contract if the employee-

(1) Normally performs support work, such as indirect or overhead functions; and

(2) Does not perform any substantial duties applicable to the contract.

Subcontract means any contract, as defined in 2.101, entered into by a subcontractor to furnish supplies or services for performance of a prime contract or a subcontract. It includes but is not limited to purchase orders, and changes and modifications to purchase orders.

Continues on page 163

Subcontractor means any supplier, distributor, vendor, or firm that furnishes supplies or services to or for a prime Contractor or another subcontractor.

United States, as defined in 8 U.S.C. 1101(a)(38), means the 50 States, the District of Columbia, Puerto Rico, Guam, the Commonwealth of the Northern Mariana Islands, and the U.S. Virgin Islands.

(b) *Enrollment and verification requirements*.

(1) If the Contractor is not enrolled as a Federal Contractor in E-Verify at time of contract award, the Contractor shall-

(i) *Enroll*. Enroll as a Federal Contractor in the E-Verify program within 30 calendar days of contract award;

(ii) *Verify all new employees*. Within 90 calendar days of enrollment in the E-Verify program, begin to use E-Verify to initiate verification of employment eligibility of all new hires of the Contractor, who are working in the United States, whether or not assigned to the contract, within 3 business days after the date of hire (but see paragraph (b)(3) of this section); and

(iii) *Verify employees assigned to the contract*. For each employee assigned to the contract, initiate verification within 90 calendar days after date of enrollment or within 30 calendar days of the employee's assignment to the contract, whichever date is later (but see paragraph (b)(4) of this section).

(2) If the Contractor is enrolled as a Federal Contractor in E-Verify at time of contract award, the Contractor shall use E-Verify to initiate verification of employment eligibility of-

(i) *All new employees*.

(A) *Enrolled 90 calendar days or more*. The Contractor shall initiate verification of all new hires of the Contractor, who are working in the United States, whether or not assigned to the contract, within 3 business days after the date of hire (but see paragraph (b)(3) of this section); or

Continues on page 164

(B) *Enrolled less than 90 calendar days.* Within 90 calendar days after enrollment as a Federal Contractor in E-Verify, the Contractor shall initiate verification of all new hires of the Contractor, who are working in the United States, whether or not assigned to the contract, within 3 business days after the date of hire (but see paragraph (b)(3) of this section); or

(ii) *Employees assigned to the contract.* For each employee assigned to the contract, the Contractor shall initiate verification within 90 calendar days after date of contract award or within 30 days after assignment to the contract, whichever date is later (but see paragraph (b)(4) of this section).

(3) If the Contractor is an institution of higher education (as defined at 20 U.S.C. 1001(a)); a State or local government or the government of a Federally recognized Indian tribe; or a surety performing under a takeover agreement entered into with a Federal agency pursuant to a performance bond, the Contractor may choose to verify only employees assigned to the contract, whether existing employees or new hires. The Contractor shall follow the applicable verification requirements at (b) (1) or (b)(2) respectively, except that any requirement for verification of new employees applies only to new employees assigned to the contract.

(4) *Option to verify employment eligibility of all employees.* The Contractor may elect to verify all existing employees hired after November 6, 1986 (after November 27, 2009, in the Commonwealth of the Northern Mariana Islands), rather than just those employees assigned to the contract. The Contractor shall initiate verification for each existing employee working in the United States who was hired after November 6, 1986 (after November 27, 2009, in the Commonwealth of the Northern Mariana Islands), within 180 calendar days of-

(i) Enrollment in the E-Verify program; or

(ii) Notification to E-Verify Operations of the Contractor's decision to exercise this option, using the contact information provided in the E-Verify program Memorandum of Understanding (MOU).

(5) The Contractor shall comply, for the period of performance of this contract, with the requirements of the E-Verify program MOU.

(i) The Department of Homeland Security (DHS) or the Social Security Administration (SSA) may terminate the Contractor's MOU and deny access to the E-Verify system in accordance with the terms of the MOU. In such case, the Contractor will be referred to a suspension or debarment official.

Continues on page 165

(ii) During the period between termination of the MOU and a decision by the suspension or debarment official whether to suspend or debar, the Contractor is excused from its obligations under paragraph (b) of this clause. If the suspension or debarment official determines not to suspend or debar the Contractor, then the Contractor must reenroll in E-Verify.

(c) *Web site*. Information on registration for and use of the E-Verify program can be obtained via the Internet at the Department of Homeland Security Web site: https://www.e-Verify.gov.

(d) *Individuals previously verified.* The Contractor is not required by this clause to perform additional employment verification using E-Verify for any employee-

(1) Whose employment eligibility was previously verified by the Contractor through the E-Verify program;

(2) Who has been granted and holds an active U.S. Government security clearance for access to confidential, secret, or top secret information in accordance with the National Industrial Security Program Operating Manual; or

(3) Who has undergone a completed background investigation and been issued credentials pursuant to Homeland Security Presidential Directive (HSPD)-12, Policy for a Common Identification Standard for Federal Employees and Contractors.

(e) *Subcontracts*. The Contractor shall include the requirements of this clause, including this paragraph (e) (appropriately modified for identification of the parties), in each subcontract that-

(1) Is for—

(i) Services (except for commercial services that are part of the purchase of a COTS item (or an item that would be a COTS item, but for minor modifications), performed by the COTS provider, and are normally provided for that COTS item); or

(ii) Construction;

(2) Has a value of more than $3,500; and

(3) Includes work performed in the United States.

5.0 Liquidated Damages

Most federal government contracts contain a liquidated damages clause. This clause alleviates you of liability for actual damages flowing from a breach and fixes your liability at an established amount for each day that project completion is inexcusably delayed. Liquidated damages must approximate the foreseeable actual damages, and if it appears to act as a penalty, the courts have held that the provision is unenforceable. This clause can act to your benefit in cases where the potential for actual damages could be very high. Liquidated damages continue until the substantial completion of the project or the "Beneficial Occupancy Date" by the government. The government can also withhold all payments otherwise due to you once the project goes into liquidated damages. The "Beneficial Occupancy Date" is the actual date that the facility can be used for its intended purpose and should not be confused with the date the government "accepts" the facility. This determines the actual date liquidated damages terminates.

FAR Clause 52.211-12 Liquidated Damages-Construction.

As prescribed in 11.503(b), insert the following clause in solicitations and contracts:

Liquidated Damages-Construction (Sept 2000)

(a) If the Contractor fails to complete the work within the time specified in the contract, the Contractor shall pay liquidated damages to the Government in the amount of ___________ *[Contracting Officer insert amount]* for each calendar day of delay until the work is completed or accepted.

(b) If the Government terminates the Contractor's right to proceed, liquidated damages will continue to accrue until the work is completed. These liquidated damages are in addition to excess costs of repurchase under the Termination clause.

6.0 Order of Precedence

The order of precedence for a government design-build contract is of primary importance to you and is shown in section 00 73 00 of the RFP. When you submitted a proposal in accordance with an RFP solicitation from the government detailing how you will meet the requirements of the RFP, the government accepted that proposal and now expects you to provide all that you proposed. The contract requires that the solicitation (RFP) and the "Accepted Proposal" constitute the "Contract." To complicate the process, however, the government includes

"Betterments" and design products as part of the "Order of Precedence," which for this contract is:

1. Betterments: Any portions of the accepted proposal that both conform to and exceed the provisions of the solicitation, defined as any component or system that exceeds the minimum requirements stated in the RFP

2. The provisions of the solicitation

3. All other provisions of the accepted proposal.

4. Any design products including, but not limited to, plans, specifications, engineering studies and analyses, shop drawings, equipment installation drawings, etc. These are "deliverables" under the contract and are not part of the contract itself. Design products must conform to all provisions of the contract in order of precedence.

FAR Clause 52.214-29 Order of Precedence-Sealed Bidding.

As prescribed in 14.201-7(d), insert the following clause:

Order of Precedence-Sealed Bidding (Jan 1986)

Any inconsistency in this solicitation or contract shall be resolved by giving precedence in the following order:

(a) The Schedule (excluding the specifications);

(b) Representations and other instructions;

(c) Contract clauses;

(d) Other documents, exhibits, and attachments; and

(e) The specifications.

7.0 Price Evaluation Preferences

Many solicitations that are not set-asides will contain these clauses. These are designed to give HUBZone small business concerns and small disadvantaged business concerns a price preference in winning federal contracts. These are socio-economic programs designed to assist firms owned and controlled by economically and socially disadvantaged individuals to enter the economic mainstream. This preference is one way the federal government assists these firms.

The price evaluation preference is used only to determine whether a HUBZone small business concern or a small, disadvantaged business concern can be considered the low bidder but not necessarily the lowest most responsive, responsible bidder. If the HUBZone small business concern or the small disadvantaged business concern does not waive its right to this price evaluation preference, then the 10% adjustment (for the HUBZone small business concern) or the designated percentage as shown in FAR Clause 52.219-23 Notice of Price Evaluation Adjustment for Small Disadvantaged Business Concerns will be added to the price of all offers, except offers from HUBZone small business concerns that have not waived the evaluation preference and otherwise successful offers from small business concerns.

The solicitation can contain both the FAR Clause 52.219-4 Notice of Price Evaluation Preference for HUBZone Small Business Concerns and FAR Clause 52.219-23 Notice of Price Evaluation Adjustment for Small Disadvantaged Business Concerns. However, the price evaluation preference for the small, disadvantaged business concerns will be added separately after all other factors have been added. If a contractor is certified as both a HUBZone small business concern and a small, disadvantaged business concern then both factors may be added.

The contractor may waive the price evaluation preference as either a HUBZone small business concern or a small, disadvantaged business concern, and if it does, then the contractor does not have to comply with the agreements in paragraph (d) of either FAR clause. If the contractor does not waive the price evaluation preference, then it must comply with the agreements shown in paragraph (d).

This process does not necessarily determine the firm that will be awarded the contract because the other evaluation factors included in the solicitation could weigh more on the contract award than the price.

FAR Clause 52.219-4 Notice of Price Evaluation Preference for HUBZone Small Business Concerns.

As prescribed in 19.1309(b), insert the following clause:

Notice of Price Evaluation preference for HUBZone Small Business Concerns (Oct 2022)

(a) Evaluation preference.

(1) Offers will be evaluated by adding a factor of 10 percent to the price of all offers, except-

(i) Offers from HUBZone small business concerns that have not waived the evaluation preference; and

(ii) Otherwise successful offers from small business concerns.

(2) The factor of 10 percent shall be applied on a line item basis or to any group of items on which award may be made. Other evaluation factors described in the solicitation shall be applied before application of the factor.

(3) When the two highest rated offerors are a HUBZone small business concern and a large business, and the evaluated offer of the HUBZone small business concern is equal to the evaluated offer of the large business after considering the price evaluation preference, award will be made to the HUBZone small business concern.

(b) *Waiver of evaluation preference.* A HUBZone small business concern may elect to waive the evaluation preference, in which case the factor will be added to its offer for evaluation purposes.

☐ Offeror elects to waive the evaluation preference.

(c) *Joint venture.* A HUBZone joint venture agrees that, in the performance of the contract, at least 40 percent of the aggregate work performed by the joint venture shall be completed by the HUBZone small business parties to the joint venture. Work performed by the HUBZone small business parties to the joint venture must be more than administrative functions.

(End of clause)

8.0 Small Business Subcontracting Plan

This plan is required by FAR Clause 52.219-9 Small Business Subcontracting Plan for contracts awarded to large businesses. Some contracts also may require that small businesses also develop this plan. Normally the goals for subcontractor participation by small business, HUBZone small, small disadvantaged, women-owned small business, veteran owned and service-disabled veteran-owned small businesses will be mandated by the contract. Sometimes the solicitation will require that the contractor meet these minimum goals and then give the contractor the option of increasing these targets in the proposal as a means of strengthening an evaluation factor for small business participation. This should be considered carefully as the penalties for not meeting the goals can be severe.

As the contractor, you must make a "good faith effort" to subcontract with the various small businesses and small disadvantaged businesses. Proper documentation and record keeping is of paramount importance in showing a "good faith effort." The following is recommended to comply with the "good faith effort":

Develop and promote company policy statements that demonstrate the company's support for awarding contracts and subcontracts to small, HUBZone small, small disadvantaged, women-owned small business concerns, veteran-owned and service- disabled veteran-owned small businesses.

Develop and maintain bidders' lists of all the above small business concerns from all possible sources.

Ensure periodic rotation of potential subcontractors on bidders' lists.

Ensure that all these businesses are included on the bidders' list for every subcontract solicitation for products and services they can provide.

Ensure that subcontract procurement "packages" are designed to permit the maximum possible participation of said small businesses.

Review subcontract solicitations to remove statements, clauses, etc., that might tend to restrict or prohibit these small businesses' participation.

Ensure that the subcontract bid proposal reviewer documents its reasons for not selecting any low bids submitted by these business concerns.

Oversee the establishment and maintenance of contract and subcontract award records.

Attend or arrange for the attendance of company counselors at business opportunity workshops, minority business enterprise seminars, trade fairs, etc.

Request sources from the SBA's Procurement Marketing and Access Network (PRO- Net).

Directly or indirectly counsel these small business concerns on subcontracting opportunities and how to prepare bids to the company.

Provide notice to subcontractors concerning penalties for misrepresentations of business status as small, HUBZone small, small disadvantaged, women-owned small business concerns, veteran-owned and service-disabled veteran-owned small businesses for the purpose of obtaining a subcontract that is to be included as part or all of a goal contained in the contractor's subcontracting plan.

Conduct or arrange training for purchasing personnel regarding the intent and impact of Public Law 95-907 on purchasing procedures.

Develop and maintain an incentive program for buyers that supports the sub- contracting program.

Monitor the company's performance and make any adjustments necessary to achieve the subcontract plan goals.

Prepare and submit timely reports.

Coordinate the company's activities during compliance reviews by federal agencies.

8.1 Clause Inclusion and Flowdown

FAR Clause 52.219-9(d)(9) requires that you provide assurances that you will include the FAR Clause 52.219-8, Utilization of Small Business Concerns, in all subcontracts that offer further subcontracting opportunities.

FAR Clause 52.219-9(d)(9) also requires that you agree in this plan to require all sub-contractors, except small business concerns, that receive subcontracts more than $1 million for construction to adopt a plan that complies with the requirements of FAR Clause 52.219-9 Small Business Subcontracting Plan.

8.2 Recordkeeping

FAR Clause 52.219-9(d) (11) requires a list of the types of records your company will maintain to demonstrate the procedures adopted to comply with the requirements and goals in the subcontracting plan. These records include, but are not limited to, the following:

Small, HUBZone small, small disadvantaged, women-owned small business concerns, veteran-owned and service-disabled veteran-owned small businesses source lists, guides, and other data identifying such vendors

Organizations contacted for these same small businesses' sources

On a contract-by-contract basis, records on all subcontract solicitations over $100,000 that indicate for each solicitation:

Whether small business concerns were solicited, and if not, why not.

Whether HUBZone small business concerns were solicited, and if not, why not.

Whether small, disadvantaged business concerns were solicited, and if not, why not.

Whether women-owned small business concerns were solicited, and if not, why not.

Whether service-disabled veteran-owned small business concerns were solicited, and if not, why not.

Reasons for the failure of said solicited business concerns to receive the subcontract award.

Records to support other outreach efforts, e.g., contacts with minority and small business trade associations, attendance at small, HUBZone small, minority, women- owned small business concerns, veteran-owned and service-disabled veteran-owned small businesses procurement conference and trade fairs.

Records to support internal activities to (1) guide and encourage purchasing personnel, e.g., workshops, seminars, training programs, incentive awards; and (2) monitor activities to evaluate compliance.

On a contract-by-contract basis, records to support subcontract award data including the name, address, and business size of each subcontractor. Note: This item is not required for company commercial plans.

Other records to support your compliance with the subcontracting plan:

Paragraph (d) (10) (iii) of this clause requires that the SF Form 294 be submitted to the government semi-annually and at project completion. This form is to be used for each individual project. This same clause also requires that the SF Form 295 be submitted semi-annually on March 31 and September 30 of each year. Correctly completing these forms is essential. Every attempt should be made to meet the goals as agreed to in the contract. The FAR clause 52.219-16 Liquidated Damages – Subcontracting Plan allows the government to assess liquidated damages in an amount equal to the actual dollar amount by which you as the contractor failed to achieve each subcontract goal.

The instructions on the back side of these forms explain how to fill them out; however, it is very important that the instructions for blocks 10a through 16 should be read very carefully and followed very closely. There are numerous places where a subcontractor may overlap into more than one block; i.e. a woman-owned small business that may also qualify as a HUBZone small business would be added to Blocks 12 and 14. By not following these instructions carefully, the report may become skewed and erroneously show you as not making your goals when in fact you may have met them.

Standard Form 295 is a summary subcontract report that encompasses all the active federal contracts you currently have. It will have the same dollars and percentages that the SF 294 has if you have only one federal contract. Distribution is as shown on the forms.

(End of clause)

FAR Clause 52.219-9 Small Business Subcontracting Plan.

As prescribed in 19.708(b), insert the following clause:

Small Business Subcontracting Plan (Sep 2023)

(a) This clause does not apply to small business concerns.

(b) *Definitions*. As used in this clause—

Alaska Native Corporation (ANC) means any Regional Corporation, Village Corporation, Urban Corporation, or Group Corporation organized under the laws of the State of Alaska in accordance with the Alaska Native Claims Settlement Act, as amended (43 U.S.C. 1601, *et seq.*) and which is considered a minority and economically disadvantaged concern under the criteria at 43 U.S.C. 1626(e)(1). This definition also includes ANC direct and indirect subsidiary corporations, joint ventures, and partnerships that meet the requirements of 43 U.S.C. 1626(e)(2).

Commercial plan means a subcontracting plan (including goals) that covers the offeror's fiscal year and that applies to the entire production of commercial products and commercial services sold by either the entire company or a portion thereof (*e.g.,* division, plant, or product line).

Commercial product means a product that satisfies the definition of "commercial product" in Federal Acquisition Regulation (FAR) 2.101.

Commercial service means a service that satisfies the definition of "commercial service" in FAR 2.101.

Continues on page 174

Electronic Subcontracting Reporting System (eSRS) means the government-wide, electronic, web-based system for small business subcontracting program reporting. The eSRS is located at http://www.esrs.gov.

Indian tribe means any Indian tribe, band, group, pueblo, or community, including native villages and native groups (including corporations organized by Kenai, Juneau, Sitka, and Kodiak) as defined in the Alaska Native Claims Settlement Act (43 U.S.C. 1601 et seq.), that is recognized by the Federal Government as eligible for services from the Bureau of Indian Affairs in accordance with 25 U.S.C. 1452(c). This definition also includes Indian-owned economic enterprises that meet the requirements of 25 U.S.C. 1452(e).

Individual subcontracting plan means a subcontracting plan that covers the entire contract period (including option periods), applies to a specific contract, and has goals that are based on the offeror's planned subcontracting in support of the specific contract, except that indirect costs incurred for common or joint purposes may be allocated on a prorated basis to the contract.

Master subcontracting plan means a subcontracting plan that contains all the required elements of an individual subcontracting plan, except goals, and may be incorporated into individual subcontracting plans, provided the master subcontracting plan has been approved.

Reduced payment means a payment that is for less than the amount agreed upon in a subcontract in accordance with its terms and conditions, for supplies and services for which the Government has paid the prime contractor.

Subcontract means any agreement (other than one involving an employer-employee relationship) entered into by a Federal Government prime Contractor or subcontractor calling for supplies or services required for performance of the contract or subcontract.

Total contract dollars means the final anticipated dollar value, including the dollar value of all options.

Untimely payment means a payment to a subcontractor that is more than 90 days past due under the terms and conditions of a subcontract for supplies and services for which the Government has paid the prime contractor.

(c)

(1) The Offeror, upon request by the Contracting Officer, shall submit and negotiate a subcontracting plan, where applicable, that separately addresses subcontracting with small business, veteran-owned small business, service-disabled veteran-owned small business,

Continues on page 175

HUBZone small business, small, disadvantaged business, and women-owned small business concerns. If the Offeror is submitting an individual subcontracting plan, the plan must separately address subcontracting with small business, veteran-owned small business, service-disabled veteran-owned small business, HUBZone small business, small, disadvantaged business, and women-owned small business concerns, with a separate part for the basic contract and separate parts for each option (if any). The subcontracting plan shall be included in and made a part of the resultant contract. The subcontracting plan shall be negotiated within the time specified by the Contracting Officer. Failure to submit and negotiate the subcontracting plan shall make the Offeror ineligible for award of a contract.

(2)

(i) The Contractor may accept a subcontractor's written representations of its size and socioeconomic status as a small business, small disadvantaged business, veteran-owned small business, service-disabled veteran-owned small business, or a women-owned small business if the subcontractor represents that the size and socioeconomic status representations with its offer are current, accurate, and complete as of the date of the offer for the subcontract.

(ii) The Contractor may accept a subcontractor's representations of its size and socioeconomic status as a small business, small, disadvantaged business, veteran-owned small business, service-disabled veteran-owned small business, or a women-owned small business in the System for Award Management (SAM) if–

(A) The subcontractor is registered in SAM; and

(B) The subcontractor represents that the size and socioeconomic status representations made in SAM are current, accurate, and complete as of the date of the offer for the subcontract.

(iii) The Contractor may not require the use of SAM for the purposes of representing size or socioeconomic status in connection with a subcontract.

(iv) In accordance with 13 CFR 121.411, 126.900, 127.700, and 128.600, a contractor acting in good faith is not liable for misrepresentations made by its subcontractors regarding the subcontractor's size or socioeconomic status.

(d) The Offeror's subcontracting plan shall include the following:

Continues on page 176

(1) Separate goals, expressed in terms of total dollars subcontracted, and as a percentage of total planned subcontracting dollars, for the use of small business, veteran-owned small business, service-disabled veteran-owned small business, HUBZone small business, small, disadvantaged business, and women-owned small business concerns as subcontractors. For individual subcontracting plans, and if required by the Contracting Officer, goals shall also be expressed in terms of percentage of total contract dollars, in addition to the goals expressed as a percentage of total subcontract dollars. The Offeror shall include all subcontracts that contribute to contract performance and may include a proportionate share of products and services that are normally allocated as indirect costs. In accordance with 43 U.S.C. 1626:

(i) Subcontracts awarded to an ANC or Indian tribe shall be counted towards the subcontracting goals for small business and small disadvantaged business concerns, regardless of the size or Small Business Administration certification status of the ANC or Indian tribe; and

(ii) Where one or more subcontractors are in the subcontract tier between the prime Contractor and the ANC or Indian tribe, the ANC or Indian tribe shall designate the appropriate Contractor(s) to count the subcontract towards its small business and small disadvantaged business subcontracting goals.

(A) In most cases, the appropriate Contractor is the Contractor that awarded the subcontract to the ANC or Indian tribe.

(B) If the ANC or Indian tribe designates more than one Contractor to count the subcontract toward its goals, the ANC or Indian tribe shall designate only a portion of the total subcontract award to each Contractor. The sum of the amounts designated to various Contractors cannot exceed the total value of the subcontract.

(C) The ANC or Indian tribe shall give a copy of the written designation to the Contracting Officer, the prime Contractor, and the subcontractors in between the prime Contractor and the ANC or Indian tribe within 30 days of the date of the subcontract award.

(D) If the Contracting Officer does not receive a copy of the ANC's or the Indian tribe's written designation within 30 days of the subcontract award, the Contractor that awarded the subcontract to the ANC or Indian tribe will be considered the designated Contractor.

Continues on page 177

(2) A statement of–

(i) Total dollars planned to be subcontracted for an individual subcontracting plan; or the Offeror's total projected sales, expressed in dollars, and the total value of projected subcontracts, including all indirect costs except as described in paragraph (g) of this clause, to support the sales for a commercial plan;

(ii) Total dollars planned to be subcontracted to small business concerns (including ANC and Indian tribes);

(iii) Total dollars planned to be subcontracted to veteran-owned small business concerns;

(iv) Total dollars planned to be subcontracted to service-disabled veteran-owned small business;

(v) Total dollars planned to be subcontracted to HUBZone small business concerns;

(vi) Total dollars planned to be subcontracted to small, disadvantaged business concerns (including ANCs and Indian tribes); and

(vii) Total dollars planned to be subcontracted to women-owned small business concerns.

(3) A description of the principal types of supplies and services to be subcontracted, and an identification of the types planned for subcontracting to-

(i) Small business concerns;

(ii) Veteran-owned small business concerns;

(iii) Service-disabled veteran-owned small business concerns;

(iv) HUBZone small business concerns;

(v) Small disadvantaged business concerns; and

(vi) Women-owned small business concerns.

(4) A description of the method used to develop the subcontracting goals in paragraph (d) (1) of this clause.

Continues on page 178

(5) A description of the method used to identify potential sources for solicitation purposes (*e.g.*, existing company source lists, SAM, veterans service organizations, the National Minority Purchasing Council Vendor Information Service, the Research and Information Division of the Minority Business Development Agency in the Department of Commerce, or small, HUBZone, small disadvantaged, and women-owned small business trade associations). A firm may rely on the information contained in SAM as an accurate representation of a concern's size and ownership characteristics for the purposes of maintaining a small, veteran-owned small, service-disabled veteran-owned small, HUBZone small, small disadvantaged, and women-owned small business source list. Use of SAM as its source list does not relieve a firm of its responsibilities (*e.g.*, outreach, assistance, counseling, or publicizing subcontracting opportunities) in this clause.

(6) A statement as to whether or not the Offeror included indirect costs in establishing subcontracting goals, and a description of the method used to determine the proportionate share of indirect costs to be incurred with–

(i) Small business concerns (including ANC and Indian tribes);

(ii) Veteran-owned small business concerns;

(iii) Service-disabled veteran-owned small business concerns;

(iv) HUBZone small business concerns;

(v) Small disadvantaged business concerns (including ANC and Indian tribes); and

(vi) Women-owned small business concerns.

(7) The name of the individual employed by the Offeror who will administer the Offeror's subcontracting program, and a description of the duties of the individual.

(8) A description of the efforts the Offeror will make to assure that small business, veteran-owned small business, service-disabled veteran-owned small business, HUBZone small business, small, disadvantaged business, and women-owned small business concerns have an equitable opportunity to compete for subcontracts.

(9) Assurances that the Offeror will include the clause of this contract entitled "Utilization of Small Business Concerns" in all subcontracts that offer further subcontracting opportunities, and that the Offeror will require all subcontractors (except small business concerns) that receive subcontracts in excess of the applicable threshold specified in FAR 19.702(a) on the date of subcontract award, with further subcontracting possibilities to adopt a subcontracting plan that complies with the requirements of this clause.

Continues on page 179

(10) Assurances that the Offeror will–

(i) Cooperate in any studies or surveys as may be required;

(ii) Submit periodic reports so that the Government can determine the extent of compliance by the Offeror with the subcontracting plan;

(iii) After November 30, 2017, include subcontracting data for each order when reporting subcontracting achievements for indefinite-delivery, indefinite-quantity *contracts with* individual subcontracting plans *where the contract is intended* for use by multiple agencies;

(iv) Submit the Individual Subcontract Report (ISR) and/or the Summary Subcontract Report (SSR), in accordance with paragraph (l) of this clause using the Electronic Subcontracting Reporting System (eSRS) at http://www.esrs.gov. The reports shall provide information on subcontract awards to small business concerns (including ANCs and Indian tribes that are not small businesses), veteran-owned small business concerns, service-disabled veteran-owned small business concerns, HUBZone small business concerns, small disadvantaged business concerns (including ANCs and Indian tribes that have not been certified by the Small Business Administration as small disadvantaged businesses), women-owned small business concerns, and for NASA only, Historically Black Colleges and Universities and Minority Institutions. Reporting shall be in accordance with this clause, or as provided in agency regulations;

(v) Ensure that its subcontractors with subcontracting plans agree to submit the ISR and/or the SSR using eSRS;

(vi) Provide its prime contract number, its unique entity identifier, and the e-mail address of the Offeror's official responsible for acknowledging receipt of or rejecting the ISRs, to all first-tier subcontractors with subcontracting plans so they can enter this information into the eSRS when submitting their ISRs; and

(vii) Require that each subcontractor with a subcontracting plan provide the prime contract number, its own unique entity identifier, and the e-mail address of the subcontractor's official responsible for acknowledging receipt of or rejecting the ISRs, to its subcontractors with subcontracting plans.

(11) A description of the types of records that will be maintained concerning procedures that have been adopted to comply with the requirements and goals in the plan, including establishing source lists; and a description of the offeror's efforts to locate small business,

Continues on page 180

veteran-owned small business, service-disabled veteran-owned small business, HUBZone small business, small disadvantaged business, and women-owned small business concerns and award subcontracts to them. The records shall include at least the following (on a plant-wide or company-wide basis, unless otherwise indicated):

(i) Source lists (*e.g.,* SAM), guides, and other data that identify small business, veteran-owned small business, service-disabled veteran-owned small business, HUBZone small business, small, disadvantaged business, and women-owned small business concerns.

(ii) Organizations contacted in an attempt to locate sources that are small business, veteran-owned small business, service-disabled veteran-owned small business, HUBZone small business, small, disadvantaged business, or women-owned small business concerns.

(iii) Records on each subcontract solicitation resulting in an award of more than the simplified acquisition threshold, as defined in FAR 2.101 on the date of subcontract award, indicating-

(A) Whether small business concerns were solicited and, if not, why not;

(B) Whether veteran-owned small business concerns were solicited and, if not, why not;

(C) Whether service-disabled veteran-owned small business concerns were solicited and, if not, why not;

(D) Whether HUBZone small business concerns were solicited and, if not, why not;

(E) Whether small, disadvantaged business concerns were solicited and, if not, why not;

(F) Whether women-owned small business concerns were solicited and, if not, why not; and

(G) If applicable, the reason award was not made to a small business concern.

(iv) Records of any outreach efforts to contact-

(A) Trade associations;

Continues on page 181

(B) Business development organizations;

(C) Conferences and trade fairs to locate small, HUBZone small, small disadvantaged, service-disabled veteran-owned, and women-owned small business sources; and

(D) Veterans service organizations.

(v) Records of internal guidance and encouragement provided to buyers through-

(A) Workshops, seminars, training, etc.; and

(B) Monitoring performance to evaluate compliance with the program's requirements.

(vi) On a contract-by-contract basis, records to support award data submitted by the offeror to the Government, including the name, address, and business size of each subcontractor. Contractors having commercial plans need not comply with this requirement.

(12) Assurances that the Offeror will make a good faith effort to acquire articles, equipment, supplies, services, or materials, or obtain the performance of construction work from the small business concerns that it used in preparing the bid or proposal, in the same or greater scope, amount, and quality used in preparing and submitting the bid or proposal. Responding to a request for a quote does not constitute use in preparing a bid or proposal. The Offeror used a small business concern in preparing the bid or proposal if–

(i) The Offeror identifies the small business concern as a subcontractor in the bid or proposal or associated small business subcontracting plan, to furnish certain supplies or perform a portion of the subcontract; or

(ii) The Offeror used the small business concern's pricing or cost information or technical expertise in preparing the bid or proposal, where there is written evidence of an intent or understanding that the small business concern will be awarded a subcontract for the related work if the Offeror is awarded the contract.

(13) Assurances that the Contractor will provide the Contracting Officer with a written explanation if the Contractor fails to acquire articles, equipment, supplies, services or materials or obtain the performance of construction work as described in (d)(12) of this clause. This written explanation must be submitted to the Contracting Officer within 30 days of contract completion.

Continues on page 182

(14) Assurances that the Contractor will not prohibit a subcontractor from discussing with the Contracting Officer any material matter pertaining to payment to or utilization of a subcontractor.

(15) Assurances that the offeror will pay its small business subcontractors on time and in accordance with the terms and conditions of the underlying subcontract and notify the contracting officer when the prime contractor makes either a reduced or an untimely payment to a small business subcontractor (see 52.242-5).

(e) In order to effectively implement this plan to the extent consistent with efficient contract performance, the Contractor shall perform the following functions:

(1) Assist small business, veteran-owned small business, service-disabled veteran-owned small business, HUBZone small business, small, disadvantaged business, and women-owned small business concerns by arranging solicitations, time for the preparation of bids, quantities, specifications, and delivery schedules so as to facilitate the participation by such concerns. Where the Contractor's lists of potential small business, veteran-owned small business, service-disabled veteran-owned small business, HUBZone small business, small, disadvantaged business, and women-owned small business subcontractors are excessively long, reasonable effort shall be made to give all such small business concerns an opportunity to compete over a period of time.

(2) Provide adequate and timely consideration of the potentialities of small business, veteran-owned small business, service-disabled veteran-owned small business, HUBZone small business, small, disadvantaged business, and women-owned small business concerns in all "make-or-buy" decisions.

(3) Counsel and discuss subcontracting opportunities with representatives of small business, veteran-owned small business, service-disabled veteran-owned small business, HUBZone small business, small, disadvantaged business, and women-owned small business firms.

(4) Confirm that a subcontractor representing itself as a HUBZone small business concern is certified by SBA as a HUBZone small business concern by accessing SAM or by accessing the Dynamic Small Business Search (DSBS) at *https://web.sba.gov/ pro-net/ search/ dsp_dsbs.cfm.*

(5) Provide notice to subcontractors concerning penalties and remedies for misrepresentations of business status as small, veteran-owned small business, HUBZone small, small disadvantaged, or women-owned small business for the purpose of obtaining

Continues on page 183

a subcontract that is to be included as part or all of a goal contained in the Contractor's subcontracting plan.

(6) For all competitive subcontracts over the simplified acquisition threshold, as defined in FAR 2.101 on the date of subcontract award, in which a small business concern received a small business preference, upon determination of the successful subcontract offeror, prior to award of the subcontract the Contractor must inform each unsuccessful small business subcontract offeror in writing of the name and location of the apparent successful offeror and if the successful subcontract offeror is a small business, veteran-owned small business, service-disabled veteran-owned small business, HUBZone small business, small disadvantaged business, or women-owned small business concern.

(7) Assign each subcontract the NAICS code and corresponding size standard that best describes the principal purpose of the subcontract.

(f) A master subcontracting plan on a plant or division-wide basis that contains all the elements required by paragraph (d) of this clause, except goals, may be incorporated by reference as a part of the subcontracting plan required of the Offeror by this clause; provided-

(1) The master subcontracting plan has been approved;

(2) The Offeror ensures that the master subcontracting plan is updated as necessary and provides copies of the approved master subcontracting plan, including evidence of its approval, to the Contracting Officer; and

(3) Goals and any deviations from the master subcontracting plan deemed necessary by the Contracting Officer to satisfy the requirements of this contract are set forth in the individual subcontracting plan.

(g) A commercial plan is the preferred type of subcontracting plan for contractors furnishing commercial products and commercial services. The commercial plan shall relate to the offeror's planned subcontracting generally, for both commercial and Government business, rather than solely to the Government contract. Once the Contractor's commercial plan has been approved, the Government will not require another subcontracting plan from the same Contractor while the plan remains in effect, as long as the product or service being provided by the Contractor continues to meet the definition of a commercial product or commercial service. A Contractor with a commercial plan shall comply with the reporting requirements stated in paragraph (d) (10) of this clause by submitting one SSR in eSRS for all contracts covered by its commercial plan.

Continues on page 184

A Contractor authorized to use a commercial subcontracting plan shall include in its subcontracting goals and in its SSR all indirect costs, with the exception of those such as the following: Employee salaries and benefits; payments for petty cash; depreciation; interest; income taxes; property taxes; lease payments; bank fees; fines, claims, and dues; original equipment manufacturer relationships during warranty periods (negotiated up front with the product); utilities and other services purchased from a municipality or an entity solely authorized by the municipality to provide those services in a particular geographical region; and philanthropic contributions. This report shall be acknowledged or rejected in eSRS by the Contracting Officer who approved the plan. This report shall be submitted within 30 days after the end of the Government's fiscal year.

(h) Prior compliance of the offeror with other such subcontracting plans under previous contracts will be considered by the Contracting Officer in determining the responsibility of the offeror for award of the contract.

(i) A contract may have no more than one subcontracting plan. When a contract modification exceeds the subcontracting plan threshold in FAR 19.702(a), or an option is exercised, the goals of the existing subcontracting plan shall be amended to reflect any new subcontracting opportunities. When the goals in a subcontracting plan are amended, these goal changes do not apply retroactively.

(j) Subcontracting plans are not required from subcontractors when the prime contract contains the clause at FAR 52.212-5, Contract Terms and Conditions Required to Implement Statutes or Executive Orders-Commercial Products and Commercial Services, or when the subcontractor provides a commercial product or commercial service subject to the clause at FAR 52.244-6, Subcontracts for Commercial Products and Commercial Services, under a prime contract.

(k) The failure of the Contractor or subcontractor to comply in good faith with (1) the clause of this contract entitled "Utilization of Small Business Concerns;" or (2) an approved plan required by this clause, shall be a material breach of the contract and may be considered in any past performance evaluation of the Contractor.

(l) The Contractor shall submit ISRs and SSRs using the web-based eSRS at http://www.esrs.gov. Purchases from a corporation, company, or subdivision that is an affiliate of the Contractor or subcontractor are not included in these reports. Subcontract awards by affiliates shall be treated as subcontract awards by the Contractor. Subcontract award data reported by the Contractor and subcontractors shall be limited to awards made to their immediate next-tier subcontractors. Credit cannot be taken for awards made to lower tier subcontractors, unless the Contractor or subcontractor has been designated to receive a small business or small disadvantaged business

Continues on page 185

credit from an ANC or Indian tribe. Only subcontracts involving performance in the United States, or its outlying areas should be included in these reports with the exception of subcontracts under a contract awarded by the State Department or any other agency that has statutory or regulatory authority to require subcontracting plans for subcontracts performed outside the United States and its outlying areas.

(1) *ISR.* This report is not required for commercial plans. The report is required for each contract containing an individual subcontracting plan.

(i) The report shall be submitted semi-annually during contract performance for the periods ending March 31 and September 30. A report is also required for each contract within 30 days of contract completion. Reports are due 30 days after the close of each reporting period, unless otherwise directed by the Contracting Officer. Reports are required when due, regardless of whether there has been any subcontracting activity since the inception of the contract or the previous reporting period. When the Contracting Officer rejects an ISR, the Contractor shall submit a corrected report within 30 days of receiving the notice of ISR rejection.

(ii)

(A) When a subcontracting plan contains separate goals for the basic contract and each option, as prescribed by FAR 19.704(c), the dollar goal inserted on this report shall be the sum of the base period through the current option; for example, for a report submitted after the second option is exercised, the dollar goal would be the sum of the goals for the basic contract, the first option, and the second option.

(B) If a subcontracting plan has been added to the contract pursuant to 19.702 a)(1)(iii) or 19.301-2(e), the Contractor's achievements must be reported in the ISR on a cumulative basis from the date of incorporation of the subcontracting plan into the contract.

(iii) When a subcontracting plan includes indirect costs in the goals, these costs must be included in this report.

(iv) The authority to acknowledge receipt or reject the ISR resides–

(A) In the case of the prime Contractor, with the Contracting Officer; and

(B) In the case of a subcontract with a subcontracting plan, with the entity that awarded the subcontract.

Continues on page 186

(2) *SSR.*

(i) Reports submitted under individual contract plans–

(A) This report encompasses all subcontracting under prime contracts and subcontracts with an executive agency, regardless of the dollar value of the subcontracts. This report also includes indirect costs on a prorated basis when the indirect costs are excluded from the subcontracting goals.

(B) The report may be submitted on a corporate, company or subdivision (*e.g.* plant or division operating as a separate profit center) basis, unless otherwise directed by the agency.

(C) If the Contractor or a subcontractor is performing work for more than one executive agency, a separate report shall be submitted to each executive agency covering only that agency's contracts, provided at least one of that agency's contracts is over the applicable threshold specified in FAR 19.702(a), and the contract and contains a subcontracting plan. For DoD, a consolidated report shall be submitted for all contracts awarded by military departments/agencies and/or subcontracts awarded by DoD prime contractors.

(D) The report shall be submitted annually by October 30 for the twelve-month period ending September 30. When a Contracting Officer rejects an SSR, the Contractor shall submit a revised report within 30 days of receiving the notice of SSR rejection.

(E) Subcontract awards that are related to work for more than one executive agency shall be appropriately allocated.

(F) The authority to acknowledge or reject SSRs in eSRS, including SSRs submitted by subcontractors with subcontracting plans, resides with the Government agency awarding the prime contracts unless stated otherwise in the contract.

(ii) *Reports submitted under a commercial plan-*

(A) The report shall include all subcontract awards under the commercial plan in effect during the Government's fiscal year and all indirect costs.

(B) The report shall be submitted annually, within thirty days after the end of the Government's fiscal year.

Continues on page 187

(C) If a Contractor has a commercial plan and is performing work for more than one executive agency, the Contractor shall specify the percentage of dollars attributable to each agency.

(D) The authority to acknowledge or reject SSRs for commercial plans resides with the Contracting Officer who approved the commercial plan.

(End of clause)

Alternate I (Nov 2016). As prescribed in 19.708 (b) (1)(i), substitute the following paragraph (c)(1) for paragraph (c)(1) of the basic clause:

(c)(1) The apparent low bidder, upon request by the Contracting Officer, shall submit a subcontracting plan, where applicable, that separately addresses subcontracting with small business, veteran-owned small business, service-disabled veteran-owned small business, HUBZone small business, small, disadvantaged business, and women-owned small business concerns. If the bidder is submitting an individual subcontracting plan, the plan must separately address subcontracting with small business, veteran-owned small business, service-disabled veteran-owned small business, HUBZone small business, small, disadvantaged business, and women-owned small business concerns, with a separate part for the basic contract and separate parts for each option (if any). The plan shall be included in and made a part of the resultant contract. The subcontracting plan shall be submitted within the time specified by the Contracting Officer. Failure to submit the subcontracting plan shall make the bidder ineligible for the award of a contract

Alternate II (Nov 2016). As prescribed in 19.708 (b) (1)(ii), substitute the following paragraph (c)(1) for paragraph (c)(1) of the basic clause:

(c)(1) Proposals submitted in response to this solicitation shall include a subcontracting plan that separately addresses subcontracting with small business, veteran-owned small business, service-disabled veteran-owned small business, HUBZone small business, small, disadvantaged business, and women-owned small business concerns. If the Offeror is submitting an individual subcontracting plan, the plan must separately address subcontracting with small business, veteran-owned small business, service-disabled veteran-owned small business, HUBZone small business, small, disadvantaged business, and women-owned small business concerns, with a separate part for the basic contract and separate parts for each option (if any). The plan shall be included in and made a part of the resultant contract. The subcontracting plan shall be negotiated within the time specified by the Contracting Officer. Failure to submit and negotiate a subcontracting plan shall make the Offeror ineligible for award of a contract.

Continues on page 188

Alternate III (Jun 2020). As prescribed in 19.708 (b) (1)(iii), substitute the following paragraphs (d)(10) and (l) for paragraphs (d)(10) and (l) in the basic clause:

(d)(10) Assurances that the offeror will—

(i) Cooperate in any studies or surveys as may be required;

(ii) Submit periodic reports so that the Government can determine the extent of compliance by the Offeror with the subcontracting plan;

(iii) Submit Standard Form (SF) 294 Subcontracting Report for Individual Contract in accordance with paragraph (l) of this clause. Submit the Summary Subcontract Report (SSR), in accordance with paragraph (l) of this clause using the Electronic Subcontracting Reporting System (eSRS) at http://www.esrs.gov. The reports shall provide information on subcontract awards to small business concerns (including ANCs and Indian tribes that are not small businesses), veteran-owned small business concerns, service-disabled veteran-owned small business concerns, HUBZone small business concerns, small disadvantaged business concerns (including ANCs and Indian tribes that have not been certified by the Small Business Administration as small disadvantaged businesses), women-owned small business concerns, and for NASA only, Historically Black Colleges and Universities and Minority Institutions. Reporting shall be in accordance with this clause, or as provided in agency regulations; and

(iv) Ensure that its subcontractors with subcontracting plans agree to submit the SF 294 in accordance with paragraph (l) of this clause. Ensure that its subcontractors with subcontracting plans agree to submit the SSR in accordance with paragraph (l) of this clause using the eSRS.

(l) The Contractor shall submit a SF 294. The Contractor shall submit SSRs using the web-based eSRS at http://www.esrs.gov. Purchases from a corporation, company, or subdivision that is an affiliate of the Contractor or subcontractor are not included in these reports. Subcontract awards by affiliates shall be treated as subcontract awards by the Contractor. Subcontract award data reported by the Contractor and subcontractors shall be limited to awards made to their immediate next-tier subcontractors. Credit cannot be taken for awards made to lower tier subcontractors, unless the Contractor or subcontractor has been designated to receive a small business or small disadvantaged business credit from an ANC or Indian tribe. Only subcontracts involving performance in the U.S., or its outlying areas should be included in these reports with the exception of subcontracts under a contract awarded by the State Department or any other agency that has statutory or regulatory authority to require subcontracting plans for subcontracts performed outside the United States and its outlying areas.

Continues on page 189

(1) *SF 294*. This report is not required for commercial plans. The report is required for each contract containing an individual subcontracting plan. For Contractors the report shall be submitted to the Contracting Officer, or as specified elsewhere in this contract. In the case of a subcontract with a subcontracting plan, the report shall be submitted to the entity that awarded the subcontract.

(i) The report shall be submitted semi-annually during contract performance for the periods ending March 31 and September 30. A report is also required for each contract within 30 days of contract completion. Reports are due 30 days after the close of each reporting period, unless otherwise directed by the Contracting Officer. Reports are required when due, regardless of whether there has been any subcontracting activity since the inception of the contract or the previous reporting period. When a Contracting Officer rejects a report, the Contractor shall submit a revised report within 30 days of receiving the notice of report rejection.

(ii)

(A) When a subcontracting plan contains separate goals for the basic contract and each option, as prescribed by FAR 19.704(c), the dollar goal inserted on this report shall be the sum of the base period through the current option; for example, for a report submitted after the second option is exercised, the dollar goal would be the sum of the goals for the basic contract, the first option, and the second option.

(B) If a subcontracting plan has been added to the contract pursuant to 19.702(a)(1)(iii) or 19.301-2(e), the Contractor's achievements must be reported in the report on a cumulative basis from the date of incorporation of the subcontracting plan into the contract.

(iii) When a subcontracting plan includes indirect costs in the goals, these costs must be included in this report.

(2) SSR. (i) *Reports submitted under individual contract plans-*

(A) This report encompasses all subcontracting under prime contracts and subcontracts with an executive agency, regardless of the dollar value of the subcontracts. This report also includes indirect costs on a prorated basis when the indirect costs are excluded from the subcontracting goals.

Continues on page 190

(B) The report may be submitted on a corporate, company or subdivision (*e.g.*, plant or division operating as a separate profit center) basis, unless otherwise directed by the agency.

(C) If the Contractor and/or a subcontractor is performing work for more than one executive agency, a separate report shall be submitted to each executive agency covering only that agency's contracts, provided at least one of that agency's contracts is over the applicable threshold specified in FAR 19.702(a), and the contract contains a subcontracting plan. For DoD, a consolidated report shall be submitted for all contracts awarded by military departments/agencies and/or subcontracts awarded by DoD prime contractors.

(D) The report shall be submitted annually by October 30, for the twelve month period ending September 30. When a Contracting Officer rejects an SSR, the Contractor is required to submit a revised SSR within 30 days of receiving the notice of report rejection.

(E) Subcontract awards that are related to work for more than one executive agency shall be appropriately allocated.

(F) The authority to acknowledge or reject SSRs in the eSRS, including SSRs submitted by subcontractors with subcontracting plans, resides with the Government agency awarding the prime contracts unless stated otherwise in the contract.

(ii) *Reports submitted under a commercial plan-*

(A) The report shall include all subcontract awards under the commercial plan in effect during the Government's fiscal year and all indirect costs.

(B) The report shall be submitted annually, within 30 days after the end of the Government's fiscal year.

(C) If a Contractor has a commercial plan and is performing work for more than one executive agency, the Contractor shall specify the percentage of dollars attributable to each agency.

(D) The authority to acknowledge or reject SSRs for commercial plans resides with the Contracting Officer who approved the commercial plan.

Continues on page 191

Alternate IV (Sep 2023). As prescribed in 19.708 (b) (1) (iv), substitute the following paragraphs (c) and (d) for paragraphs (c) and (d) of the basic clause:

(c)

(1) The Contractor, upon request by the Contracting Officer, shall submit and negotiate a subcontracting plan, where applicable, that separately addresses subcontracting with small business, veteran-owned small business, service-disabled veteran-owned small business, HUBZone small business, small, disadvantaged business, and women-owned small business concerns. If the Contractor is submitting an individual subcontracting plan, the plan shall separately address subcontracting with small business, veteran-owned small business, service-disabled veteran-owned small business, HUBZone small business, small, disadvantaged business, and women-owned small business concerns, with a separate part for the basic contract and separate parts for each option (if any). The subcontracting plan shall be incorporated into the contract. The subcontracting plan shall be negotiated within the time specified by the Contracting Officer. The subcontracting plan does not apply retroactively.

(2)

(i) The prime Contractor may accept a subcontractor's written representations of its size and socioeconomic status as a small business, small disadvantaged business, veteran-owned small business, service-disabled veteran-owned small business, or a women-owned small business if the subcontractor represents that the size and socioeconomic status representations with its offer are current, accurate, and complete as of the date of the offer for the subcontract.

(ii) The Contractor may accept a subcontractor's representations of its size and socioeconomic status as a small business, small, disadvantaged business, veteran-owned small business, service-disabled veteran-owned small business, or a women-owned small business in the System for Award Management (SAM) if–

(A) The subcontractor is registered in SAM; and

(B) The subcontractor represents that the size and socioeconomic status representations made in SAM are current, accurate, and complete as of the date of the offer for the subcontract.

(iii) The Contractor may not require the use of SAM for the purposes of representing size or socioeconomic status in connection with a subcontract.

Continues on page 192

(iv) In accordance with 13 CFR 121.411, 126.900, 127.700, and 128.600, a contractor acting in good faith is not liable for misrepresentations made by its subcontractors regarding the subcontractor's size or socioeconomic status.

(d) The Contractor's subcontracting plan shall include the following:

(1) Separate goals, expressed in terms of total dollars subcontracted and as a percentage of total planned subcontracting dollars, for the use of small business, veteran-owned small business, service-disabled veteran-owned small business, HUBZone small business, small, disadvantaged business, and women-owned small business concerns as subcontractors. For individual subcontracting plans, and if required by the Contracting Officer, goals shall also be expressed in terms of percentage of total contract dollars, in addition to the goals expressed as a percentage of total subcontract dollars. The Contractor shall include all subcontracts that contribute to contract performance and may include a proportionate share of products and services that are normally allocated as indirect costs. In accordance with 43 U.S.C. 1626–

(i) Subcontracts awarded to an ANC or Indian tribe shall be counted towards the subcontracting goals for small business and small disadvantaged business concerns, regardless of the size or Small Business Administration certification status of the ANC or Indian tribe; and

(ii) Where one or more subcontractors are in the subcontract tier between the prime Contractor and the ANC or Indian tribe, the ANC or Indian tribe shall designate the appropriate Contractor(s) to count the subcontract towards its small business and small disadvantaged business subcontracting goals.

(A) In most cases, the appropriate Contractor is the Contractor that awarded the subcontract to the ANC or Indian tribe.

(B) If the ANC or Indian tribe designates more than one Contractor to count the subcontract toward its goals, the ANC or Indian tribe shall designate only a portion of the total subcontract award to each Contractor. The sum of the amounts designated to various Contractors cannot exceed the total value of the subcontract.

(C) The ANC or Indian tribe shall give a copy of the written designation to the Contracting Officer, the Contractor, and the subcontractors in between the prime Contractor and the ANC or Indian tribe within 30 days of the date of the subcontract award.

Continues on page 193

(D) If the Contracting Officer does not receive a copy of the ANC's or the Indian tribe's written designation within 30 days of the subcontract award, the Contractor that awarded the subcontract to the ANC or Indian tribe will be considered the designated Contractor.

(2) A statement of–

(i) Total dollars planned to be subcontracted for an individual subcontracting plan; or the Contractor's total projected sales, expressed in dollars, and the total value of projected subcontracts to support the sales for a commercial plan, including all indirect costs, with the exception of those such as the following: Employee salaries and benefits; payments for petty cash; depreciation; interest; income taxes; property taxes; lease payments; bank fees; fines, claims, and dues; original equipment manufacturer relationships during warranty periods (negotiated up front with the product); utilities and other services purchased from a municipality or an entity solely authorized by the municipality to provide those services in a particular geographical region; and philanthropic contributions;

(iii) Total dollars planned to be subcontracted to veteran-owned small business concerns; (iv) Total dollars planned to be subcontracted to service-disabled veteran-owned small business; (v) Total dollars planned to be subcontracted to HUBZone small business concerns; (vi) Total dollars planned to be subcontracted to small disadvantaged business concerns (including ANCs and Indian tribes); and (vii) Total dollars planned to be subcontracted to women-owned small business concerns.

(3) A description of the principal types of supplies and services to be subcontracted, and an identification of the types planned for subcontracting to

(i) Small business concerns;

(ii) Veteran-owned small business concerns;

(iii) Service-disabled veteran-owned small business concerns;

(iv) HUBZone small business concerns;

(v) Small disadvantaged business concerns; and

(vi) Women-owned small business concerns.

Continues on page 194

(4) A description of the method used to develop the subcontracting goals in paragraph (d)(1) of this clause.

(5) A description of the method used to identify potential sources for solicitation purposes (e.g., existing company source lists, SAM, veterans service organizations, the National Minority Purchasing Council Vendor Information Service, the Research and Information Division of the Minority Business Development Agency in the Department of Commerce, or small, HUBZone, small disadvantaged, and women-owned small business trade associations). The Contractor may rely on the information contained in SAM as an accurate representation of a concern's size and ownership characteristics for the purposes of maintaining a small, veteran-owned small, service-disabled veteran-owned small, HUBZone small, small disadvantaged, and women-owned small business source list. Use of SAM as its source list does not relieve a firm of its responsibilities (e.g., outreach, assistance, counseling, or publicizing subcontracting opportunities) in this clause.

(6) A statement as to whether or not the Contractor included indirect costs in establishing subcontracting goals, and a description of the method used to determine the proportionate share of indirect costs to be incurred with–

(i) Small business concerns (including ANC and Indian tribes);

(ii) Veteran-owned small business concerns;

(iii) Service-disabled veteran-owned small business concerns;

(iv) HUBZone small business concerns;

(v) Small disadvantaged business concerns (including ANC and Indian tribes); and

(vi) Women-owned small business concerns.

(7) The name of the individual employed by the Contractor who will administer the Contractor's subcontracting program, and a description of the duties of the individual.

(8) A description of the efforts the Contractor will make to assure that small business, veteran-owned small business, service-disabled veteran-owned small business, HUBZone small business, small, disadvantaged business, and women-owned small business concerns have an equitable opportunity to compete for subcontracts.

Continues on page 195

(9) Assurances that the Contractor will include the clause of this contract entitled "Utilization of Small Business Concerns" in all subcontracts that offer further subcontracting opportunities, and that the Contractor will require all subcontractors (except small business concerns) that receive subcontracts in excess of the applicable threshold specified in FAR 19.702(a) on the date of subcontract award, with further subcontracting possibilities to adopt a subcontracting plan that complies with the requirements of this clause.

(10) Assurances that the Contractor will–

(i) Cooperate in any studies or surveys as may be required;

(ii) Submit periodic reports so that the Government can determine the extent of compliance by the Contractor with the subcontracting plan;

(iii) After November 30, 2017, include subcontracting data for each order when reporting subcontracting achievements for an indefinite-delivery, indefinite-quantity *contracts with* individual subcontracting plans *where the contract is intended* for use by multiple agencies;

(iv) Submit the Individual Subcontract Report (ISR) and/or the Summary Subcontract Report (SSR), in accordance with paragraph (l) of this clause using the Electronic Subcontracting Reporting System (eSRS) at http://www.esrs.gov. The reports shall provide information on subcontract awards to small business concerns (including ANCs and Indian tribes that are not small businesses), veteran-owned small business concerns, service-disabled veteran-owned small business concerns, HUBZone small business concerns, small disadvantaged business concerns (including ANCs and Indian tribes that have not been certified by SBA as small disadvantaged businesses), women-owned small business concerns, and for NASA only, Historically Black Colleges and Universities and Minority Institutions. Reporting shall be in accordance with this clause, or as provided in agency regulations;

(v) Ensure that its subcontractors with subcontracting plans agree to submit the ISR and/or the SSR using eSRS;

(vi) Provide its prime contract number, its unique entity identifier, and the e-mail address of the Contractor's official responsible for acknowledging receipt of or rejecting the ISRs, to all first-tier subcontractors with subcontracting plans so they can enter this information into the eSRS when submitting their ISRs; and

Continues on page 196

(vii) Require that each subcontractor with a subcontracting plan provide the prime contract number, its own unique entity identifier, and the e-mail address of the subcontractor's official responsible for acknowledging receipt of or rejecting the ISRs, to its subcontractors with subcontracting plans.

(11) A description of the types of records that will be maintained concerning procedures that have been adopted to comply with the requirements and goals in the plan, including establishing source lists; and a description of the Contractor's efforts to locate small business, veteran-owned small business, service-disabled veteran-owned small business, HUBZone small business, small disadvantaged business, and women-owned small business concerns and award subcontracts to them. The records shall include at least the following (on a plant-wide or company-wide basis, unless otherwise indicated):

(i) Source lists (e.g., SAM), guides, and other data that identify small business, veteran-owned small business, service-disabled veteran-owned small business, HUBZone small business, small, disadvantaged business, and women-owned small business concerns.

(ii) Organizations contacted in an attempt to locate sources that are small business, veteran-owned small business, service-disabled veteran-owned small business, HUBZone small business, small, disadvantaged business, or women-owned small business concerns.

(iii) Records on each subcontract solicitation resulting in an award of more than the simplified acquisition threshold, as defined in FAR 2.101 on the date of subcontract award, indicating–

(A) Whether small business concerns were solicited and, if not, why not;

(B) Whether veteran-owned small business concerns were solicited and, if not, why not;

(C) Whether service-disabled veteran-owned small business concerns were solicited and, if not, why not;

(D) Whether HUBZone small business concerns were solicited and, if not, why not;

(E) Whether small, disadvantaged business concerns were solicited and, if not, why not;

Continues on page 197

(F) Whether women-owned small business concerns were solicited and, if not, why not; and

(G) If applicable, the reason award was not made to a small business concern.

(iv) Records of any outreach efforts to contact–

(A) Trade associations;

(B) Business development organizations;

(C) Conferences and trade fairs to locate small, HUBZone small, small disadvantaged, service-disabled veteran-owned, and women-owned small business sources; and

(D) Veterans service organizations.

(v) Records of internal guidance and encouragement provided to buyers through–

(A) Workshops, seminars, training, etc.; and

(B) Monitoring performance to evaluate compliance with the program's requirements.

(vi) On a contract-by-contract basis, records to support award data submitted by the Contractor to the Government, including the name, address, and business size of each subcontractor. Contractors having commercial plans need not comply with this requirement.

(12) Assurances that the Contractor will make a good faith effort to acquire articles, equipment, supplies, services, or materials, or obtain the performance of construction work from the small business concerns that it used in preparing the proposal for the modification, in the same or greater scope, amount, and quality used in preparing and submitting the modification proposal. Responding to a request for a quote does not constitute use in preparing a proposal. The Contractor used a small business concern in preparing the proposal for a modification if–

(i) The Contractor identifies the small business concern as a subcontractor in the proposal or associated small business subcontracting plan, to furnish certain supplies or perform a portion of the subcontract; or(ii) The Contractor used the small business concern's pricing or cost information or technical expertise in preparing the proposal, where there is written evidence of an intent or understanding that the small business concern will be awarded a subcontract for the related work when the modification is executed.

Continues on page 198

(13) Assurances that the Contractor will provide the Contracting Officer with a written explanation if the Contractor fails to acquire articles, equipment, supplies, services or materials or obtain the performance of construction work as described in (d)(12) of this clause. This written explanation must be submitted to the Contracting Officer within 30 days of contract completion.

(14) Assurances that the Contractor will not prohibit a subcontractor from discussing with the contracting officer any material matter pertaining to the payment to or utilization of a subcontractor.

(15) Assurances that the offeror will pay its small business subcontractors on time and in accordance with the terms and conditions of the underlying subcontract and notify the contracting officer when the prime contractor makes either a reduced or an untimely payment to a small business subcontractor (see 52.242-5).

FAR Clause 52.219-16 Liquidated Damages-Subcontracting Plan.

As prescribed in 19.708(b) (2), insert the following clause:

Liquidated Damages-Subcontracting Plan (Sep 2021)

(a) "Failure to make a good faith effort to comply with the subcontracting plan," as used in this clause, means a willful or intentional failure to perform in accordance with the requirements of the subcontracting plan approved under the clause in this contract entitled "Small Business Subcontracting Plan," or willful or intentional action to frustrate the plan.

(b) Performance shall be measured by applying the percentage goals to the total actual subcontracting dollars or, if a commercial plan is involved, to the pro rata share of actual subcontracting dollars attributable to Government contracts covered by the commercial plan. If, at contract completion or, in the case of a commercial plan, at the close of the fiscal year for which the plan is applicable, the Contractor has failed to meet its subcontracting goals, and the Contracting Officer decides in accordance with paragraph (c) of this clause that the Contractor failed to make a good faith effort to comply with its subcontracting plan (see 19.705-7), established in accordance with the clause in this contract entitled "Small Business Subcontracting Plan," the Contractor shall pay the Government liquidated damages in an amount stated. The amount of probable damages attributable to the Contractor's failure to comply shall be an amount equal to the actual dollar amount by which the Contractor failed to achieve each subcontract goal.

Continues on page 199

(c) Before the Contracting Officer makes a final decision that the Contractor has failed to make such good faith effort, the Contracting Officer shall give the Contractor written notice specifying the failure and permitting the Contractor to demonstrate what good faith efforts have been made and to discuss the matter. Failure to respond to the notice may be taken as an admission that no valid explanation exists. If, after consideration of all the pertinent data, the Contracting Officer finds that the Contractor failed to make a good faith effort to comply with the subcontracting plan, the Contracting Officer shall issue a final decision to that effect and require that the Contractor pay the Government liquidated damages as provided in paragraph (b) of this clause.

(d) With respect to commercial plans, the Contracting Officer who approved the plan will perform the functions of the Contracting Officer under this clause on behalf of all agencies with contracts covered by the commercial plan.

(e) The Contractor shall have the right of appeal, under the clause in this contract entitled, Disputes, from any final decision of the Contracting Officer.

(f) Liquidated damages shall be in addition to any other remedies that the Government may have.

(End of clause)

9.0 Davis-Bacon Act (Prevailing Wages)

The Davis-Bacon Act of 1931 is a United States federal law that established the requirement for paying prevailing wages on public works projects. All federal government construction contracts—and most contracts for federally assisted construction over $2,000—must include provisions for paying workers onsite no less than the locally prevailing wages and benefits paid on similar projects.

9.1 General FAR Requirements

The following FAR clauses (all offshoot clauses from the Davis-Bacon Act of 1931) constitute the requirements for labor, labor payroll/reporting, and penalties incurred in all federally funded construction projects: 52.222-3, Convict Labor; 52.222-4, Contract Work Hours and Safety Standards Act—Overtime Compensation; 52.222-5, Davis-Bacon Act—Secondary Site of the Work; 52.222-6, Davis-Bacon Act; 52.222-7, Withholding of Funds; 52.222-8, Payrolls and Basic Records; 52.222-9, Apprentices and Trainees; 52.222-11, Subcontracts.

9.2 Who is allowed to work?

All persons except convict labor (see FAR clause 52.222-3 Convict Labor). Persons that have served their sentences, are out of prison on parole or probation, in a work-release program, have been pardoned or are otherwise legally authorized to work, are allowed to work on government contracts.

9.3 Site of the Work

This is defined as primary and secondary sites as follows:

1. The primary site of the work is the physical place(s) where the construction called for in the contract will remain when work on it is completed.

2. The secondary site of the work, if any, as well as any other site where a significant portion of the building or work is constructed, provided that such site is located in the United States and is established specifically for the performance of the contract or project. This includes any fabrication plants, mobile factories, batch plants, borrow pits, job headquarters, tool yards, etc., provided they are dedicated exclusively, or nearly so, to performance of the contract or project.

3. Does not include permanent home offices, branch plant establishments, fabrication plants, or tool yards of a contractor or sub- contractor whose locations and continuance in operation are determined wholly without regard to a particular federal contract or project. In addition, fabrication plants, batch plants, borrow pits, job headquarters, yards, etc., of a commercial or material supplier established by a supplier of materials for the project before opening of bids and not on the project site, are not included in the "site of the work." Such permanent, previously established facilities are not a part of this site even if the operations for a period of time may be dedicated exclusively, or nearly so, to the performance of a contract.

9.4 Wage Determination

Each federally funded contract will have at least one and as many as three wage determinations. They are delineated as "Heavy-Highway," "Building," and "Residential." The wage determination in effect on the date of award of the contract will be the wage determination that will be used for the entire contract. A new wage determination cannot be used unless added by contract modification and a cost increase. Wage determinations only dictate the "minimum" hourly rate and fringe benefits that must be paid.

9.5 Pay Determination

Each employee of the contractor, subcontractor, or lower tier subcontractor that performs work at the project site or secondary site of the work as defined above must be paid according to the applicable wage determination. Site management personnel, such as project managers, superintendents, project engineers, foremen, administrative personnel, etc., are exempt from this requirement unless they spend 20% or more of the workweek performing craftsman type work for the project. All workers must be paid weekly.

Determining the proper worker classification and pay rate is critical to avoiding a Department of Labor audit and penalties. Subcontractors quite often see this as a way to save money, but it can be devastating for you as the contractor. If a worker is to be paid without any benefits, then the "fringes" as shown in the wage determination for a particular work classification must be added to the hourly wage rate. You can pay some of the fringe benefits but must clearly show what the fringe benefit is and what it costs. The rest of the fringe benefit must be made up in the hourly rate of pay.

9.6 Work Hours

The work hours are generally limited to between 7 a.m. and 4 p.m., Monday through Friday. Federal holidays are stipulated in the contract. The workers can work forty hours per week before overtime, for which one and a half times the regular rate of pay must be given. There is no limit as to how many hours per day can be worked, and federal holidays do not count toward the forty-hour workweek. The workweek must be yours or the subcontractor's normal stated workweek and cannot change during the contract period.

9.7 Payrolls and Basic Records

As the contractor, you must maintain payrolls and basic records relating to the contract during the work. These records should contain the name, address, and SSN of each worker, his or her correct classification, hourly rates of wages paid (including rates of contributions or costs anticipated for bona fide fringe benefits or cash equivalents of the types described in section 1(b)(2)(B) of the Davis-Bacon Act), daily and weekly number of hours worked, deductions made, and actual wages paid. You should maintain records showing that the commitment to provide such benefits is enforceable, that the plan or program is financially responsible, and that it has been communicated in writing to the laborers or mechanics affected, as well as records that show the costs anticipated or the actual cost incurred in providing such benefits. If you employ apprentices or trainees under approved programs, you should maintain written evidence of the registration of apprenticeship programs and certification of trainee programs, the registration of the apprentices and trainees, and the ratios and wage rates prescribed in the applicable programs.

You must submit weekly, for each week in which any contract work is performed, a copy of all payrolls to the CO. The payrolls submitted should set out accurately and completely all the information required to be maintained as required above. This information may be submitted in any form desired. Optional Form WH-347 (Federal Stock Number 029-005-00014-1) is available for this purpose and can be downloaded from the Internet. As the prime contractor, you are responsible for the submission of copies of payrolls by all subcontractors.

Each payroll submitted must be accompanied by a "Statement of Compliance" signed by you or the subcontractor or his/her agent who pays or supervises the payment of the persons employed under the contract and should certify:

> That the payroll for the payroll period contains the information required to be maintained under paragraph A above and that it is correct and complete
>
> That each laborer or mechanic (including each helper, apprentice, and trainee) employed on the contract during the payroll period has been paid the full weekly wages earned, without rebate, either directly or indirectly, and that no deductions have been made either directly or indirectly from the full wages earned, other than permissible deductions

That each laborer or mechanic has been paid not less than the applicable wage rates and fringe benefits or cash equivalents for the classification of work performed, as specified in the applicable wage determination incorporated into the contract.

The weekly submission of a properly executed certification set forth on the reverse side of Optional Form WH-347 satisfies the requirement for submission of the required "Statement of Compliance." The falsification of any of the certifications in this clause may subject you or your subcontractor to civil or criminal prosecution under Section 1001 of Title 18 and Section 3729 of Title 31 of the *United States Code*.

You or your subcontractor must make the required records available for inspection, copying, or transcription by the CO or his/her authorized representatives or the Department of Labor. You or your subcontractor should permit the CO or his/her representatives or the Department of Labor to interview employees during working hours on the job. If you or your subcontractor fails to submit these required records or to make them available, the CO may, after written notice to you, take any action as may be necessary to suspend any further payments, which can lead to debarment.

Within 14 days after award of the contract, you must deliver to the CO a completed Standard Form (SF) 1413 Statement and Acknowledgment for each subcontract for construction within the United States, including the subcontractor's signed and dated acknowledgment that the clauses in FAR 52.222-11 paragraph (b) have been included in the subcontract. Within 14 days after the award of any subsequently awarded subcontract, you must deliver to the CO an updated completed SF 1413 for this additional subcontract.

You should perform random weekly labor interviews of subcontractors and lower tier subcontractors. This should be used as a check against the certified payroll to eliminate potential fraud. Remember, as the prime contractor, you are ultimately responsible for payment of all workers.

9.8 Apprentices and Trainees

Apprentices

An apprentice will be permitted to work at less than the predetermined rate for the work performed when employed:

Pursuant to and individually registered in a bona fide apprenticeship program registered with the U.S. Department of Labor, Employment and Training Administration, Office of Apprenticeship Training, Employer, and Labor Services (OATELS) or with a State Apprenticeship Agency recognized by the OATELS; or

In the first 90 days of probationary employment as an apprentice in such an apprenticeship program, even though not individually registered in the program, if certified by the OATELS or a State Apprenticeship Agency (where appropriate) to be eligible for probationary employment as an apprentice.

The allowable ration of apprentices to journeymen on the job site in any craft classification may not be greater than the ratio permitted to the contractor for the entire workforce under the registered program. The contractor must watch this very closely as subcontractors sometimes will use the wrong ratio of apprentices to journeymen to save money.

Any worker listed on a payroll at an apprentice wage rate who is not registered or otherwise employed as stated above must be paid not less than the applicable wage determination for the classification of work performed. In addition, any apprentice performing work on the job site more than the ration permitted under the registered program must be not less than the applicable wage rate on the wage determination for the work performed.

Where a contractor is performing construction on a project in a locality other than that in which its program is registered, the ratios and wage rates specified in the contractor's or subcontractor's registered program must be observed. Every apprentice must be paid at not less than the rate specified in the registered program for the apprentice's level of progress, expressed as a percentage of the journeyman hourly rate specified in the applicable wage determination.

Apprentices must be paid fringe benefits in accordance with the provisions of the apprenticeship program. If the apprenticeship program does not specify fringe benefits, apprentices must be paid the full amount of fringe benefits listed on the wage determination for the applicable apprentice classification; fringes must be paid in accordance with that determination.

In the event OATELS, or a State Apprenticeship Agency recognized by OATELS, withdraws approval of an apprenticeship program, the contractor will no longer be permitted to utilize apprentices at less than the applicable predetermined rate for the work performed until an acceptable program is approved.

Trainees.

Trainees may not be permitted to work at less than the predetermined rate for the work performed unless they are employed pursuant to and individually registered in a program which has received prior approval, evidenced by formal certification by the U.S. Department of Labor, Employment, and Training Administration, Office of Apprenticeship Training, Employer, and Labor Services (OATELS). The ratio of trainees to journeymen on the job site shall not be greater than permitted under the plan approved by OATELS.

Every trainee must be paid at not less than the rate specified in the approved program for the trainee's level of progress, expressed as a percentage of the journeyman's hourly rate specified in the applicable wage determination. Trainees shall be paid fringe benefits in accordance with the provisions of the trainee program. If the trainee program does not mention fringe benefits, trainees shall be paid the full amount of fringe benefits listed in the wage determination unless the administrator of the Wage and Hour Division determines that there is an apprenticeship program associated with the corresponding journeyman wage rate in the wage determination that provides for less than full fringe benefits for apprentices. Any employee listed on the pay- roll at a trainee rate who is not registered and participating in a training plan approved by OATELS shall be paid not less than the applicable wage rate in the wage determination for the classification of work performed. In addition, any trainee performing work on the job site more than the ratio permitted under the registered program shall be paid not less than the applicable wage rate in the wage determination for the work performed.

In the event OATELS withdraws approval of a training program, the contractor will no longer be permitted to utilize trainees at less than the applicable predetermined rate for the work performed until an acceptable program is approved.

9.9 Withholding of Funds

The Contracting Officer shall, upon his or her own action or upon written request of an authorized representative of the Department of Labor, withhold or cause to be withheld from the

Contractor under this contract or any other Federal contract with the same Prime Contractor, or any other Federally assisted contract subject to Davis-Bacon prevailing wage requirements, which is held by the same Prime Contractor, so much of the accrued payments or advances as may be considered necessary to pay laborers and mechanics, including apprentices, trainees, and helpers, employed by the Contractor or any subcontractor the full amount of wages required by the contract. In the event of failure to pay any laborer or mechanic, including any apprentice, trainee, or helper, employed or working on the site of the work, all or part of the wages required by the contract, the Contracting Officer may, after written notice to the Contractor, take such action as may be necessary to cause the suspension of any further payment, advance, or guarantee of funds until such violations have ceased.

The Contracting Officer will generally require that the Contractor shows proof that the back wages owed have been paid. This generally includes a copy of the canceled check showing that the back wage amount has been received. The Contracting Officer may also request that the bonding company pay the back wages owed if no action is taken by the Contractor.

9.10 Contract Flowdown

The Contractor must insert in each subcontract the FAR clauses that are listed in FAR Clause 52.222-11 Subcontracts.

Instructions for Completing Payroll Form WH-347

This form meets needs resulting from the amendment of the Davis-Bacon Act to include fringe benefits provisions. Under this amended law, the contractor is required to pay not less than fringe benefits as predetermined by the Department of Labor, in addition to payment of not less than the predetermined rates. The contractor's obligation to pay fringe benefits may be met either by payment of the fringes to the various plans, funds or programs or by making these payments to the employees as cash in lieu of fringes.

This payroll provides for the contractor's showing on the face of the payroll all monies to the employees, whether as basic rates or as cash in lieu of fringes and provides for the contractor's representation in the statement of compliance on the rear of the pay-roll that he is paying to other fringes required by the contract and not paid as cash in lieu of fringes. Detailed instructions concerning the preparation of the payroll follow:

Contractor or Subcontractor: Fill in your firm's name and check appropriate box.

Address: Fill in your firm's address.

Column 1 - Name, Address, and Social Security Number of Employee: The employee's full name and Social Security Number must be shown on each weekly payroll submitted.

The employee's address must also be shown on the payroll covering the first week in which the employee works on the project. The address need not be shown on subsequent weekly payrolls unless the address changes.

Column 2 - Withholding Exemptions: This column is merely inserted for the employer's convenience and is not a requirement of Regulations, Part 3 and 5.

Column 3 - Work Classifications: List classification descriptive of work performed by employees. Consult classification and minimum wage schedule set forth in contract specifications. If additional classifications are deemed necessary, see Contracting Officer or Agency representative. Employees may be shown as having worked in more than one classification provided accurate breakdown or hours so worked are maintained and shown on submitted payroll by use of separate entries.

Column 4 - Hours worked: On all contracts subject to the Contract Work Hours Standard Act enter as overtime hours worked in excess of 8 hours per day and 40 hours a week.

Column 5 - Total: Self-explanatory

Column 6 - Rate of Pay, including Fringe Benefits: In straight time box, list actual hourly rate paid the employee for straight time worked plus in cash in lieu of fringes paid the employee. When recording the straight time hourly rate, any cash paid in lieu of fringes may be shown separately from the basic rate, thus $3.25/.40. This is of assistance in correctly computing overtime. See "Fringe Benefits" below. In the overtime box show overtime hourly rate paid, plus any cash in lieu of fringes paid the employee. See "Fringe Benefits" below. Payment of not less than time and one-half the basic or regular rate paid is required for overtime under the Contract Work Hours Standard Act of 1962. In addition to paying no less than the predetermined rate for the classification which the employee works, the contractor shall pay to approved plans, funds or programs or shall pay as cash in lieu of fringes amounts predetermined as fringe benefits in the wage decision made part of the contract. See "FRINGE BENEFITS" below.

FRINGE BENEFITS - Contractors who pay all required fringe benefits: A contractor who pays fringe benefits to approved plans, funds, or programs in amounts not less than were determined in the applicable wage decision of the Secretary of labor shall continue to show on the face of the payroll the basic cash hourly rate and overtime rate paid to his employees just as he has always done. Such a contractor shall check paragraph 4(a) of the statement on the reverse of the payroll to indicate that he is also paying to approved plans, funds or programs not less than the amount predetermined as fringe benefits for each craft. Any exceptions shall be noted in section 4(c).

Contractors who pay no fringe benefits: A contractor who pays no fringe benefits shall pay to the employee and insert in the straight time hourly rate column of the payroll, an amount not less than the predetermined rate for each classification plus the amount of fringe benefits determined for each classification in the applicable wage decision. Inasmuch as it is not necessary to pay time and a half on cash paid in lieu of fringes, the overtime rate shall be not less than the sum of the basic predetermined rate, plus the half time premium on basic or regular rate, plus the required cash in lieu of fringes at the straight time rate. In addition, the contractor shall check paragraph 4(b) of the statement on the reverse of the payroll to indicate that he is paying fringe benefits in cash directly to his employees. Any exceptions shall be noted in Section 4(c).

Use of Section 4(c), Exceptions

Any contractor who is making payment to approved plans, funds, or programs in amounts less than the wage determination requires is obliged to pay the deficiency directly to the employees as cash in lieu of fringes. Any exceptions to Section 4(a) or 4(b), whichever the contractor may check, shall be entered in section 4(c). Enter the Exception column the craft and enter in the Explanation column the hourly amount paid the employee as cash in lieu of fringes and the hourly amount paid to plans, funds, or programs as fringes. The contractor shall pay and shall show that he is paying to each such employee for all hours (unless otherwise provided by applicable determination) worked on Federal or Federally assisted project an amount not less than the predetermined rate plus cash in lieu of fringes as shown in Section 4(c). The rate paid and amount of cash paid in lieu of fringe benefits per hour should be entered in column 6 on the payroll. See paragraph on "Contractors who pay no fringe benefits" for computation of overtime rate.

Column 7 - Gross Amount Earned: Enter gross amount earned on this project. If part of the employees' weekly wage was earned on projects other than the project described on this payroll, enter in column 7 first the amount earned on the Federal or Federally assisted project and then the gross amount earned during the week on all projects, thus $63.00/$120.00.

Column 8 - Deductions: Five columns are provided for showing deductions made. If more than five deductions should be involved, use first 4 columns; show the balance deductions under "Other" column; show actual total under "Total Deductions" column: and in the attachment to the payroll describe the deduction contained in the "Other" column. All deductions must be in accordance with the provisions of the Copeland Act Regulations, 29 CFR, Part 3. If the employee worked on other jobs in addition to this project, show actual deductions from his weekly gross wage, but indicate that deductions are based on his gross wages.

Column 9 - Net Wages Paid for Week: Self-explanatory

Totals - Space has been left at the bottom of the columns so that totals may be shown if the contractor so desires.

Statement Required by Regulations, Parts 3 and 5: While this form needs not be notarized, the statement on the back of the payroll is subject to the penalties provided by 18 USC 1001, namely, possible imprisonment of 5 years or $10,000.00 fine or both. Accordingly, the party signing this statement should have knowledge of the facts represented as true.

Space has been provided between items (1) and (2) of the statement for describing any deductions made. If all deductions made are adequately described in the "Deductions" column above, state "See Deductions column in this payroll." See paragraph entitled "FRINGE BENEFITS" above for instructions concerning filling out paragraph 4 of the statement.

10.0 Contract Flowdown

Many FAR clauses have a requirement that they be specifically included in any subcontracts. The FAR clause 52.222-11 Subcontracts (Labor Standards) requires that specific clauses be included in all subcontracts.

To properly protect you as the contractor, it is highly recommended that the subcontracts should include all FAR clauses. This is because there are many FAR clauses that require flowdown and it is easy to miss one of them. This also ties the subcontractor to all the FAR clauses for which you are responsible for.

FAR Clause 52.222-11 Subcontracts (Labor Standards).

As prescribed in 22.407(a), insert the following clause:

Subcontracts (Labor Standards) (May 2014)

(a) *Definition.* "Construction, alteration or repair," as used in this clause, means all types of work done by laborers and mechanics employed by the construction Contractor or construction subcontractor on a particular building or work at the site thereof, including without limitation-

(1) Altering, remodeling, installation (if appropriate) on the site of the work of items fabricated off-site;

(2) Painting and decorating;

(3) Manufacturing or furnishing of materials, articles, supplies, or equipment on the site of the building or work;

(4) Transportation of materials and supplies between the site of the work within the meaning of paragraphs (a)(1)(i) and (ii) of the "site of the work" as defined in the FAR clause at 52.222-6, Construction Wage Rate Requirements of this contract, and a facility which is dedicated to the construction of the building or work and is deemed part of the site of the work within the meaning of paragraph (2) of the "site of the work" definition; and

(5) Transportation of portions of the building or work between a secondary site where a significant portion of the building or work is constructed, which is part of the "site of the work" definition in paragraph (a)(1)(ii) of the FAR clause at 52.222-6, Construction Wage Rate Requirements, and the physical place or places where the building or work will remain (paragraph (a)(1)(i) of the FAR clause at 52.222-6, in the "site of the work" definition).

(b) The Contractor shall insert in any subcontracts for construction, alterations, and repairs within the United States the clauses entitled-

(1) Construction Wage Rate Requirements;

(2) Contract Work Hours and Safety Standards-Overtime Compensation (if the clause is included in this contract);

(3) Apprentices and Trainees;

(4) Payrolls and Basic Records;

Continues on page 210

(5) Compliance with Copeland Act Requirements;

(6) Withholding of Funds;

(7) Subcontracts (Labor Standards);

(8) Contract Termination-Debarment;

(9) Disputes Concerning Labor Standards;

(10) Compliance with Construction Wage Rate Requirements and Related Regulations; and

(11) Certification of Eligibility.

(c) The prime Contractor shall be responsible for compliance by any subcontractor or lower tier subcontractor performing construction within the United States with all the contract clauses cited in paragraph (b).

(d)

(1) Within 14 days after award of the contract, the Contractor shall deliver to the Contracting Officer a completed Standard Form (SF) 1413, Statement and Acknowledgment, for each subcontract for construction within the United States, including the subcontractor's signed and dated acknowledgment that the clauses set forth in paragraph (b) of this clause have been included in the subcontract.

(2) Within 14 days after the award of any subsequently awarded subcontract the Contractor shall deliver to the Contracting Officer an updated completed SF 1413 for such additional subcontract.

(e) The Contractor shall insert the substance of this clause, including this paragraph (e) in all subcontracts for construction within the United States.

(End of clause)

11.0 Buy American Act

There are three "Buy American Act" FAR clauses: 52.225-3 Buy American Act—Free Trade Agreements—Israeli Trade Act; 52.225-9 Buy American Act—Construction Materials; 52.225-11 Buy American Act—Construction Materials under Trade Agreements, and two "Recovery Act," "Buy American Act" FAR Clauses: FAR Clause 52.225-21 Required Use of American

Iron, Steel, and Other Manufactured Goods-Buy American Act-Construction Materials; and FAR Clause 52.225-23 Required Use of American Iron, Steel, and Other Manufactured Goods-Buy American Act-Construction Materials Under Trade Agreements. A contract could have any one of these clauses inserted into a contract /RFP. The CO has very specific criteria to determine which of these FAR clauses it must include in a solicitation/RFP.

FAR Clause 52.225-9 Buy American Act—Construction Materials is the most restrictive of the clauses. It allows only U.S. manufactured construction materials and products, but foreign materials may be used if the cost for a domestically produced product is at least 20% more than the foreign produced material.

FAR Clause 52.225-21 Required Use of American Iron, Steel, and Other Manufactured Goods-Buy American Act-Construction Materials implements the Buy American Act-Construction Materials and Section 1605 of the American Recovery and Reinvestment Act of 2009(P.L. 111-5). This clause mandates the use of only manufactured goods and materials and mandates the difference in cost limitation between domestic and foreign material to a 25% increase in cumulative cost of the entire contract. This is a very restrictive clause and effectively denies the use of any non-domestic products, including NAFTA manufactured products.

FAR Clause 52.225-3, Buy American Act—Free Trade Agreements—Israeli Trade Act includes the U.S. Australia, Bahrain, Chile, Columbia, Costa Rica, Dominican Republic, El Salvador, Guatemala, Honduras, Korea (Republic of) Morocco, Nicaragua, Oman, Peru, or Singapore. This act allows the use of products from "Free Trade Agreement" countries.

FAR Clause 52.225-11 Buy American Act—Construction Materials under Trade Agreements is the most liberal of the acts. This clause allows use of products from most countries in the world including U.S., Armenia, Australia, Aruba, Austria, Belgium, Bulgaria, Canada, Croatia, Cyprus, Czech Republic, Denmark, Estonia, Finland, France, Germany, Greece, Hong Kong, Hungary, Iceland, Ireland, Israel, Italy, Japan, Korea (Republic of), Latvia, Liechtenstein, Lithuania, Luxembourg, Malta, Moldova, Montenegro, Netherlands, New Zealand, North Macedonia, Norway, Poland, Portugal, Romania, Singapore, Slovak Republic, Slovenia, Spain, Sweden, Switzerland, Taiwan, Ukraine, United Kingdom, Bahrain, Chile, Costa Rica, Dominican Republic, El Salvador, Guatemala, Honduras, Israel, Mexico, Morocco, Nicaragua, Oman, Panama, Peru, Singapore, Afghanistan, Angola, Bangladesh, Benin, Bhutan, Burkina Faso, Burundi, Cambodia, Central African Republic, Chad, Comoros, Democratic Republic of Congo, Djibouti, Equatorial Guinea, Eritrea, Ethiopia, Gambia, Guinea, Guinea- Bissau, Haiti, Kiribati, Laos, Lesotho, Liberia, Madagascar, Malawi, Mali, Mauritania, Mozambique, Nepal, Niger, Rwanda, Samoa, Sao Tome and Principe, Senegal, Sierra Leone, Solomon Islands, Somalia, South Sudan, Tanzania, Timor-Leste, Togo, Tuvalu, Uganda, Vanuatu, Yemen, Zambia, Antigua and Barbuda, Bahamas, Barbados, Belize, Bonaire, British Virgin Islands, Curacao, Dominica, Grenada, Guyana, Haiti, Jamaica, Montserrat, Saba, St. Kitts and Nevis, St. Lucia, St. Vincent and the Grenadines, Sint Eustatius, or Trinidad and Tobago manufactured products.

FAR Clause 52.225-23, Required Use of American Iron, Steel, and Other Manufactured Goods-Buy American Act-Construction Materials Under Trade Agreements lifts the restrictions of the Buy American Act and Section 1605 of the American Recovery and Reinvestment Act of 2009(P.L. 111-5). This clause mandates the use of only U.S., Armenia, Australia, Aruba, Austria, Belgium, Bulgaria, Canada, Croatia, Cyprus, Czech Republic, Denmark, Estonia, Finland, France, Germany, Greece, Hong Kong, Hungary, Iceland, Ireland, Israel, Italy, Japan, Korea (Republic of), Latvia, Liechtenstein, Lithuania, Luxembourg, Malta, Moldova, Montenegro, Netherlands, New Zealand, North Macedonia, Norway, Poland, Portugal, Romania, Singapore, Slovak Republic, Slovenia, Spain, Sweden, Switzerland, Taiwan, Ukraine, United Kingdom, Bahrain, Chile, Costa Rica, Dominican Republic, El Salvador, Guatemala, Honduras, Israel, Mexico, Morocco, Nicaragua, Oman, Panama, Peru, Singapore, Afghanistan, Angola, Bangladesh, Benin, Bhutan, Burkina Faso, Burundi, Cambodia, Central African Republic, Chad, Comoros, Democratic Republic of Congo, Djibouti, Equatorial Guinea, Eritrea, Ethiopia, Gambia, Guinea, Guinea- Bissau, Haiti, Kiribati, Laos, Lesotho, Liberia, Madagascar, Malawi, Mali, Mauritania, Mozambique, Nepal, Niger, Rwanda, Samoa, Sao Tome and Principe, Senegal, Sierra Leone, Solomon Islands, Somalia, South Sudan, Tanzania, Timor-Leste, Togo, Tuvalu, Uganda, Vanuatu, Yemen, Zambia, Antigua and Barbuda, Bahamas, Barbados, Belize, Bonaire, British Virgin Islands, Curacao, Dominica, Grenada, Guyana, Haiti, Jamaica, Montserrat, Saba, St. Kitts and Nevis, St. Lucia, St. Vincent and the Grenadines, Sint Eustatius, or Trinidad and Tobago manufactured products.

The end product must be at least 50% by cost of a material made either in the U.S. or another designated country as appropriate. "Construction Material" also includes an item brought to the site preassembled from articles, materials, or supplies. As long as the cost of the preassembled item has at least 50% made in the U.S. or a trade agreements country, as appropriate, then the item is considered to meet the requirements of the Buy American Act. Emergency life safety systems, such as emergency lighting, fire alarm, and audio evacuation systems, that are discrete systems incorporated into a public building or work and that are produced as complete systems, are evaluated as a single and distinct construction material regardless of when or how the individual parts or components of those systems are delivered to the construction site. Each Buy American Act clause is significantly different; however, they all allow for a foreign material to be used if the cost of the domestic material exceeds the cost of the foreign material by more than twenty (20) percent. However, the "American Recovery and Reinvestment Act of 2009," section 1605, mandates the use of the Buy American Act and changes the 20% requirement for domestic and foreign cost differential to a 25% contract cumulative contract increase. If the FAR Clause 52.225-21 Required Use of American Iron, Steel, and Other Manufactured Goods-Buy American Act-Construction Materials is included in the contract, then care must be taken during the bidding process to ascertain that all the materials are manufactured in the United States.

The Buy American Act FAR clauses have a procedure that must be followed to obtain the waiver. That procedure is as follows: Any contractor request to use foreign construction material must include adequate information for government evaluation of the request, including:

A description of the foreign and domestic construction materials

Unit of measure

Quantity

Cost

Time of delivery or availability

Location of the construction project

Name and address of the proposed supplier

A detailed justification of the reason for use of foreign construction material

A request based on unreasonable cost must include a reasonable survey of the market and a completed cost comparison table (see below). The cost of construction material must include all delivery costs to the construction site and any applicable duty. Any contractor requests for a determination submitted after contract award must explain why the contractor could not reasonably foresee the need for such a determination and could not have requested the determination before contract award. If the contractor does not submit a satisfactory explanation, the CO need not make a determination.

If the government determines after contract award that an exception to section 1605 of the Recovery Act or the Buy American Act applies and the CO and the contractor negotiate adequate consideration, the CO will modify the contract to allow use of the foreign construction material. However, when the basis for the exception is the unreasonable cost of a domestic construction material, adequate consideration is not less than the differential established above. Note: A contractor seldom knows whether a product is domestic or foreign manufactured when the project is bid, thus there will be no savings to the contractor by using the foreign product. This must be emphasized when requesting a CO's decision.

Unless the government determines that an exception to section 1605 of the Recovery Act or the Buy American Act applies, use of foreign construction material other than that covered by trade agreements is noncompliant with the applicable act.

The DAR Buy American clauses follow.

FAR Clause 52.225-10 Notice of Buy American Requirement-Construction Materials.

As prescribed in 25.1102(b) (1), insert the following provision:

Notice of Buy American Requirement-Construction Materials (May 2014)

(a) *Definitions*. "Commercially available off-the-shelf (COTS) item," "construction material," "domestic construction material," and "foreign construction material," as used in this provision, are defined in the clause of this solicitation entitled "Buy American-Construction Materials" (Federal Acquisition Regulation (FAR) clause 52.225-9).

(b) *Requests for determinations of inapplicability*. An offeror requesting a determination regarding the inapplicability of the Buy American statute should submit the request to the Contracting Officer in time to allow a determination before submission of offers. The offeror shall include the information and applicable supporting data required by paragraphs (c) and (d) of the clause at FAR 52.225-9 in the request. If an offeror has not requested a determination regarding the inapplicability of the Buy American statute before submitting its offer or has not received a response to a previous request, the offeror shall include the information and supporting data in the offer.

(c) Evaluation of offers.

(1) The Government will evaluate an offer requesting exception to the requirements of the Buy American statute, based on claimed unreasonable cost of domestic construction material, by adding to the offered price the appropriate percentage of the cost of such foreign construction material, as specified in paragraph (b)(3)(i) of the clause at FAR 52.225-9.

(2) If evaluation results in a tie between an offeror that requested the substitution of foreign construction material based on unreasonable cost and an offeror that did not request an exception, the Contracting Officer will award to the offeror that did not request an exception based on unreasonable cost.

(d) Alternate offers.

(1) When an offer includes foreign construction material not listed by the Government in this solicitation in paragraph (b) (2) of the clause at FAR 52.225-9, the offeror also may submit an alternate offer based on use of equivalent domestic construction material.

Continues on page 215

(2) If an alternate offer is submitted, the offeror shall submit a separate Standard Form 1442 for the alternate offer, and a separate price comparison table prepared in accordance with paragraphs (c) and (d) of the clause at FAR 52.225-9 for the offer that is based on the use of any foreign construction material for which the Government has not yet determined an exception applies.

(3) If the Government determines that a particular exception requested in accordance with paragraph (c) of the clause at FAR 52.225-9 does not apply, the Government will evaluate only those offers based on use of the equivalent domestic construction material, and the offeror shall be required to furnish such domestic construction material. An offer based on use of the foreign construction material for which an exception was requested-

(i) Will be rejected as nonresponsive if this acquisition is conducted by sealed bidding; or

(ii) May be accepted if revised during negotiations.

(End of Provision)

Alternate I (May 2014). As prescribed in 25.1102 (b) (2), substitute the following paragraph (b) for paragraph (b) of the basic provision:

(b) *Requests for determinations of inapplicability.* An offeror requesting a determination regarding the inapplicability of the Buy American statute shall submit the request with its offer, including the information and applicable supporting data required by paragraphs (c) and (d) of the clause at FAR 52.225-9.

FAR Clause 52.225-3 Buy American-Free Trade Agreements-Israeli Trade Act.

As prescribed in 25.1101 (b) (1)(i), insert the following clause:

Buy American-Free Trade Agreements-Israeli Trade Act (Nov 2023)

(a) *Definitions*. As used in this clause—

Bahraini, Moroccan, Omani, Panamanian, or Peruvian end product means an article that—

(1) Is wholly the growth, product, or manufacture of Bahrain, Morocco, Oman, Panama, or Peru; or

Continues on page 216

(2) In the case of an article that consists in whole or in part of materials from another country, has been substantially transformed in Bahrain, Morocco, Oman, Panama, or Peru into a new and different article of commerce with a name, character, or use distinct from that of the article or articles from which it was transformed. The term refers to a product offered for purchase under a supply contract, but for purposes of calculating the value of the end product includes services (except transportation services) incidental to the article, provided that the value of those incidental services does not exceed that of the article itself.

Commercially available off-the-shelf (COTS) item—

(1) Means any item of supply (including construction material) that is-

(i) A commercial product (as defined in paragraph (1) of the definition of "commercial product" at Federal Acquisition Regulation (FAR) 2.101);

(ii) Sold in substantial quantities in the commercial marketplace; and

(iii) Offered to the Government, under a contract or subcontract at any tier, without modification, in the same form in which it is sold in the commercial marketplace; and

(2) Does not include bulk cargo, as defined in 46 U.S.C. 40102(4), such as agricultural products and petroleum products.

Component means an article, material, or supply incorporated directly into an end product.

Cost of components means—

(1) For components purchased by the Contractor, the acquisition cost, including transportation costs to the place of incorporation into the end product (whether or not such costs are paid to a domestic firm), and any applicable duty (whether or not a duty-free entry certificate is issued); or

(2) For components manufactured by the Contractor, all costs associated with the manufacture of the component, including transportation costs as described in paragraph (1) of this definition, plus allocable overhead costs, but excluding profit. Cost of components does not include any costs associated with the manufacture of the end product.

Critical component means a component that is mined, produced, or manufactured in the United States and deemed critical to the U.S. supply chain. The list of critical components is at FAR 25.105.

Domestic end product means—

Continues on page 217

(1) For an end product that does not consist wholly or predominantly of iron or steel or a combination of both–

(i) An unmanufactured end product mined or produced in the United States;

(ii) An end product manufactured in the United States, if—

(A) The cost of its components mined, produced, or manufactured in the United States exceeds 60 percent of the cost of all its components, except that the percentage will be 65 percent for items delivered in calendar years 2024 through 2028 and 75 percent for items delivered starting in calendar year 2029. Components of foreign origin of the same class or kind as those that the agency determines are not mined, produced, or manufactured in sufficient and reasonably available commercial quantities of a satisfactory quality are treated as domestic. Components of unknown origin are treated as foreign. Scrap generated, collected, and prepared for processing in the United States is considered domestic; or

(B) The end product is a COTS item; or

(2) For an end product that consists wholly or predominantly of iron or steel or a combination of both, an end product manufactured in the United States, if the cost of foreign iron and steel constitutes less than 5 percent of the cost of all the components used in the end product. The cost of foreign iron and steel includes but is not limited to the cost of foreign iron or steel mill products (such as bar, billet, slab, wire, plate, or sheet), castings, or forgings utilized in the manufacture of the end product and a good faith estimate of the cost of all foreign iron or steel components excluding COTS fasteners. Iron or steel components of unknown origin are treated as foreign. If the end product contains multiple components, the cost of all the materials used in such end product is calculated in accordance with the definition of "cost of components".

End product means those articles, materials, and supplies to be acquired under the contract for public use.

Fastener means a hardware device that mechanically joins or affixes two or more objects together. Examples of fasteners are nuts, bolts, pins, rivets, nails, clips, and screws.

Foreign end product means an end product other than a domestic end product.

Foreign iron and steel means iron or steel products not produced in the United States. Produced in the United States means that all manufacturing processes of the iron or steel must take place

Continues on page 218

in the United States, from the initial melting stage through the application of coatings, except metallurgical processes involving refinement of steel additives. The origin of the elements of the iron or steel is not relevant to the determination of whether it is domestic or foreign.

Free Trade Agreement country means Australia, Bahrain, Chile, Colombia, Costa Rica, Dominican Republic, El Salvador, Guatemala, Honduras, Korea (Republic of), Mexico, Morocco, Nicaragua, Oman, Panama, Peru, or Singapore.

Free Trade Agreement country end product means an article that-

(1) Is wholly the growth, product, or manufacture of a Free Trade Agreement country; or

(2) In the case of an article that consists in whole or in part of materials from another country, has been substantially transformed in a Free Trade Agreement country into a new and different article of commerce with a name, character, or use distinct from that of the article or articles from which it was transformed. The term refers to a product offered for purchase under a supply contract, but for purposes of calculating the value of the end product includes services (except transportation services) incidental to the article, provided that the value of those incidental services does not exceed that of the article itself.

Israeli end product means an article that—

(1) Is wholly the growth, product, or manufacture of Israel; or

(2) In the case of an article that consists in whole or in part of materials from another country, has been substantially transformed in Israel into a new and different article of commerce with a name, character, or use distinct from that of the article or articles from which it was transformed.

Predominantly of iron or steel or a combination of both means that the cost of the iron and steel content exceeds 50 percent of the total cost of all its components. The cost of iron and steel is the cost of the iron or steel mill products (such as bar, billet, slab, wire, plate, or sheet), castings, or forgings utilized in the manufacture of the product and a good faith estimate of the cost of iron or steel components excluding COTS fasteners.

Steel means an alloy that includes at least 50 percent iron, between 0.02 and 2 percent carbon, and may include other elements.

United States means the 50 States, the District of Columbia, and outlying areas.

Continues on page 219

(b) *Components of foreign origin.* Offerors may obtain from the Contracting Officer a list of foreign articles that the Contracting Officer will treat as domestic for this contract.

(c) *Delivery of end products.* 41 U.S.C.chapter 83, Buy American statute, provides a preference for domestic end products for supplies acquired for use in the United States. In accordance with 41 U.S.C. 1907, the domestic content test of the Buy American statute is waived for an end product that is a COTS item (see 12.505(a)(1)), except that for an end product that consists wholly or predominantly of iron or steel or a combination of both, the domestic content test is applied only to the iron and steel content of the end product, excluding COTS fasteners. Unless otherwise specified, these trade agreements apply to all items in the Schedule. The Contractor shall deliver under this contract only domestic end products except to the extent that, in its offer, it specified delivery of foreign end products in the provision entitled "Buy American-Free Trade Agreements-Israeli Trade Act Certificate." If the Contractor specified in its offer that the Contractor would supply a Free Trade Agreement country end product (other than a Bahraini, Moroccan, Omani, Panamanian, or Peruvian end product) or an Israeli end product, then the Contractor shall supply a Free Trade Agreement country end product (other than a Bahraini, Moroccan, Omani, Panamanian, or Peruvian end product), an Israeli end product or, at the Contractor's option, a domestic end product.

(End of clause)

Alternate I [Reserved]

Alternate II (Dec 2022). As prescribed in 25.1101 (b) (1) (ii), substitute the following paragraph (c) for paragraph (c) of the basic clause:

(c) *Delivery of end products.* 41 U.S.C.chapter 83 provides a preference for domestic end products for supplies acquired for use in the United States. In accordance with 41 U.S.C. 1907, the domestic content test of the Buy American statute is waived for an end product that is a COTS item (see 12.505(a) (1)), except that for an end product that consists wholly or predominantly of iron or steel or a combination of both, the domestic content test is applied only to the iron and steel content of the end product, excluding COTS fasteners. In addition, the Contracting Officer has determined that the Israeli Trade Act applies to this acquisition. Unless otherwise specified, this trade agreement applies to all items in the Schedule. The Contractor shall deliver under this contract only domestic end products except to the extent that, in its offer, it specified delivery of foreign end products in the provision entitled "Buy American—Free Trade Agreements—Israeli Trade Act." If the Contractor specified in its offer that the Contractor would supply an Israeli end product, then the Contractor shall supply an Israeli end product or, at the Contractor's option, a domestic end product.

Continues on page 220

Alternate III (Nov 2023). As prescribed in 25.1101 (b)(1)(iii), delete the definition of "Bahraini, Moroccan, Omani, Panamanian, or Peruvian end product" and add in its place the following definition of "Bahraini, Korean, Moroccan, Omani, Panamanian, or Peruvian end product" in paragraph (a) of the basic clause; and substitute the following paragraph (c) for paragraph (c) of the basic clause:

Bahraini, Korean, Moroccan, Omani, Panamanian, or Peruvian end product means an article that-

(1) Is wholly the growth, product, or manufacture of Bahrain, Korea (Republic of), Morocco, Oman, Panama, or Peru; or

(2) In the case of an article that consists in whole or in part of materials from another country, has been substantially transformed in Bahrain, Korea (Republic of), Morocco, Oman, Panama, or Peru into a new and different article of commerce with a name, character, or use distinct from that of the article or articles from which it was transformed. The term refers to a product offered for purchase under a supply contract, but for purposes of calculating the value of the end product includes services (except transportation services) incidental to the article, provided that the value of those incidental services does not exceed that of the article itself.

(c) *Delivery of end products.* 41 U.S.C.chapter 83 provides a preference for domestic end products for supplies acquired for use in the United States. In accordance with 41 U.S.C.1907, the domestic content test of the Buy American statute is waived for an end product that is a COTS item (see 12.505(a)(1)), except that for an end product that consists wholly or predominantly of iron or steel or a combination of both, the domestic content test is applied only to the iron and steel content of the end product, excluding COTS fasteners. In addition, the Contracting Officer has determined that FTAs (except the Bahrain, Korea (Republic of), Morocco, Oman, Panama, and Peru FTAs) and the Israeli Trade Act apply to this acquisition. Unless otherwise specified, these trade agreements apply to all items in the Schedule. The Contractor shall deliver under this contract only domestic end products except to the extent that, in its offer, it specified delivery of foreign end products in the provision entitled "Buy American-Free Trade Agreements-Israeli Trade Act Certificate." If the Contractor specified in its offer that the Contractor would supply a Free Trade Agreement country end product (other than a Bahraini, Korean, Moroccan, Omani, Panamanian, or Peruvian end product) or an Israeli end product, then the Contractor shall supply a Free Trade Agreement country end product (other than a Bahraini, Korean, Moroccan, Omani, Panamanian, or Peruvian end product), an Israeli end product or, at the Contractor's option, a domestic end product.

Continues on page 221

Alternate IV (Oct 2022). As prescribed in 25.1101 (b) (1)(iv) substitute the following sentence for the first sentence of paragraph (1)(ii)(A) of the definition of *domestic end product* in paragraph (a):

> (A) The cost of its components mined, produced, or manufactured in the United States exceeds __ percent of the cost of all its components. *[Contracting officer to insert the percentage.]*

FAR Clause 52.225-9 Buy American-Construction Materials.

As prescribed in 25.1102(a), insert the following clause:

Buy American-Construction Materials (Oct 2022)

(a) *Definitions*. As used in this clause—

Commercially available off-the-shelf (COTS) item—

(1) Means any item of supply (including construction material) that is–

(i) A commercial product (as defined in paragraph (1) of the definition of "commercial product" at Federal Acquisition Regulation (FAR) 2.101);

(ii) Sold in substantial quantities in the commercial marketplace; and

(iii) Offered to the Government, under a contract or subcontract at any tier, without modification, in the same form in which it is sold in the commercial marketplace; and

(2) Does not include bulk cargo, as defined in 46 U.S.C. 40102(4), such as agricultural products and petroleum products.

"Construction material" means an article, material, or supply brought to the construction site by the Contractor or a subcontractor for incorporation into the building or work. The term also includes an item brought to the site preassembled from articles, materials, or supplies. However, emergency life safety systems, such as emergency lighting, fire alarm, and audio evacuation systems, that are discrete systems incorporated into a public building or work and that are produced as complete systems, are evaluated as a single and distinct construction material regardless of when or how the individual parts or components of those systems are delivered to the construction site. Materials purchased directly by the Government are supplies, not construction material.

Continues on page 222

Cost of components means—

(1) For components purchased by the Contractor, the acquisition cost, including transportation costs to the place of incorporation into the construction material (whether or not such costs are paid to a domestic firm), and any applicable duty (whether or not a duty-free entry certificate is issued); or

(2) For components manufactured by the Contractor, all costs associated with the manufacture of the component, including transportation costs as described in paragraph (1) of this definition, plus allocable overhead costs, but excluding profit. Cost of components does not include any costs associated with the manufacture of the construction material.

Critical component means a component that is mined, produced, or manufactured in the United States and deemed critical to the U.S. supply chain. The list of critical components is at FAR 25.105.

Critical item means a domestic construction material or domestic end product that is deemed critical to U.S. supply chain resiliency. The list of critical items is at FAR 25.105.

Domestic construction material means—

(1) For construction material that does not consist wholly or predominantly of iron or steel or a combination of both-

(i) An unmanufactured construction material mined or produced in the United States; or

(ii) A construction material manufactured in the United States, if–

(A) The cost of its components mined, produced, or manufactured in the United States exceeds 60 percent of the cost of all its components, except that the percentage will be 65 percent for items delivered in calendar years 2024 through 2028 and 75 percent for items delivered starting in calendar year 2029. Components of foreign origin of the same class or kind for which non availability determinations have been made are treated as domestic. Components of unknown origin are treated as foreign; or

(B) The construction material is a COTS item; or

Continues on page 223

(2) For construction material that consists wholly or predominantly of iron or steel or a combination of both, a construction material manufactured in the United States if the cost of foreign iron and steel constitutes less than 5 percent of the cost of all components used in such construction material. The cost of foreign iron and steel includes but is not limited to the cost of foreign iron or steel mill products (such as bar, billet, slab, wire, plate, or sheet), castings, or forgings utilized in the manufacture of the construction material and a good faith estimate of the cost of all foreign iron or steel components excluding COTS fasteners. Iron or steel components of unknown origin are treated as foreign. If the construction material contains multiple components, the cost of all the materials used in such construction material is calculated in accordance with the definition of "cost of components".

Fastener means a hardware device that mechanically joins or affixes two or more objects together. Examples of fasteners are nuts, bolts, pins, rivets, nails, clips, and screws.

Foreign construction material means a construction material other than a domestic construction material.

Foreign iron and steel means iron or steel products not produced in the United States. Produced in the United States means that all manufacturing processes of the iron or steel must take place in the United States, from the initial melting stage through the application of coatings, except metallurgical processes involving refinement of steel additives. The origin of the elements of the iron or steel is not relevant to the determination of whether it is domestic or foreign.

Predominantly of iron or steel or a combination of both means that the cost of the iron and steel content exceeds 50 percent of the total cost of all its components. The cost of iron and steel is the cost of the iron or steel mill products (such as bar, billet, slab, wire, plate, or sheet), castings, or forgings utilized in the manufacture of the product and a good faith estimate of the cost of iron or steel components excluding COTS fasteners.

Steel means an alloy that includes at least 50 percent iron, between 0.02 and 2 percent carbon, and may include other elements.

"United States" means the 50 States, the District of Columbia, and outlying areas.

(b) Domestic preference.

Continues on page 224

(1) This clause implements 41 U.S.C.chapter 83, Buy American, by providing a preference for domestic construction material. In accordance with 41 U.S.C. 1907, the domestic content test of the Buy American statute is waived for construction material that is a COTS item, except that for construction material that consists wholly or predominantly of iron or steel or a combination of both, the domestic content test is applied only to the iron and steel content of the construction materials, excluding COTS fasteners. (See FAR 12.505(a) (2)). The Contractor shall use only domestic construction material in performing this contract, except as provided in paragraphs (b) (2) and (b) (3) of this clause.

(2) This requirement does not apply to information technology that is a commercial product or to the construction materials or components listed by the Government as follows:

____ *[Contracting Officer to list applicable excepted materials or indicate "none"]*

(3) The Contracting Officer may add other foreign construction material to the list in paragraph (b) (2) of this clause if the Government determines that-

(i) The cost of domestic construction material would be unreasonable.

(A) *For domestic construction material that is not a critical item or does not contain critical components.*

(1) The cost of a particular domestic construction material subject to the requirements of the Buy American statute is unreasonable when the cost of such material exceeds the cost of foreign material by more than 20 percent;

(2) For construction material that is not a COTS item and does not consist wholly or predominantly of iron or steel or a combination of both, if the cost of a particular domestic construction material is determined to be unreasonable or there is no domestic offer received, and the low offer is for foreign construction material that is manufactured in the United States and does not exceed 55 percent domestic content, the Contracting Officer will treat the lowest offer of foreign construction material that exceeds 55 percent domestic content as a domestic offer and determine whether the cost of that offer is unreasonable by applying the evaluation factor listed in paragraph (b)(3)(i)(A)*(1)* of this clause.

(3) The procedures in paragraph (b) (3) (i)(A)*(2)* of this clause will no longer apply as of January 1, 2030.

Continues on page 225

(B) *For domestic construction material that is a critical item or contains critical components.*

(1) The cost of a particular domestic construction material that is a critical item or contains critical components, subject to the requirements of the Buy American statute, is unreasonable when the cost of such material exceeds the cost of foreign material by more than 20 percent plus the additional preference factor identified for the critical item or construction material containing critical components listed at FAR 25.105.

(2) For construction material that does not consist wholly or predominantly of iron or steel or a combination of both, if the cost of a particular domestic construction material is determined to be unreasonable or there is no domestic offer received, and the low offer is for foreign construction material that does not exceed 55 percent domestic content, the Contracting Officer will treat the lowest foreign offer of construction material that is manufactured in the United States and exceeds 55 percent domestic content as a domestic offer, and determine whether the cost of that offer is unreasonable by applying the evaluation factor listed in paragraph (b)(3)(i)(B)*(1)* of this clause.

(3) The procedures in paragraph (b)(3)(i)(B)*(2)* of this clause will no longer apply as of January 1, 2030.

(ii) The application of the restriction of the Buy American statute to a particular construction material would be impracticable or inconsistent with the public interest; or

(iii) The construction material is not mined, produced, or manufactured in the United States in sufficient and reasonably available commercial quantities of a satisfactory quality.

(c) Request for determination of inapplicability of the Buy American statute.

(1)

(i) Any Contractor request to use foreign construction material in accordance with paragraph (b)(3) of this clause shall include adequate information for Government evaluation of the request, including-

Continues on page 226

(A) A description of the foreign and domestic construction materials;

(B) Unit of measure;

(C) Quantity;

(D) Price;

(E) Time of delivery or availability;

(F) Location of the construction project;

(G) Name and address of the proposed supplier; and

(H) A detailed justification of the reason for use of foreign construction materials cited in accordance with paragraph (b) (3) of this clause.

(ii) A request based on unreasonable cost shall include a reasonable survey of the market and a completed price comparison table in the format in paragraph (d) of this clause.

(iii) The price of construction material shall include all delivery costs to the construction site and any applicable duty (whether or not a duty-free certificate may be issued).

(iv) Any Contractor request for a determination submitted after contract award shall explain why the Contractor could not reasonably foresee the need for such determination and could not have requested the determination before contract award. If the Contractor does not submit a satisfactory explanation, the Contracting Officer need not make a determination.

(2) If the Government determines after contract award that an exception to the Buy American statute applies and the Contracting Officer and the Contractor negotiate adequate consideration, the Contracting Officer will modify the contract to allow use of the foreign construction material. However, when the basis for the exception is the unreasonable price of a domestic construction material, adequate consideration is not less than the differential established in paragraph (b)(3)(i) of this clause.

(3) Unless the Government determines that an exception to the Buy American statute applies, use of foreign construction material is noncompliant with the Buy American statute.

Continues on page 227

(d) *Data.* To permit evaluation of requests under paragraph (c) of this clause based on unreasonable cost, the Contractor shall include the following information and any applicable supporting data based on the survey of suppliers:

	Foreign and Domestic Construction Materials Price Comparison				
	Construction Material Description	Unit of Measure	Quantity	Price (dollars)*	
	Item1:				
	Foreign construction material	____	____	____	
	Domestic construction material	____	____	____	
	Item2:				
	Foreign construction material	____	____	____	
	Domestic construction material	____	____	____	

[* *Include all delivery costs to the construction site and any applicable duty (whether or not a duty-free entry certificate is issued)*].

[*List name, address, telephone number, and contact for suppliers surveyed. Attach copy of response; if oral, attach summary.*]

[*Include other applicable supporting information.*]

(End of clause)

Alternate I (Oct 2022). As prescribed in 25.1102 (a) (3) substitute the following sentence for the first sentence in paragraph (1) (ii) (A) of the definition of "domestic construction material" in paragraph (a):

Continues on page 228

(A) The cost of its components mined, produced, or manufactured in the United States exceeds __ percent of the cost of all its components. [*Contracting officer to insert the percentage.*]

FAR Clause 52.225-11 Buy American-Construction Materials under Trade Agreements.

As prescribed in 25.1102(c), insert the following clause:

Buy American-Construction Materials under Trade Agreements (Nov 2023)

(a) *Definitions*. As used in this clause—

Caribbean Basin country construction material means a construction material that—

(1) Is wholly the growth, product, or manufacture of a Caribbean Basin country; or

(2) In the case of a construction material that consists in whole or in part of materials from another country, has been substantially transformed in a Caribbean Basin country into a new and different construction material distinct from the materials from which it was transformed.

Commercially available off-the-shelf (COTS) item—

(1) Means any item of supply (including construction material) that is–

(i) A commercial product (as defined in paragraph (1) of the definition of "commercial product" at Federal Acquisition Regulation (FAR) 2.101);

(ii) Sold in substantial quantities in the commercial marketplace; and

(iii) Offered to the Government, under a contract or subcontract at any tier, without modification, in the same form in which it is sold in the commercial marketplace; and

(2) Does not include bulk cargo, as defined in 46 U.S.C.40102(4), such as agricultural products and petroleum products.

Component means an article, material, or supply incorporated directly into a construction material.

Continues on page 229

Construction material means an article, material, or supply brought to the construction site by the Contractor or subcontractor for incorporation into the building or work. The term also includes an item brought to the site preassembled from articles, materials, or supplies. However, emergency life safety systems, such as emergency lighting, fire alarm, and audio evacuation systems, that are discrete systems incorporated into a public building or work and that are produced as complete systems, are evaluated as a single and distinct construction material regardless of when or how the individual parts or components of those systems are delivered to the construction site. Materials purchased directly by the Government are supplies, not construction material.

Cost of components means—

(1) For components purchased by the Contractor, the acquisition cost, including transportation costs to the place of incorporation into the construction material (whether or not such costs are paid to a domestic firm), and any applicable duty (whether or not a duty-free entry certificate is issued); or

(2) For components manufactured by the Contractor, all costs associated with the manufacture of the component, including transportation costs as described in paragraph (1) of this definition, plus allocable overhead costs, but excluding profit. Cost of components does not include any costs associated with the manufacture of the construction material.

Critical component means a component that is mined, produced, or manufactured in the United States and deemed critical to the U.S. supply chain. The list of critical components is at FAR 25.105.

Critical item means a domestic construction material or domestic end product that is deemed critical to U.S. supply chain resiliency. The list of critical items is at FAR 25.105.

Designated country means any of the following countries:

(1) A World Trade Organization Government Procurement Agreement (WTO GPA) country (Armenia, Aruba, Australia, Austria, Belgium, Bulgaria, Canada, Croatia, Cyprus, Czech Republic, Denmark, Estonia, Finland, France, Germany, Greece, Hong Kong, Hungary, Iceland, Ireland, Israel, Italy, Japan, Korea (Republic of), Latvia, Liechtenstein, Lithuania, Luxembourg, Malta, Moldova, Montenegro, Netherlands, New Zealand, North Macedonia, Norway, Poland, Portugal, Romania, Singapore, Slovak Republic, Slovenia, Spain, Sweden, Switzerland, Taiwan, Ukraine, or United Kingdom);

Continues on page 230

(2) A Free Trade Agreement (FTA) country (Australia, Bahrain, Chile, Colombia, Costa Rica, Dominican Republic, El Salvador, Guatemala, Honduras, Korea (Republic of), Mexico, Morocco, Nicaragua, Oman, Panama, Peru, or Singapore);

(3) A least developed country (Afghanistan, Angola, Bangladesh, Benin, Bhutan, Burkina Faso, Burundi, Cambodia, Central African Republic, Chad, Comoros, Democratic Republic of Congo, Djibouti, Equatorial Guinea, Eritrea, Ethiopia, Gambia, Guinea, Guinea-Bissau, Haiti, Kiribati, Laos, Lesotho, Liberia, Madagascar, Malawi, Mali, Mauritania, Mozambique, Nepal, Niger, Rwanda, Samoa, Sao Tome and Principe, Senegal, Sierra Leone, Solomon Islands, Somalia, South Sudan, Tanzania, Timor-Leste, Togo, Tuvalu, Uganda, Vanuatu, Yemen, or Zambia); or

(4) A Caribbean Basin country (Antigua and Barbuda, Aruba, Bahamas, Barbados, Belize, Bonaire, British Virgin Islands, Curacao, Dominica, Grenada, Guyana, Haiti, Jamaica, Montserrat, Saba, St. Kitts and Nevis, St. Lucia, St. Vincent and the Grenadines, Sint Eustatius, Sint Maarten, or Trinidad and Tobago).

Designated country construction material means a construction material that is a WTO GPA country construction material, an FTA country construction material, a least developed country construction material, or a Caribbean Basin country construction material.

Domestic construction material means—

(1) For construction material that does not consist wholly or predominantly of iron or steel or a combination of both-

(i) An unmanufactured construction material mined or produced in the United States; or

(ii) A construction material manufactured in the United States, if—

(A) The cost of its components mined, produced, or manufactured in the United States exceeds 60 percent of the cost of all its components, except that the percentage will be 65 percent for items delivered in calendar years 2024 through 2028 and 75 percent for items delivered starting in calendar year 2029.

(B) The construction material is a COTS item; or

Continues on page 231

(2) For construction material that consists wholly or predominantly of iron or steel or a combination of both, a construction material manufactured in the United States if the cost of foreign iron and steel constitutes less than 5 percent of the cost of all components used in such construction material. The cost of foreign iron and steel includes but is not limited to the cost of foreign iron or steel mill products (such as bar, billet, slab, wire, plate, or sheet), castings, or forgings utilized in the manufacture of the construction material and a good faith estimate of the cost of all foreign iron or steel components excluding COTS fasteners. Iron or steel components of unknown origin are treated as foreign. If the construction material contains multiple components, the cost of all the materials used in such construction material is calculated in accordance with the definition of "cost of components."

Fastener means a hardware device that mechanically joins or affixes two or more objects together. Examples of fasteners are nuts, bolts, pins, rivets, nails, clips, and screws.

Foreign construction material means a construction material other than a domestic construction material.

Foreign iron and steel means iron or steel products not produced in the United States. Produced in the United States means that all manufacturing processes of the iron or steel must take place in the United States, from the initial melting stage through the application of coatings, except metallurgical processes involving refinement of steel additives. The origin of the elements of the iron or steel is not relevant to the determination of whether it is domestic or foreign.

Free Trade Agreement country construction material means a construction material that-

(1) Is wholly the growth, product, or manufacture of a Free Trade Agreement (FTA) country; or

(2) In the case of a construction material that consists in whole or in part of materials from another country, has been substantially transformed in a FTA country into a new and different construction material distinct from the materials from which it was transformed.

Least developed country construction material means a construction material that-

(1) Is wholly the growth, product, or manufacture of a least developed country; or

(2) In the case of a construction material that consists in whole or in part of materials from another country, has been substantially transformed in a least developed country into a new and different construction material distinct from the materials from which it was transformed.

Continues on page 232

Predominantly of iron or steel or a combination of both means that the cost of the iron and steel content exceeds 50 percent of the total cost of all its components. The cost of iron and steel is the cost of the iron or steel mill products (such as bar, billet, slab, wire, plate, or sheet), castings, or forgings utilized in the manufacture of the product and a good faith estimate of the cost of iron or steel components excluding COTS fasteners.

Steel means an alloy that includes at least 50 percent iron, between 0.02 and 2 percent carbon, and may include other elements.

United States means the 50 States, the District of Columbia, and outlying areas.

WTO GPA country construction material means a construction material that-

(1) Is wholly the growth, product, or manufacture of a WTO GPA country; or

(2) In the case of a construction material that consists in whole or in part of materials from another country, has been substantially transformed in a WTO GPA country into a new and different construction material distinct from the materials from which it was transformed.

(b) Construction materials.

(1) This clause implements 41 U.S.C.chapter 83, Buy American, by providing a preference for domestic construction material. In accordance with 41 U.S.C.1907, the domestic content test of the Buy American statute is waived for construction material that is a COTS item, except that for construction material that consists wholly or predominantly of iron or steel or a combination of both, the domestic content test is applied only to the iron and steel content of the construction material, excluding COTS fasteners. (See FAR 12.505(a)(2)). In addition, the Contracting Officer has determined that the WTO GPA and Free Trade Agreements (FTAs) apply to this acquisition. Therefore, the Buy American restrictions are waived for designated country construction materials.

(2) The Contractor shall use only domestic or designated country construction material in performing this contract, except as provided in paragraphs (b) (3) and (b) (4) of this clause.

(3) The requirement in paragraph (b) (2) of this clause does not apply to information technology that is a commercial product or to the construction materials or components listed by the Government as follows:

[Contracting Officer to list applicable excepted materials or indicate "none"]

Continues on page 233

(4) The Contracting Officer may add other foreign construction material to the list in paragraph (b) (3) of this clause if the Government determines that-

(i) The cost of domestic construction material would be unreasonable.

(A) *For domestic construction material that is not a critical item or does not contain critical components.*

(1) The cost of a particular domestic construction material subject to the restrictions of the Buy American statute is unreasonable when the cost of such material exceeds the cost of foreign material by more than 20 percent;

(2) For construction material that is not a COTS item and does not consist wholly or predominantly of iron or steel or a combination of both, if the cost of a particular domestic construction material is determined to be unreasonable or there is no domestic offer received, and the low offer is for foreign construction material that does not exceed 55 percent domestic content, the Contracting Officer will treat the lowest offer of foreign construction material that is manufactured in the United States and exceeds 55 percent domestic content as a domestic offer and determine whether the cost of that offer is unreasonable by applying the evaluation factor listed in paragraph (b)(4)(i)(A)*(1)* of this clause.

(3) The procedures in paragraph (b) (4)(i)(A)*(2)* of this clause will no longer apply as of January 1, 2030.

(B) *For domestic construction material that is a critical item or contains critical components.*

(1) The cost of a particular domestic construction material that is a critical item or contains critical components, subject to the requirements of the Buy American statute, is unreasonable when the cost of such material exceeds the cost of foreign material by more than 20 percent plus the additional preference factor identified for the critical item or construction material containing critical components listed at FAR 25.105.

(2) For construction material that does not consist wholly or predominantly of iron or steel or a combination of both, if the cost of a particular domestic construction material is determined to be unreasonable or there is no domestic offer received, and the low offer is for foreign construction material that does not exceed 55 percent domestic content, the Contracting

Continues on page 234

Officer will treat the lowest offer of foreign construction material that is manufactured in the United States and exceeds 55 percent domestic content as a domestic offer, and determine whether the cost of that offer is unreasonable by applying the evaluation factor listed in paragraph (b)(4)(i)(B)*(1)* of this clause.

(3) The procedures in paragraph (b) (4)(i)(B)*(2)* of this clause will no longer apply as of January 1, 2030.

(ii) The application of the restriction of the Buy American Act to a particular construction material would be impracticable or inconsistent with the public interest; or

(iii) The construction material is not mined, produced, or manufactured in the United States in sufficient and reasonably available commercial quantities of a satisfactory quality.

(c) Request for determination of inapplicability of the Buy American statute.

(1)

(i) Any Contractor request to use foreign construction material in accordance with paragraph (b)(4) of this clause shall include adequate information for Government evaluation of the request, including-

(A) A description of the foreign and domestic construction materials;

(B) Unit of measure;

(C) Quantity;

(D) Price;

(E) Time of delivery or availability;

(F) Location of the construction project;

(G) Name and address of the proposed supplier; and

(H) A detailed justification of the reason for use of foreign construction materials cited in accordance with paragraph (b) (3) of this clause.

Continues on page 235

(ii) A request based on unreasonable cost shall include a reasonable survey of the market and a completed price comparison table in the format in paragraph (d) of this clause.

(iii) The price of construction material shall include all delivery costs to the construction site and any applicable duty (whether or not a duty-free certificate may be issued).

(iv) Any Contractor request for a determination submitted after contract award shall explain why the Contractor could not reasonably foresee the need for such determination and could not have requested the determination before contract award. If the Contractor does not submit a satisfactory explanation, the Contracting Officer need not make a determination.

(2) If the Government determines after contract award that an exception to the Buy American statute applies and the Contracting Officer and the Contractor negotiate adequate consideration, the Contracting Officer will modify the contract to allow use of the foreign construction material. However, when the basis for the exception is the unreasonable price of a domestic construction material, adequate consideration is not less than the differential established in paragraph (b)(4)(i) of this clause.

(3) Unless the Government determines that an exception to the Buy American statute applies, use of foreign construction material is noncompliant with the Buy American statute.

Continues on page 236

(d) *Data.* To permit evaluation of requests under paragraph (c) of this clause based on unreasonable cost, the Contractor shall include the following information and any applicable supporting data based on the survey of suppliers:

Foreign and Domestic Construction Materials Price Comparison			
Construction Material Description	Unit of Measure	Quantity	Price (Dollars)*
Item1			
Foreign construction material	______	______	______
Domestic construction material	______	______	______
Item1			
Foreign construction material	______	______	______
Domestic construction material	______	______	______

[Include all delivery costs to the construction site and any applicable duty (whether or not a duty-free entry certificate is issued)].*

[List name, address, telephone number, and contact for suppliers surveyed. Attach copy of response; if oral, attach summary.]

[Include other applicable supporting information.]

(End of clause)

Alternate I (Nov 2023). As prescribed in 25.1102 (c)(3), add the following definition of "Bahraini, Mexican, or Omani construction material" to paragraph (a) of the basic clause, and substitute the following paragraphs (b)(1) and (b)(2) for paragraphs (b)(1) and (b)(2) of the basic clause:

"Bahraini, Mexican, or Omani construction material" means a construction material that-

(1) Is wholly the growth, product, or manufacture of Bahrain, Mexico, or Oman; or

Continues on page 237

(2) In the case of a construction material that consists in whole or in part of materials from another country, has been substantially transformed in Bahrain, Mexico, or Oman into a new and different construction material distinct from the materials from which it was transformed.

(b) Construction materials. (1) This clause implements 41 U.S.C. chapter 83, Buy American, by providing a preference for domestic construction material. In accordance with 41 U.S.C. 1907, the domestic content test of the Buy American statute is waived for construction material that is a COTS item, except that for construction material that consists wholly or predominantly of iron or steel or a combination of both, the domestic content test is applied only to the iron and steel content of the construction material, excluding COTS fasteners. (See 12.505(a) (2)). In addition, the Contracting Officer has determined that the WTO GPA and all the Free Trade Agreements except the Bahrain FTA, United States-Mexico-Canada Agreement, and the Oman FTA apply to this acquisition. Therefore, the Buy American statute restrictions are waived for designated country construction materials other than Bahraini, Mexican, or Omani construction materials.

(2) The Contractor shall use only domestic or designated country construction material other than Bahraini, Mexican, or Omani construction material in performing this contract, except as provided in paragraphs (b)(3) and (b)(4) of this clause.

Alternate II (Oct 2022). As prescribed in 25.1102 (c)(4) substitute the following sentence for the first sentence of paragraph (1)(ii)(A) of the definition of *domestic construction material* in paragraph (a):

(A) The cost of its components mined, produced, or manufactured in the United States exceeds __ percent of the cost of all its components. [*Contracting officer to insert the percentage.]*

FAR Clause 52.225-21 Required Use of American Iron, Steel, and Manufactured Goods-Buy American Statute-Construction Materials.

As prescribed in 25.1102(e), insert the following clause:

Required Use of American Iron, Steel, and Manufactured Goods-Buy American Statute-Construction Materials (Jan 2021)

(a) *Definitions*. As used in this clause-

Component means an article, material, or supply incorporated directly into a construction material.

Continues on page 238

Construction material means an article, material, or supply brought to the construction site by the Contractor or a subcontractor for incorporation into the building or work. The term also includes an item brought to the site preassembled from articles, materials, or supplies. However, emergency life safety systems, such as emergency lighting, fire alarm, and audio evacuation systems, that are discrete systems incorporated into a public building or work and that are produced as complete systems, are evaluated as a single and distinct construction material regardless of when or how the individual parts or components of those systems are delivered to the construction site.

Domestic construction material means the following-

(1) An unmanufactured construction material mined or produced in the United States. (The Buy American statute applies.)

(2) A manufactured construction material that is manufactured in the United States and, if the construction material consists wholly or predominantly of iron or steel, the iron or steel was produced in the United States. (Section 1605 of the Recovery Act applies.)

Foreign construction material means a construction material other than a domestic construction material.

Manufactured construction material means any construction material that is not unmanufactured construction material.

Steel means an alloy that includes at least 50 percent iron, between 0.02 and 2 percent carbon, and may include other elements.

United States means the 50 States, the District of Columbia, and outlying areas.

Unmanufactured construction material means raw material brought to the construction site for incorporation into the building or work that has not been-

(1) Processed into a specific form and shape; or

(2) Combined with other raw material to create a material that has different properties than the properties of the individual raw materials.

(b) Domestic preference.

(1) This clause implements-

Continues on page 239

(i) Section 1605 of the American Recovery and Reinvestment Act of 2009 (Recovery Act) (Pub. L. 111-5), by requiring, unless an exception applies, that all manufactured construction material in the project is manufactured in the United States and, if the construction material consists wholly or predominantly of iron or steel, the iron or steel was produced in the United States (produced in the United States means that all manufacturing processes of the iron or steel must take place in the United States, except metallurgical processes involving refinement of steel additives); and

(ii) 41 U.S.C chapter 83, Buy American, by providing a preference for unmanufactured construction material mined or produced in the United States over unmanufactured construction material mined or produced in a foreign country.

(2) The Contractor shall use only domestic construction material in performing this contract, except as provided in paragraph (b) (3) and (b) (4) of this clause.

(3) This requirement does not apply to the construction material or components listed by the Government as follows:

____

____*[Contracting Officer to list applicable excepted materials or indicate "none"]*

(4) The Contracting Officer may add other foreign construction material to the list in paragraph (b) (3) of this clause if the Government determines that-

(i) The cost of domestic construction material would be unreasonable;

(A) The cost of domestic manufactured construction material, when compared to the cost of comparable foreign manufactured construction material, is unreasonable when the cumulative cost of such material will increase the cost of the contract by more than 25 percent;

(B) The cost of domestic unmanufactured construction material is unreasonable when the cost of such material exceeds the cost of comparable foreign unmanufactured construction material by more than 20 percent;

(ii) The construction material is not mined, produced, or manufactured in the United States in sufficient and reasonably available quantities and of a satisfactory quality;

Continues on page 240

(iii) The application of the restriction of section 1605 of the Recovery Act to a particular manufactured construction material would be inconsistent with the public interest or the application of the Buy American statute to a particular unmanufactured construction material would be impracticable or inconsistent with the public interest.

(c) Request for determination of inapplicability of section 1605 of the Recovery Act or the Buy American statute.

(1)

(i) Any Contractor request to use foreign construction material in accordance with paragraph (b)(4) of this clause shall include adequate information for Government evaluation of the request, including-

(A) A description of the foreign and domestic construction materials;

(B) Unit of measure;

(C) Quantity;

(D) Cost;

(E) Time of delivery or availability;

(F) Location of the construction project;

(G) Name and address of the proposed supplier; and

(H) A detailed justification of the reason for use of foreign construction materials cited in accordance with paragraph (b) (4) of this clause.

(ii) A request based on unreasonable cost shall include a reasonable survey of the market and a completed cost comparison table in the format in paragraph (d) of this clause.

(iii) The cost of construction material shall include all delivery costs to the construction site and any applicable duty.

(iv) Any Contractor request for a determination submitted after contract award shall explain why the Contractor could not reasonably foresee the need for such determination and could not have requested the determination before contract award.

Continues on page 241

If the Contractor does not submit a satisfactory explanation, the Contracting Officer need not make a determination.

(2) If the Government determines after contract award that an exception to section 1605 of the Recovery Act or the Buy American statute applies and the Contracting Officer and the Contractor negotiate adequate consideration, the Contracting Officer will modify the contract to allow use of the foreign construction material. However, when the basis for the exception is the unreasonable cost of a domestic construction material, adequate consideration is not less than the differential established in paragraph (b)(4)(i) of this clause.

(3) Unless the Government determines that an exception to section 1605 of the Recovery Act or the Buy American statute applies, use of foreign construction material is noncompliant with section 1605 of the American Recovery and Reinvestment Act or the Buy American statute.

Continues on page 242

(d) *Data.* To permit evaluation of requests under paragraph (c) of this clause based on unreasonable cost, the Contractor shall include the following information and any applicable supporting data based on the survey of suppliers:

Foreign and Domestic Construction Materials Cost Comparison			
Construction Material Description	Unit of Measure	Quantity	Cost (Dollars)*
Item 1:			
Foreign construction material	______	______	______
Domestic construction material	______	______	______
Item 2:			
Foreign construction material	______	______	______
Domestic construction material	______	______	______
[*List name, address, telephone number, and contact for suppliers surveyed. Attach copy of response; if oral, attach summary.*] [*Include other applicable supporting information.*] [* *Include all delivery costs to the construction site.*]			

(End of clause)

Continues on page 243

52.225-23 Required Use of American Iron, Steel, and Manufactured Goods-Buy American Statute-Construction Materials under Trade Agreements.

As prescribed in 25.1102(e), insert the following clause:

Required Use of American Iron, Steel, and Manufactured Goods-Buy American Statute-Construction Materials under Trade Agreements (Nov 2023)

(a) *Definitions*. As used in this clause—

Component means an article, material, or supply incorporated directly into a construction material.

Construction material means an article, material, or supply brought to the construction site by the Contractor or subcontractor for incorporation into the building or work. The term also includes an item brought to the site preassembled from articles, materials, or supplies. However, emergency life safety systems, such as emergency lighting, fire alarm, and audio evacuation systems, that are discrete systems incorporated into a public building or work and that are produced as complete systems, are evaluated as a single and distinct construction material regardless of when or how the individual parts or components of those systems are delivered to the construction site.

Designated country means any of the following countries:

(1) A World Trade Organization Government Procurement Agreement (WTO GPA) country (Armenia, Aruba, Australia, Austria, Belgium, Bulgaria, Canada, Croatia, Cyprus, Czech Republic, Denmark, Estonia, Finland, France, Germany, Greece, Hong Kong, Hungary, Iceland, Ireland, Israel, Italy, Japan, Korea (Republic of), Latvia, Liechtenstein, Lithuania, Luxembourg, Malta, Moldova, Montenegro, Netherlands, New Zealand, North Macedonia, Norway, Poland, Portugal, Romania, Singapore, Slovak Republic, Slovenia, Spain, Sweden, Switzerland, Taiwan, Ukraine, or United Kingdom);

(2) A Free Trade Agreement (FTA) country (Australia, Bahrain, Chile, Colombia, Costa Rica, Dominican Republic, El Salvador, Guatemala, Honduras, Korea (Republic of), Mexico, Morocco, Nicaragua, Oman, Panama, Peru, or Singapore);

(3) A least developed country (Afghanistan, Angola, Bangladesh, Benin, Bhutan, Burkina Faso, Burundi, Cambodia, Central African Republic, Chad, Comoros, Democratic Republic of Congo, Djibouti, Equatorial Guinea, Eritrea, Ethiopia, Gambia, Guinea, Guinea-Bissau,

Continues on page 244

Haiti, Kiribati, Laos, Lesotho, Liberia, Madagascar, Malawi, Mali, Mauritania, Mozambique, Nepal, Niger, Rwanda, Samoa, Sao Tome and Principe, Senegal, Sierra Leone, Solomon Islands, Somalia, South Sudan, Tanzania, Timor-Leste, Togo, Tuvalu, Uganda, Vanuatu, Yemen, or Zambia); or

(4) A Caribbean Basin country (Antigua and Barbuda, Aruba, Bahamas, Barbados, Belize, Bonaire, British Virgin Islands, Curacao, Dominica, Grenada, Guyana, Haiti, Jamaica, Montserrat, Saba, St. Kitts and Nevis, St. Lucia, St. Vincent and the Grenadines, Sint Eustatius, Sint Maarten, or Trinidad and Tobago).

Designated country construction material means a construction material that is a WTO GPA country construction material, an FTA country construction material, a least developed country construction material, or a Caribbean Basin country construction material.

Domestic construction material means the following:

(1) An unmanufactured construction material mined or produced in the United States. (The Buy American statute applies.)

(2) A manufactured construction material that is manufactured in the United States and, if the construction material consists wholly or predominantly of iron or steel, the iron or steel was produced in the United States. (Section 1605 of the Recovery Act applies.)

Foreign construction material means a construction material other than a domestic construction material.

Free trade agreement (FTA) country construction material means a construction material that-

(1) Is wholly the growth, product, or manufacture of an FTA country; or

(2) In the case of a construction material that consists in whole or in part of materials from another country, has been substantially transformed in an FTA country into a new and different construction material distinct from the materials from which it was transformed.

Least developed country construction material means a construction material that-

(1) Is wholly the growth, product, or manufacture of a least developed country; or

(2) In the case of a construction material that consists in whole or in part of materials from another country, has been substantially transformed in a least developed country into a new and different construction material distinct from the materials from which it was transformed.

Continues on page 245

Manufactured construction material means any construction material that is not unmanufactured construction material.

Non-designated country means a country other than the United States or a designated country.

Recovery Act designated country means any of the following countries:

(1) A World Trade Organization Government Procurement Agreement (WTO GPA) country (Armenia, Aruba, Australia, Austria, Belgium, Bulgaria, Canada, Croatia, Cyprus, Czech Republic, Denmark, Estonia, Finland, France, Germany, Greece, Hong Kong, Hungary, Iceland, Ireland, Israel, Italy, Japan, Korea (Republic of), Latvia, Liechtenstein, Lithuania, Luxembourg, Malta, Moldova, Montenegro, Netherlands, New Zealand, Norway, Poland, Portugal, Romania, Singapore, Slovak Republic, Slovenia, Spain, Sweden, Switzerland, Taiwan, Ukraine, or United Kingdom);

(2) A Free Trade Agreement country (FTA) (Australia, Bahrain, Chile, Colombia, Costa Rica, Dominican Republic, El Salvador, Guatemala, Honduras, Korea (Republic of), Mexico, Morocco, Nicaragua, Oman, Panama, Peru, or Singapore); or

(3) A least developed country (Afghanistan, Angola, Bangladesh, Benin, Bhutan, Burkina Faso, Burundi, Cambodia, Central African Republic, Chad, Comoros, Democratic Republic of Congo, Djibouti, Equatorial Guinea, Eritrea, Ethiopia, Gambia, Guinea, Guinea-Bissau, Haiti, Kiribati, Laos, Lesotho, Liberia, Madagascar, Malawi, Mali, Mauritania, Mozambique, Nepal, Niger, Rwanda, Samoa, Sao Tome and Principe, Senegal, Sierra Leone, Solomon Islands, Somalia, South Sudan, Tanzania, Timor-Leste, Togo, Tuvalu, Uganda, Vanuatu, Yemen, or Zambia).

Recovery Act designated country construction material means a construction material that is a WTO GPA country construction material, an FTA country construction material, or a least developed country construction material.

Steel means an alloy that includes at least 50 percent iron, between 0.02 and 2 percent carbon, and may include other elements.

United States means the 50 States, the District of Columbia, and outlying areas.

Unmanufactured construction material means raw material brought to the construction site for incorporation into the building or work that has not been-

(1) Processed into a specific form and shape; or

Continues on page 246

(2) Combined with other raw material to create a material that has different properties than the properties of the individual raw materials.

WTO GPA country construction material means a construction material that-

(1) Is wholly the growth, product, or manufacture of a WTO GPA country; or

(2) In the case of a construction material that consists in whole or in part of materials from another country, has been substantially transformed in a WTO GPA country into a new and different construction material distinct from the materials from which it was transformed.

(b) *Construction materials.*

(1) The restrictions of section 1605 of the American Recovery and Reinvestment Act of 2009 (Pub. L. 111-5) (Recovery Act) do not apply to Recovery Act designated country manufactured construction material. The restrictions of the Buy American statute do not apply to designated country unmanufactured construction material. Consistent with U.S. obligations under international agreements, this clause implements-

(i) Section 1605 of the Recovery Act by requiring, unless an exception applies, that all manufactured construction material in the project is manufactured in the United States and, if the construction material consists wholly or predominantly of iron or steel, the iron or steel was produced in the United States (produced in the United States means that all manufacturing processes of the iron or steel must take place in the United States, except metallurgical processes involving refinement of steel additives); and.

(ii) The Buy American statute by providing a preference for unmanufactured construction material mined or produced in the United States over unmanufactured construction material mined or produced in a non-designated country.

(2) The Contractor shall use only domestic construction material, Recovery Act designated country manufactured construction material, or designated country unmanufactured construction material in performing this contract, except as provided in paragraphs (b)(3) and (b)(4) of this clause.

(3) The requirement in paragraph (b) (2) of this clause does not apply to the construction materials or components listed by the Government as follows:

[Contracting Officer to list applicable excepted materials or indicate "none."]

Continues on page 247

(4) The Contracting Officer may add other construction material to the list in paragraph (b)(3) of this clause if the Government determines that-

(i) The cost of domestic construction material would be unreasonable;

(A) The cost of domestic manufactured construction material is unreasonable when the cumulative cost of such material, when compared to the cost of comparable foreign manufactured construction material, other than Recovery Act designated country construction material, will increase the overall cost of the contract by more than 25 percent;

(B) The cost of domestic unmanufactured construction material is unreasonable when the cost of such material exceeds the cost of comparable foreign unmanufactured construction material, other than designated country construction material, by more than 20 percent;

(ii) The construction material is not mined, produced, or manufactured in the United States in sufficient and reasonably available commercial quantities of a satisfactory quality; or

(iii) The application of the restriction of section 1605 of the Recovery Act to a particular manufactured construction material would be inconsistent with the public interest or the application of the Buy American statute to a particular unmanufactured construction material would be impracticable or inconsistent with the public interest.

(c) *Request for determination of inapplicability of section 1605 of the Recovery Act or the Buy American statute.*

(1)

(i) Any Contractor request to use foreign construction material in accordance with paragraph (b)(4) of this clause shall include adequate information for Government evaluation of the request, including-

(A) A description of the foreign and domestic construction materials;

(B) Unit of measure;

(C) Quantity;

(D) Cost;

Continues on page 248

(E) Time of delivery or availability;

(F) Location of the construction project;

(G) Name and address of the proposed supplier; and

(H) A detailed justification of the reason for use of foreign construction materials cited in accordance with paragraph (b) (4) of this clause.

(ii) A request based on unreasonable cost shall include a reasonable survey of the market and a completed cost comparison table in the format in paragraph (d) of this clause.

(iii) The cost of construction material shall include all delivery costs to the construction site and any applicable duty.

(iv) Any Contractor request for a determination submitted after contract award shall explain why the Contractor could not reasonably foresee the need for such determination and could not have requested the determination before contract award. If the Contractor does not submit a satisfactory explanation, the Contracting Officer need not make a determination.

(2) If the Government determines after contract award that an exception to section 1605 of the Recovery Act or the Buy American statute applies and the Contracting Officer and the Contractor negotiate adequate consideration, the Contracting Officer will modify the contract to allow use of the foreign construction material. However, when the basis for the exception is the unreasonable cost of a domestic construction material, adequate consideration is not less than the differential established in paragraph (b)(4)(i) of this clause.

(3) Unless the Government determines that an exception to section 1605 of the Recovery Act or the Buy American statute applies, use of foreign construction material other than manufactured construction material from a Recovery Act designated country or unmanufactured construction material from a designated country is noncompliant with the applicable statute.

(d) *Data.* To permit evaluation of requests under paragraph (c) of this clause based on unreasonable cost, the Contractor shall include the following information and any applicable supporting data based on the survey of suppliers:

Continues on page 249

Foreign (Non-designated Country) and Domestic Construction Materials Cost Comparison

Construction Material Description	Unit of Measure	Quantity	Cost (Dollars)*
Item 1:			
Foreign construction material	______	______	______
Domestic construction material	______	______	______
Item 2:			
Foreign construction material	______	______	______
Domestic construction material	______	______	______

[*List name, address, telephone number, and contact for suppliers surveyed. Attach copy of response; if oral, attach summary.*]

[*Include other applicable supporting information.*]

[* *Include all delivery costs to the construction site.*]

(End of clause)

Alternate I (Nov 2023). As prescribed in 25.1102 (e), add the following definition of "Bahraini, Mexican, or Omani construction material" to paragraph (a) of the basic clause, and substitute the following paragraphs (b)(1) and (b)(2) for paragraphs (b)(1) and (b)(2) of the basic clause:

Bahraini, Mexican, or Omani construction material means a construction material that-

Continues on page 250

(1)(1) Is wholly the growth, product, or manufacture of Bahrain, Mexico, or Oman; or

(2)(2) In the case of a construction material that consists in whole or in part of materials from another country, has been substantially transformed in Bahrain, Mexico, or Oman into a new and different construction material distinct from the materials from which it was transformed.

(b) *Construction materials.* (1) The restrictions of section 1605 of the American Recovery and Reinvestment Act of 2009 (Pub. L. 111-5) (Recovery Act) do not apply to Recovery Act designated country manufactured construction material. The restrictions of the Buy American statute do not apply to designated country unmanufactured construction material. Consistent with U.S. obligations under international agreements, this clause implements-

(i) Section 1605 of the Recovery Act, by requiring, unless an exception applies, that all manufactured construction material in the project is manufactured in the United States and, if the construction material consists wholly or predominantly of iron or steel, the iron or steel was produced in the United States (produced in the United States means that all manufacturing processes of the iron or steel must take place in the United States, except metallurgical processes involving refinement of steel additives); and

(ii) The Buy American statute by providing a preference for unmanufactured construction material mined or produced in the United States over unmanufactured construction material mined or produced in a non-designated country.

(2) The Contractor shall use only domestic construction material, Recovery Act designated country manufactured construction material, or designated country unmanufactured construction material, other than Bahraini, Mexican, or Omani construction material, in performing this contract, except as provided in paragraphs (b)(3) and (b)(4) of this clause.

12.0 Prompt Payment Act

When FAR clause 52.232-27 Prompt Payment for Construction Contracts is included in a contract, it sets out the requirements for an acceptable invoice and allows payment within 14 calendar days. The key element is that the invoice must be an "acceptable" invoice. There are several types of invoice payments that may occur under construction contracts. The contract may also have other requirements in various sections that mandate additional requirements for an acceptable invoice, i.e. QC system and schedules.

12.1 Progress Payments

Progress payments are based on CO approval of the estimated amount and value of work or services performed, including payments for reaching milestones in any project.

The due date for making such payments is fourteen days after the designated billing office receives a proper payment request. If the designated billing office fails to annotate the payment request with the actual date of receipt at the time of receipt, the payment due date is the fourteenth day after the date of the contractor's payment request, provided the designated billing office receives a proper payment request and there is no disagreement over quantity, quality, or contractor compliance with contract requirements.

The due date for payment of any amounts retained by the CO in accordance with the FAR Clause 52.232-5 Payments under Fixed-Price Construction Contracts is thirty days after approval by the CO for release to the contractor.

12.2 Final Payments

Final payments are based on completion and acceptance of all work and presentation of release of all claims against the government arising by virtue of the con- tract and payments for partial deliveries that have been accepted by the government (e.g., each separate building, public work, or other division of the contract for which the price is stated separately in the contract).

The due date for making such payments is the later of the following two events:

> The 30th day after the designated billing office receives a proper invoice from the contractor.
>
> The 30th day after the government acceptance of the work or services completed by the contractor. For a final invoice when the payment amount is subject to contract settlement actions (e.g., release of claims), acceptance is deemed to occur on the effective date of the contract settlement.

If the designated billing office fails to annotate the invoice with the date of actual receipt at the time of receipt, the invoice payment due date is the 30th day after the date of the contractor's invoice, provided the designated billing office receives a proper invoice and there is no disagreement over quantity, quality, or contractor compliance with contract requirements.

The contractor should prepare and submit the invoice to the billing office specified in the contract. A proper invoice must include the items listed below. If the invoice does not comply with these requirements, the designated billing office must return it with an explanation within seven days after receipt. When considering any interest penalty owed the contractor, the government will consider whether it has notified the contractor of an improper invoice in an untimely manner.

Name and address of the contractor.

Invoice date and invoice numbers. (The contractor should date invoices as close as possible to the date of mailing or transmission.)

Contract number or other authorization for work or services performed, including order number and contract line item numbers.

Description of work or services performed.

Delivery and payment terms (e.g., discount for prompt payment terms).

Name and address of CO to whom payment is to be sent (must be the same as in the contract or in a proper notice of assignment).

Name (where practicable), title, phone number, and mailing address of person to notify in the event of a defective invoice.

For payments described above, substantiation of the amounts requested and certification in accordance with the requirements of the clause at 52.232-5, Payments under Fixed-Price Construction Contracts.

Taxpayer Identification Number (TIN). The contractor should include the TIN on the invoice only if required elsewhere in the contract.

Any other information or documentation required by the contract.

12.3 Payment Requests – U.S. Army Corps of Engineers

All progress payment requests must be prepared using QCS. The contractor must complete the payment request worksheet, prompt payment certification, and payment invoice in QCS. The work completed under the contract, measured as percent or as specific quantities, must be updated at least monthly. After the update, the contractor will generate a payment request report using QCS. The contractor must submit the payment requests, prompt payment certification, and payment invoice with supporting data by using the government's SFTP repository built into the QCS export function. If permitted by the CO, e-mail or a CD-ROM may be used. A signed paper copy of the approved payment request is also required, which shall govern in the event of discrepancy with the electronic version. Other items such as photographs may be required.

12.4 Interest Penalty

The designated payment office will pay an interest penalty automatically, without request from the contractor, if payment is not made by the due date and a proper invoice has been accepted. However, when the due date falls on a Saturday, Sunday, or legal holiday, the designated payment office may make payment on the following working day without incurring a late payment interest penalty.

The contractor must meet the following requirements for the government to pay interest on a late payment:

The designated billing office received a proper invoice.

The government processed a receiving report or other documentation authorizing payment and there was no disagreement over quantity, quality, contractor compliance with any contract term or condition, or requested progress payment amount.

In the case of a final invoice for any balance of funds due the contractor for work or services performed, the amount was not subject to further contract settlement actions between the government and the contractor.

12.4.1 Computing Penalty Amount

The government will compute the interest penalty in accordance with the Office of Management and Budget prompt payment regulations at 5 CFR part 1315. For the sole purpose of computing an interest penalty that might be due the contractor for payments described above, government acceptance or approval is deemed to occur constructively on the seventh day after the contractor has completed the work or services in accordance with the terms and conditions of the contract. If actual acceptance or approval occurs within the constructive acceptance or approval period, the government will base the determination of an interest penalty on the actual date of acceptance or approval. Constructive acceptance or constructive approval requirements do not apply if there is a disagreement over quantity, quality, or contractor compliance with a contract provision.

12.4.2 Additional Interest Penalty

The designated payment office will pay a penalty amount, calculated in accordance with the prompt payment regulations at 5 CFR part 1315, in addition to the interest penalty amount if:

The government owes an interest penalty of $1 or more;

The designated payment office does not pay the interest penalty within ten days after the date the invoice amount is paid; and

The contractor makes a written demand to the designated payment office for additional penalty payment, postmarked no later than forty days after the date the invoice amount is paid.

The contractor must support written demands for additional penalty payments with the following data. The contractor must:

Specifically assert that late payment interest is due under a specific in-voice and request payment of all overdue late payment interest penalty and such additional penalty as may be required;

Attach a copy of the invoice on which the unpaid late payment interest was due; and

State that payment of the principal has been received, including the date of receipt.

12.5 Prompt Payment for Subcontractors

FAR Clause 52.232-5 is a payment clause that not only requires payment to the contractor but also obligates the contractor to pay the subcontractor for satisfactory performance under its subcontract. This payment must be made not later than seven days from receipt of payment out of such amounts as are paid to the contractor under the contract. Further, the contractor cannot withhold funds from the subcontractor for the work that it has certified unless the government withholds funds from the contractor.

FAR Clause 52.232-5 Payments under Fixed-Price Construction Contracts.

As prescribed in 32.111(a) (5), insert the following clause:

Payments under Fixed-Price Construction Contracts (May 2014)

(a) *Payment of price.* The Government shall pay the Contractor the contract price as provided in this contract.

(b) *Progress payments.* The Government shall make progress payments monthly as the work proceeds, or at more frequent intervals as determined by the Contracting Officer, on estimates of work accomplished which meets the standards of quality established under the contract, as approved by the Contracting Officer.

(1) The Contractor's request for progress payments shall include the following substantiation:

(i) An itemization of the amounts requested, related to the various elements of work required by the contract covered by the payment requested.

(ii) A listing of the amount included for work performed by each subcontractor under the contract.

(iii) A listing of the total amount of each subcontract under the contract.

(iv) A listing of the amounts previously paid to each such subcontractor under the contract.

(v) Additional supporting data in a form and detail required by the Contracting Officer.

(2) In the preparation of estimates, the Contracting Officer may authorize material delivered on the site and preparatory work done to be taken into consideration. Material delivered to the Contractor at locations other than the site also may be taken into consideration if-

(i) Consideration is specifically authorized by this contract; and

(ii) The Contractor furnishes satisfactory evidence that it has acquired title to such material and that the material will be used to perform this contract.

Continues on page 256

(c) *Contractor certification.* Along with each request for progress payments, the Contractor shall furnish the following certification, or payment shall not be made: (However, if the Contractor elects to delete paragraph (c) (4) from the certification, the certification is still acceptable.)

I hereby certify, to the best of my knowledge and belief, that-

(1) The amounts requested are only for performance in accordance with the specifications, terms, and conditions of the contract;

(2) All payments due to subcontractors and suppliers from previous payments received under the contract have been made, and timely payments will be made from the proceeds of the payment covered by this certification, in accordance with subcontract agreements and the requirements of Chapter 39 of Title 31, United States Code;

(3) This request for progress payments does not include any amounts which the prime contractor intends to withhold or retain from a subcontractor or supplier in accordance with the terms and conditions of the subcontract; and

(4) This certification is not to be construed as final acceptance of a subcontractor's performance.

____ (*Name*)

____ (*Title*)

____ (*Date*)

(d) *Refund of unearned amounts.* If the Contractor, after making a certified request for progress payments, discovers that a portion or all of such request constitutes a payment for performance by the Contractor that fails to conform to the specifications, terms, and conditions of this contract (hereinafter referred to as the "unearned amount"), the Contractor shall-

(1) Notify the Contracting Officer of such performance deficiency; and

(2) Be obligated to pay the Government an amount (computed by the Contracting Officer in the manner provided in paragraph (j) of this clause) equal to interest on the unearned amount from the 8th day after the date of receipt of the unearned amount until-

(i) The date the Contractor notifies the Contracting Officer that the performance deficiency has been corrected; or

Continues on page 257

(ii) The date the Contractor reduces the amount of any subsequent certified request for progress payments by an amount equal to the unearned amount.

(e) *Retainage*. If the Contracting Officer finds that satisfactory progress was achieved during any period for which a progress payment is to be made, the Contracting Officer shall authorize payment to be made in full. However, if satisfactory progress has not been made, the Contracting Officer may retain a maximum of 10 percent of the amount of the payment until satisfactory progress is achieved. When the work is substantially complete, the Contracting Officer may retain from previously withheld funds and future progress payments that amount the Contracting Officer considers adequate for protection of the Government and shall release to the Contractor all the remaining withheld funds. Also, on completion and acceptance of each separate building, public work, or other division of the contract, for which the price is stated separately in the contract, payment shall be made for the completed work without retention of a percentage.

(f) *Title, liability, and reservation of rights*. All material and work covered by progress payments made shall, at the time of payment, become the sole property of the Government, but this shall not be construed as-

(1) Relieving the Contractor from the sole responsibility for all material and work upon which payments have been made or the restoration of any damaged work; or

(2) Waiving the right of the Government to require the fulfillment of all of the terms of the contract.

(g) *Reimbursement for bond premiums*. In making these progress payments, the Government shall, upon request, reimburse the Contractor for the amount of premiums paid for performance and payment bonds (including coinsurance and reinsurance agreements, when applicable) after the Contractor has furnished evidence of full payment to the surety. The retainage provisions in paragraph (e) of this clause shall not apply to that portion of progress payments attributable to bond premiums.

(h) *Final payment*. The Government shall pay the amount due the Contractor under this contract after-

(1) Completion and acceptance of all work;

(2) Presentation of a properly executed voucher; and

Continues on page 258

(3) Presentation of release of all claims against the Government arising by virtue of this contract, other than claims, in stated amounts, that the Contractor has specifically excepted from the operation of the release. A release may also be required of the assignee if the Contractor's claim to amounts payable under this contract has been assigned under the Assignment of Claims Act of1940 (31 U.S.C.3727 and 41 U.S.C.6305).

(i) *Limitation because of undefinitized work.* Notwithstanding any provision of this contract, progress payments shall not exceed 80 percent on work accomplished on undefinitized contract actions. A "contract action" is any action resulting in a contract, as defined in FAR subpart 2.1, including contract modifications for additional supplies or services, but not including contract modifications that are within the scope and under the terms of the contract, such as contract modifications issued pursuant to the Changes clause, or funding and other administrative changes.

(j) *Interest computation on unearned amounts.* In accordance with 31 U.S.C.3903(c)(1), the amount payable under paragraph (d)(2) of this clause shall be-

(1) Computed at the rate of average bond equivalent rates of 91-day Treasury bills auctioned at the most recent auction of such bills prior to the date the Contractor receives the unearned amount; and

(2) Deducted from the next available payment to the Contractor.

(End of clause)

FAR Clause 52.232-27 Prompt Payment for Construction Contracts.

As prescribed in 32.908(b), insert the following clause:

Prompt Payment for Construction Contracts (Jan 2017)

Notwithstanding any other payment terms in this contract, the Government will make invoice payments under the terms and conditions specified in this clause. The Government considers payment as being made on the day a check is dated or the date of an electronic funds transfer. Definitions of pertinent terms are set forth in sections 2.101, 32.001, and 32.902 of the Federal Acquisition Regulation. All days referred to in this clause are calendar days, unless otherwise specified. (However, see paragraph (a) (3) concerning payments due on Saturdays, Sundays, and legal holidays.)

(a) Invoice payments-

Continues on page 259

(1) *Types of invoice payments*. For purposes of this clause, there are several types of invoice payments that may occur under this contract, as follows:

(i) Progress payments, if provided for elsewhere in this contract, based on Contracting Officer approval of the estimated amount and value of work or services performed, including payments for reaching milestones in any project.

(A) The due date for making such payments is 14 days after the designated billing office receives a proper payment request. If the designated billing office fails to annotate the payment request with the actual date of receipt at the time of receipt, the payment due date is the 14th day after the date of the Contractor's payment request, provided the designated billing office receives a proper payment request and there is no disagreement over quantity, quality, or Contractor compliance with contract requirements.

(B) The due date for payment of any amounts retained by the Contracting Officer in accordance with the clause at 52.232-5, Payments under Fixed-Price Construction Contracts, is as specified in the contract or, if not specified, 30 days after approval by the Contracting Officer for release to the Contractor.

(ii) Final payments based on completion and acceptance of all work and presentation of release of all claims against the Government arising by virtue of the contract, and payments for partial deliveries that have been accepted by the Government (*e.g.*, each separate building, public work, or other division of the contract for which the price is stated separately in the contract).

(A) The due date for making such payments is the later of the following two events:

(1) The 30th day after the designated billing office receives a proper invoice from the Contractor.

(2) The 30th day after Government acceptance of the work or services completed by the Contractor. For a final invoice when the payment amount is subject to contract settlement actions (*e.g.*, release of claims), acceptance is deemed to occur on the effective date of the contract settlement.

Continues on page 260

(B) If the designated billing office fails to annotate the invoice with the date of actual receipt at the time of receipt, the invoice payment due date is the 30th day after the date of the Contractor's invoice, provided the designated billing office receives a proper invoice and there is no disagreement over quantity, quality, or Contractor compliance with contract requirements.

(2) *Contractor's invoice*. The Contractor shall prepare and submit invoices to the designated billing office specified in the contract. A proper invoice must include the items listed in paragraphs (a) (2)(i) through (a)(2)(xi) of this clause. If the invoice does not comply with these requirements, the designated billing office must return it within 7 days after receipt, with the reasons why it is not a proper invoice. When computing any interest penalty owed the Contractor, the Government will take into account if the Government notifies the Contractor of an improper invoice in an untimely manner.

(i) Name and address of the Contractor.

(ii) Invoice date and invoice number. (The Contractor should date invoices as close as possible to the date of mailing or transmission.)

(iii) Contract number or other authorization for work or services performed (including order number and line item number).

(iv) Description of work or services performed.

(v) Delivery and payment terms (*e.g.,* discount for prompt payment terms).

(vi) Name and address of Contractor official to whom payment is to be sent (must be the same as that in the contract or in a proper notice of assignment).

(vii) Name (where practicable), title, phone number, and mailing address of person to notify in the event of a defective invoice.

(viii) For payments described in paragraph (a) (1)(i) of this clause, substantiation of the amounts requested and certification in accordance with the requirements of the clause at 52.232-5, Payments Under Fixed-Price Construction Contracts.

(ix) Taxpayer Identification Number (TIN). The Contractor shall include its TIN on the invoice only if required elsewhere in this contract.

(x) Electronic funds transfer (EFT) banking information.

Continues on page 261

(A) The Contractor shall include EFT banking information on the invoice only if required elsewhere in this contract.

(B) If EFT banking information is not required to be on the invoice, in order for the invoice to be a proper invoice, the Contractor shall have submitted correct EFT banking information in accordance with the applicable solicitation provision (*e.g.*, 52.232-38, Submission of Electronic Funds Transfer Information with Offer), contract clause (*e.g.*, 52.232-33, Payment by Electronic Funds Transfer-System for Award Management, or 52.232-34, Payment by Electronic Funds Transfer-Other Than System for Award Management), or applicable agency procedures.

(C) EFT banking information is not required if the Government waived the requirement to pay by EFT.

(xi) Any other information or documentation required by the contract.

(3) *Interest penalty*. The designated payment office will pay an interest penalty automatically, without request from the Contractor, if payment is not made by the due date and the conditions listed in paragraphs (a) (3)(i) through (a)(3)(iii) of this clause are met, if applicable. However, when the due date falls on a Saturday, Sunday, or legal holiday, the designated payment office may make payment on the following working day without incurring a late payment interest penalty.

(i) The designated billing office received a proper invoice.

(ii) The Government processed a receiving report or other Government documentation authorizing payment and there was no disagreement over quantity, quality, Contractor compliance with any contract term or condition, or requested progress payment amount.

(iii) In the case of a final invoice for any balance of funds due the Contractor for work or services performed, the amount was not subject to further contract settlement actions between the Government and the Contractor.

(4) *Computing penalty amount*. The Government will compute the interest penalty in accordance with the Office of Management and Budget prompt payment regulations at 5 CFR Part 1315.

Continues on page 262

(i) For the sole purpose of computing an interest penalty that might be due the Contractor for payments described in paragraph (a)(1)(ii) of this clause, Government acceptance or approval is deemed to occur constructively on the 7th day after the Contractor has completed the work or services in accordance with the terms and conditions of the contract. If actual acceptance or approval occurs within the constructive acceptance or approval period, the Government will base the determination of an interest penalty on the actual date of acceptance or approval. Constructive acceptance or constructive approval requirements do not apply if there is a disagreement over quantity, quality, or Contractor compliance with a contract provision. These requirements also do not compel Government officials to accept work or services, approve Contractor estimates, perform contract administration functions, or make payment prior to fulfilling their responsibilities.

(ii) The prompt payment regulations at 5 CFR1315.10(c) do not require the Government to pay interest penalties if payment delays are due to disagreement between the Government and the Contractor over the payment amount or other issues involving contract compliance, or on amounts temporarily withheld or retained in accordance with the terms of the contract. The Government and the Contractor shall resolve claims involving disputes, and any interest that may be payable in accordance with the clause at FAR 52.233-1, Disputes.

(5) *Discounts for prompt payment*. The designated payment office will pay an interest penalty automatically, without request from the Contractor, if the Government takes a discount for prompt payment improperly. The Government will calculate the interest penalty in accordance with the prompt payment regulations at 5 CFR Part 1315.

(6) Additional interest penalty.

(i) The designated payment office will pay a penalty amount, calculated in accordance with the prompt payment regulations at 5 CFR Part 1315 in addition to the interest penalty amount only if-

(A) The Government owes an interest penalty of $1 or more;

(B) The designated payment office does not pay the interest penalty within 10 days after the date the invoice amount is paid; and

(C) The Contractor makes a written demand to the designated payment office for additional penalty payment, in accordance with paragraph (a) (6)(ii) of this clause, postmarked not later than 40 days after the date the invoice amount is paid.

Continues on page 263

(ii)

(A) The Contractor shall support written demands for additional penalty payments with the following data. The Government will not request any additional data. The Contractor shall-

(1) Specifically assert that late payment interest is due under a specific invoice, and request payment of all overdue late payment interest penalty and such additional penalty as may be required;

(2) Attach a copy of the invoice on which the unpaid late payment interest was due; and

(3) State that payment of the principal has been received, including the date of receipt.

(B) If there is no postmark or the postmark is illegible-

(1) The designated payment office that receives the demand will annotate it with the date of receipt provided the demand is received on or before the 40th day after payment was made; or

(2) If the designated payment office fails to make the required annotation, the Government will determine the demand's validity based on the date the Contractor has placed on the demand, provided such date is no later than the 40th day after payment was made.

(b) *Contract financing payments*. If this contract provides for contract financing, the Government will make contract financing payments in accordance with the applicable contract financing clause.

(c) *Subcontract clause requirements*. The Contractor shall include in each subcontract for property or services (including a material supplier) for the purpose of performing this contract the following:

(1) *Prompt payment for subcontractors*. A payment clause that obligates the Contractor to pay the subcontractor for satisfactory performance under its subcontract not later than 7 days from receipt of payment out of such amounts as are paid to the Contractor under this contract.

Continues on page 264

(2) *Interest for subcontractors.* An interest penalty clause that obligates the Contractor to pay to the subcontractor an interest penalty for each payment not made in accordance with the payment clause-

(i) For the period beginning on the day after the required payment date and ending on the date on which payment of the amount due is made; and

(ii) Computed at the rate of interest established by the Secretary of the Treasury, and published in the *Federal Register*, for interest payments under 41 U.S.C. 7109 in effect at the time the Contractor accrues the obligation to pay an interest penalty.

(3) *Subcontractor clause flowdown.* A clause requiring each subcontractor to-

(i) Include a payment clause and an interest penalty clause conforming to the standards set forth in paragraphs (c) (1) and (c)(2) of this clause in each of its subcontracts; and

(ii) Require each of its subcontractors to include such clauses in their subcontracts with each lower-tier subcontractor or supplier.

(d) *Subcontract clause interpretation.* The clauses required by paragraph (c) of this clause shall not be construed to impair the right of the Contractor or a subcontractor at any tier to negotiate, and to include in their subcontract, provisions that-

(1) *Retainage permitted.* Permit the Contractor or a subcontractor to retain (without cause) a specified percentage of each progress payment otherwise due to a subcontractor for satisfactory performance under the subcontract without incurring any obligation to pay a late payment interest penalty, in accordance with terms and conditions agreed to by the parties to the subcontract, giving such recognition as the parties deem appropriate to the ability of a subcontractor to furnish a performance bond and a payment bond;

(2) *Withholding permitted.* Permit the Contractor or subcontractor to make a determination that part or all of the subcontractor's request for payment may be withheld in accordance with the subcontract agreement; and

(3) *Withholding requirements.* Permit such withholding without incurring any obligation to pay a late payment penalty if-

(i) A notice conforming to the standards of paragraph (g) of this clause previously has been furnished to the subcontractor; and

Continues on page 265

(ii) The Contractor furnishes to the Contracting Officer a copy of any notice issued by a Contractor pursuant to paragraph (d)(3)(i) of this clause.

(e) *Subcontractor withholding procedures*. If a Contractor, after making a request for payment to the Government but before making a payment to a subcontractor for the subcontractor's performance covered by the payment request, discovers that all or a portion of the payment otherwise due such subcontractor is subject to withholding from the subcontractor in accordance with the subcontract agreement, then the Contractor shall-

(1) *Subcontractor notice*. Furnish to the subcontractor a notice conforming to the standards of paragraph (g) of this clause as soon as practicable upon ascertaining the cause giving rise to a withholding, but prior to the due date for subcontractor payment;

(2) *Contracting Officer Notice*. Furnish to the Contracting Officer, as soon as practicable, a copy of the notice furnished to the subcontractor pursuant to paragraph (e) (1) of this clause;

(3) *Subcontractor progress payment reduction*. Reduce the subcontractor's progress payment by an amount not to exceed the amount specified in the notice of withholding furnished under paragraph (e)(1) of this clause;

(4) *Subsequent subcontractor payment*. Pay the subcontractor as soon as practicable after the correction of the identified subcontract performance deficiency, and-

(i) Make such payment within-

(A) Seven days after correction of the identified subcontract performance deficiency (unless the funds therefor must be recovered from the Government because of a reduction under paragraph (e) (5)(i)) of this clause; or

(B) Seven days after the Contractor recovers such funds from the Government; or

(ii) Incur an obligation to pay a late payment interest penalty computed at the rate of interest established by the Secretary of the Treasury, and published in the *Federal Register*, for interest payments under 41 U.S.C. 7109 in effect at the time the Contractor accrues the obligation to pay an interest penalty;

(5) *Notice to Contracting Officer*. Notify the Contracting Officer upon-

(i) Reduction of the amount of any subsequent certified application for payment; or

Continues on page 266

(ii) Payment to the subcontractor of any withheld amounts of a progress payment, specifying-

(A) The amounts withheld under paragraph (e) (1) of this clause; and

(B) The dates that such withholding began and ended; and

(6) *Interest to Government.* Be obligated to pay to the Government an amount equal to interest on the withheld payments (computed in the manner provided in 31 U.S.C.3903(c)(1)), from the 8th day after receipt of the withheld amounts from the Government until-

(i) The day the identified subcontractor performance deficiency is corrected; or

(ii) The date that any subsequent payment is reduced under paragraph (e)(5)(i) of this clause.

(f) Third-party deficiency reports-

(1) *Withholding from subcontractor.* If a Contractor, after making payment to a first-tier subcontractor, receives from a supplier or subcontractor of the first-tier subcontractor (hereafter referred to as a "second-tier subcontractor") a written notice in accordance with 40 U.S.C. 3133, asserting a deficiency in such first-tier subcontractor's performance under the contract for which the Contractor may be ultimately liable, and the Contractor determines that all or a portion of future payments otherwise due such first-tier subcontractor is subject to withholding in accordance with the subcontract agreement, the Contractor may, without incurring an obligation to pay an interest penalty under paragraph (e)(6) of this clause-

(i) Furnish to the first-tier subcontractor a notice conforming to the standards of paragraph (g) of this clause as soon as practicable upon making such determination; and

(ii) Withhold from the first-tier subcontractor's next available progress payment or payments an amount not to exceed the amount specified in the notice of withholding furnished under paragraph (f)(1)(i) of this clause.

(2) *Subsequent payment or interest charge.* As soon as practicable, but not later than 7 days after receipt of satisfactory written notification that the identified subcontract performance deficiency has been corrected, the Contractor shall-

Continues on page 267

(i) Pay the amount withheld under paragraph (f) (1)(ii) of this clause to such first-tier subcontractor; or

(ii) Incur an obligation to pay a late payment interest penalty to such first-tier subcontractor computed at the rate of interest established by the Secretary of the Treasury, and published in the *Federal Register*, for interest payments under 41 U.S.C. 7109 in effect at the time the Contractor accrues the obligation to pay an interest penalty.

(g) *Written notice of subcontractor withholding.* The Contractor shall issue a written notice of any withholding to a subcontractor (with a copy furnished to the Contracting Officer), specifying-

(1) The amount to be withheld;

(2) The specific causes for the withholding under the terms of the subcontract; and

(3) The remedial actions to be taken by the subcontractor in order to receive payment of the amounts withheld.

(h) *Subcontractor payment entitlement.* The Contractor may not request payment from the Government of any amount withheld or retained in accordance with paragraph (d) of this clause until such time as the Contractor has determined and certified to the Contracting Officer that the subcontractor is entitled to the payment of such amount.

(i) *Prime-subcontractor disputes.* A dispute between the Contractor and subcontractor relating to the amount or entitlement of a subcontractor to a payment or a late payment interest penalty under a clause included in the subcontract pursuant to paragraph (c) of this clause does not constitute a dispute to which the Government is a party. The Government may not be interpleaded in any judicial or administrative proceeding involving such a dispute.

(j) *Preservation of prime-subcontractor rights.* Except as provided in paragraph (i) of this clause, this clause shall not limit or impair any contractual, administrative, or judicial remedies otherwise available to the Contractor or a subcontractor in the event of a dispute involving late payment or nonpayment by the Contractor or deficient subcontract performance or nonperformance by a subcontractor.

(k) *Non-recourse for prime contractor interest penalty.* The Contractor's obligation to pay an interest penalty to a subcontractor pursuant to the clauses included in a subcontract under paragraph (c) of this clause shall not be construed to be an obligation of the Government for such interest penalty. A cost-reimbursement claim may not include any amount for reimbursement of such interest penalty.

Continues on page 268

(l) *Overpayments*. If the Contractor becomes aware of a duplicate contract financing or invoice payment or that the Government has otherwise overpaid on a contract financing or invoice payment, the Contractor shall-

(1) Remit the overpayment amount to the payment office cited in the contract along with a description of the overpayment including the-

(i) Circumstances of the overpayment (*e.g.*, duplicate payment, erroneous payment, liquidation errors, date(s) of overpayment);

(ii) Affected contract number and delivery order number if applicable;

(iii) Affected line item or subline item, if applicable; and

(iv) Contractor point of contact.

(2) Provide a copy of the remittance and supporting documentation to the Contracting Officer.

(End of clause)

13.0 Disputes

FAR clause 52.233-1 Disputes is used whenever a contractor files a claim, which means a written demand or assertion requesting an adjustment or interpretation of the contract. Normally this is for work that the government has told you to perform but you consider it out of the scope of the contract. The claim notification must be submitted to the Armed Services Board of Contract Appeals (ASBCA) no later than ninety calendar days after the CO's "Final" decision. The ASBCA has held that this notification must be strictly adhered to for it to hear the case. The claim may be filed within six years after the CO's decision.

The proper method for submitting a claim is to submit a "Request for Equitable Adjustment" and then await the CO's decision. If the CO denies the REA, then request a CO's final decision. Alternative dispute resolution can then be requested but if this is not mutually agreed upon, then you can file a claim with the Armed Services Board of Contract Appeals.

Documentation of the reasons for the claim, cost, and certification as required by the "Disputes" clause will either win or lose the claim. Prior to submitting a claim, the government will try to refute the evidence presented with the REA. Additional evidence will have to be included in a claim if it is to be upheld by the court. Daily re- ports, correspondence, documentation of verbal or written directives, schedules, etc., may need to be submitted. Proof that notifications were properly given will be critical.

The two parties should use ADR instead of going to the ASBCA as the attorney's fees can be very expensive and, under federal law, cannot be recouped. Also note that only 17% of the cases before the ASBCA are won by the contractor.

You must proceed diligently with the work in dispute pending final resolution if so directed by the CO.

Except as provided in the act, all disputes arising under or relating to the contract will be resolved under this clause.

You must proceed diligently with performance of the contract, pending final resolution of any request for relief, claim, appeal, or action arising under the contract, and comply with any decision of the CO.

FAR Clause 52.233-1 Disputes.

As prescribed in 33.215 , insert the following clause:

Disputes (May 2014)

(a) This contract is subject to 41 U.S.C chapter 71, Contract Disputes.

(b) Except as provided in 41 U.S.C chapter 71, all disputes arising under or relating to this contract shall be resolved under this clause.

(c) "Claim," as used in this clause, means a written demand or written assertion by one of the contracting parties seeking, as a matter of right, the payment of money in a sum certain, the adjustment or interpretation of contract terms, or other relief arising under or relating to this contract. However, a written demand or written assertion by the Contractor seeking the payment of money exceeding $100,000 is not a claim under 41 U.S.C chapter 71 until certified. A voucher, invoice, or other routine request for payment that is not in dispute when submitted is not a claim under 41 U.S.C chapter 71. The submission may be converted to a claim under 41 U.S.C chapter 71, by complying with the submission and certification requirements of this clause, if it is disputed either as to liability or amount or is not acted upon in a reasonable time.

(d)

Continues on page 270

(1) A claim by the Contractor shall be made in writing and, unless otherwise stated in this contract, submitted within 6 years after accrual of the claim to the Contracting Officer for a written decision. A claim by the Government against the Contractor shall be subject to a written decision by the Contracting Officer.

(2)

(i) The Contractor shall provide the certification specified in paragraph (d) (2)(iii) of this clause when submitting any claim exceeding $100,000.

(ii) The certification requirement does not apply to issues in controversy that have not been submitted as all or part of a claim.

(iii) The certification shall state as follows: "I certify that the claim is made in good faith; that the supporting data are accurate and complete to the best of my knowledge and belief; that the amount requested accurately reflects the contract adjustment for which the Contractor believes the Government is liable; and that I am authorized to certify the claim on behalf of the Contractor."

(3) The certification may be executed by any person authorized to bind the Contractor with respect to the claim.

(e) For Contractor claims of $100,000 or less, the Contracting Officer must, if requested in writing by the Contractor, render a decision within 60 days of the request. For Contractor-certified claims over $100,000, the Contracting Officer must, within 60 days, decide the claim or notify the Contractor of the date by which the decision will be made.

(f) The Contracting Officer's decision shall be final unless the Contractor appeals or files a suit as provided in 41 U.S.C chapter 71.

(g) If the claim by the Contractor is submitted to the Contracting Officer or a claim by the Government is presented to the Contractor, the parties, by mutual consent, may agree to use alternative dispute resolution (ADR). If the Contractor refuses an offer for ADR, the Contractor shall inform the Contracting Officer, in writing, of the Contractor's specific reasons for rejecting the offer.

(h) The Government shall pay interest on the amount found due and unpaid from (1) the date that the Contracting Officer receives the claim (certified, if required); or (2) the date that payment otherwise would be due, if that date is later, until the date of payment. Regarding claims having defective certifications, as defined in FAR 33.201, interest shall be paid from the date that the

Continues on page 271

Contracting Officer initially receives the claim. Simple interest on claims shall be paid at the rate, fixed by the Secretary of the Treasury as provided in the Act, which is applicable to the period during which the Contracting Officer receives the claim and then at the rate applicable for each 6-month period as fixed by the Treasury Secretary during the pendency of the claim.

(i) The Contractor shall proceed diligently with performance of this contract, pending final resolution of any request for relief, claim, appeal, or action arising under the contract, and comply with any decision of the Contracting Officer.

(End of clause)

Alternate I (Dec 1991). As prescribed in 33.215, substitute the following paragraph (i) for paragraph (i) of the basic clause:

(i) The Contractor shall proceed diligently with performance of this contract, pending final resolution of any request for relief, claim, appeal, or action arising under or relating to the contract, and comply with any decision of the Contracting Officer.

14.0 The Miller Act

The Miller Act (1935) is a federal law (40 U.S.C. Section 3131 to 3134) that requires contractors to post surety bonds on construction projects. This is implemented in government contracts by FAR Clause 52.228 - 15, Performance and Payment Bonds – Construction. The law also provides significant protection through the payment bond requirement for subcontractors and vendors that have direct contract relationships with the prime contractor and for lower tier subcontractors and vendors that have direct contract relationships with those same subcontractors and vendors.

14.1 Requirements

The Miller Act requires that a contractor on a federal project post two bonds:

A performance bond

A labor and material payment bond

The surety company issuing the bonds must be listed as a qualified surety on the Treasury List, which the U.S. Department of the Treasury issues each year. Bonds must be provided by a contractor before a contract that exceeds $150,000 in amount for construction, alteration, or repair of any building or public work of the United States is awarded. The performance bond will be in an amount the CO deems adequate to protect the interest of the United States. The bond amount is usually 100% of the contract price.

A separate payment bond for the protection of suppliers of labor and materials. The sum of the bond is equal to 50% of the contract price when the contract is less than $1 million and 40% when the contract is from $1 million to $5 million. Contracts more than $5 million require a payment bond in the amount of $2.5 million.

14.2 Alternatives to Payment Bonds

The FAR provides alternatives to payment bonds as payment protections for suppliers of labor and materials for contracts that are more than $35,000 and not more than $150,000.

> The contractor may provide an "Irrevocable letter of Credit" in accordance with FAR Clause 52.228-14 Irrevocable Letter of Credit as an alternative to a performance and payment bond.
>
> The contractor may pledge assets in accordance with FAR Clause 52.228- 4003, Individual Sureties.

The requirements for these alternatives are very stringent and must be approved by the CO.

14.3 Who is Covered by the Miller Act?

> Subcontractors and suppliers who have direct contracts with the prime contractor. These are called first tier claimants.
>
> Subcontractors and material suppliers that have contracts with a subcontractor, but not those who have contracts with a supplier. These are called second tier claimants.

14.4 Who is Not Covered by the Miller Act?

> Anyone farther down the contract chain not considered a second-tier claimant is considered too remote and cannot assert a claim against a Miller Act payment bond posted by the contractor.

14.5 Getting a Copy of the Contractor's Bond

A subcontractor or supplier can request a copy from you, and you must promptly provide a copy of the payment bond as required by FAR Clause 52.228-12 Prospective Subcontractor Requests for Bonds. The CO must furnish a certified copy of a payment bond and the contract for which it was given to any person applying for a copy who submits an affidavit that he or she has supplied labor or material for work described in the contract and payment for the work has not been made or that he or she is being sued on the bond. The applicant must pay any fees to cover the cost of preparing the certified copy.

14.6 Non-payment Recourse under the Miller Act

A person having furnished labor or material in carrying out work provided for in a contract for which a payment bond is furnished and has not been paid in full within ninety days after the day on which the last of the labor was formed or the material was furnished may file a claim. The person for which the claim is made must have a *direct contractual relationship with the contractor.* He may then bring civil action on the payment bond for the amount unpaid at the time the civil action is brought and may prosecute the action to final execution and judgment for the amount due. Note: This action does not require prior notification.

A person having a *direct contractual relationship with subcontractor but no contractual relationship with the contractor* furnishing the payment bond may bring a civil action on the payment bond on giving written notice to the contractor within 90 days from the date on which the person performed the last of the labor or furnished or supplied the last of the material for which the claim is made.

This civil action requires 90 day notification to the contractor. The action must state with substantial accuracy the amount claimed and the name of the party to whom the material was furnished or supplied or for whom the labor was performed. The notice may be served by any means that provides written, third-party verification of delivery to the contractor at any place the contractor maintains an office or conducts business or at the contractor's residence; or in any manner in which the U.S. marshal of the district in which the public improvement is situated by law may serve summons.

A civil action must be:

Brought in the name of the United States for the use of the person bringing the action.

Brought in the United States District Court for any district in which the contract was to be performed and executed, regardless of the amount in controversy.

Brought no later than one year after the day on which the last labor was performed or material was supplied by the person bringing the action.

The government is not liable for the payment of any costs or expenses of any civil suit brought under the Miller Act.

14.7 Waiver of Right to Civil Action

This is commonly called the "Release of Claims and Waiver of Lien." Contractors generally want this signed prior to making partial and final payments to a subcontractor and a supplier. This waiver is void unless:

It is in writing

Signed by the person whose right is waived

It is executed after the person whose right is waived has furnished labor or material for use in the performance of the contract.

14.8 Coverage for Taxes in the Performance Bond

Every performance bond required under the Miller Act should provide coverage for taxes the government imposes, which are collected, deducted, or withheld from wages the contractor pays in carrying out the contract with respect to which the bond is furnished.

The government must give the surety on the bond written notice, with respect to any unpaid taxes attributable to any period, within 90 days after the date when the contractor files a return for the period, except that notice must be given no later than 180 days from the date when a return was required to be filed under the Internal Revenue Code of 1986(26 U.S.C. 1 et seq.). In addition, the government may not bring a civil suit on the bond for the taxes unless the required notice is given and if more than one year after the day on which notice is given has passed.

FAR Clause 52.228-15 Performance and Payment Bonds-Construction.

As prescribed in 28.102-3(a), insert a clause substantially as follows:

Performance and Payment Bonds-Construction (Jun 2020)

(a) *Definitions*. As used in this clause-

Original contract price means the award price of the contract; or, for requirements contracts, the price payable for the estimated total quantity; or, for indefinite-quantity contracts, the price payable for the specified minimum quantity. Original contract price does not include the price of any options, except those options exercised at the time of contract award.

Continues on page 275

(b) *Amount of required bonds*. Unless the resulting contract price is valued at or below the threshold specified in Federal Acquisition Regulation 28.102-1(a) on the date of award of this contract, the successful offeror shall furnish performance and payment bonds to the Contracting Officer as follows:

(1) *Performance bonds (Standard Form 25)*. The penal amount of performance bonds at the time of contract award shall be 100 percent of the original contract price.

(2) *Payment Bonds (Standard Form 25A)*. The penal amount of payment bonds at the time of contract award shall be 100 percent of the original contract price.

(3) Additional bond protection.

(i) The Government may require additional performance and payment bond protection if the contract price is increased. The increase in protection generally will equal 100 percent of the increase in contract price.

(ii) The Government may secure the additional protection by directing the Contractor to increase the penal amount of the existing bond or to obtain an additional bond.

(c) *Furnishing executed bonds*. The Contractor shall furnish all executed bonds, including any necessary reinsurance agreements, to the Contracting Officer, within the time period specified in the Bid Guarantee provision of the solicitation, or otherwise specified by the Contracting Officer, but in any event, before starting work.

(d) *Surety or other security for bonds*. The bonds shall be in the form of firm commitment, supported by corporate sureties whose names appear on the list contained in Treasury Department Circular 570, individual sureties, or by other acceptable security such as postal money order, certified check, cashier's check, irrevocable letter of credit, or, in accordance with Treasury Department regulations, certain bonds or notes of the United States. Treasury Circular 570 is published in the *Federal Register* or may be obtained from the:

U.S. Department of the Treasury,

Financial Management,

Service Surety Bond Branch,

3700 East West Highway,

Room 6 F01,

Continues on page 276

Hyattsville, MD 20782.

Or via the internet at http://www.fms.treas.gov/c570/.

(e) *Notice of subcontractor waiver of protection* (40 U.S.C. 3133(c)). Any waiver of the right to sue on the payment bond is void unless it is in writing, signed by the person whose right is waived, and executed after such person has first furnished labor or material for use in the performance of the contract.

(End of clause)

15.0 Work by the Contractor

The federal government, to ensure adequate interest in and supervision of all work involved in larger projects, from time to time requires the contractor to perform a significant part of the contract work with its own forces. The contract will express this requirement in terms of a percentage that reflects the minimum amount of work the contractor must perform with its own forces (see FAR Clause 52.236-1 Performance of the Work by the Contractor). This percentage is as high as the contracting officer considers appropriate for the project, consistent with customary or necessary specialty subcontracting and the complexity and magnitude of the work, and ordinarily not less than 12% unless a greater percentage is required by law or agency regulation. Specialties such as plumbing, heating, and electrical work are usually subcontracted and are not normally considered in establishing the amount of work required to be performed by the contractor. This percentage sometimes will be further defined as labor only exclusive of materials and management costs.

FAR Clause 52.236-1 Performance of Work by the Contractor.

As prescribed in 36.501(b), insert the following clause: [*Complete the clause by inserting the appropriate percentage consistent with the complexity and magnitude of the work and customary or necessary specialty subcontracting (see 36.501(a)).*]

Performance of Work by the Contractor (Apr 1984)

The Contractor shall perform on the site, and with its own organization, work equivalent to at least ______ *[insert the appropriate number in words followed by numerals in parentheses]* percent of the total amount of work to be performed under the contract. This percentage may be reduced by a supplemental agreement to this contract if, during performing the work, the Contractor requests a reduction and the Contracting Officer determines that the reduction would be to the advantage of the Government.

(End of clause)

The FAR Clause 52.236-5 Material and Workmanship requires that all material be "new;" that references to product names, makes, or catalog numbers only establish a level of quality and should not be construed to limiting competition; that material and equipment including samples be submitted when required by the contract or at any other time that the CO determines and that payment will not be made for this work until the submittal is approved; requires that all work be accomplished in a skillful and workmanlike manner; and allows the CO to remove from the work any employee that he/she deems incompetent, careless, or otherwise objectionable.

The most important part of this clause is that it allows the use of equipment, materials, or patented processes that meet the level of quality of the equipment/materials, etc. shown using propriety brand names. That is why this clause is sometimes called the "or equal" clause. To prove that the product you are proposing to use is an "or equal" you must show that your product has all the same "salient" characteristics.

FAR Clause 52.236-5 Material and Workmanship.

As prescribed in 36.505 , insert the following clause:

Material and Workmanship (Apr 1984)

(a) All equipment, material, and articles incorporated into the work covered by this contract shall be new and of the most suitable grade for the purpose intended, unless otherwise specifically provided in this contract. References in the specifications to equipment, material, articles, or patented processes by trade name, make, or catalog number, shall be regarded as establishing a standard of quality and shall not be construed as limiting competition. The Contractor may, at its option, use any equipment, material, article, or process that, in the judgment of the Contracting Officer, is equal to that named in the specifications, unless otherwise specifically provided in this contract.

(b) The Contractor shall obtain the Contracting Officer's approval of the machinery and mechanical and other equipment to be incorporated into the work. When requesting approval, the Contractor shall furnish to the Contracting Officer the name of the manufacturer, the model number, and other information concerning the performance, capacity, nature, and rating of the machinery and mechanical and other equipment. When required by this contract or by the Contracting Officer, the Contractor shall also obtain the Contracting Officer's approval of the material or articles which the Contractor contemplates incorporating into the work. When requesting approval, the Contractor shall provide full information concerning the material or articles. When directed to do so, the Contractor shall submit samples for approval at the Contractor's expense, with all shipping charges prepaid. Machinery, equipment, material, and articles that do not have the required approval shall be installed or used at the risk of subsequent rejection.

(c) All work under this contract shall be performed in a skillful and workmanlike manner. The Contracting Officer may require, in writing, that the Contractor remove from the work any employee the Contracting Officer deems incompetent, careless, or otherwise objectionable.

(End of clause)

The superintendent is arguably the most important person on the jobsite as he or she directs all the on-site day to day activities and is responsible for the overall quality of the project and its on-time completion. The government understands this and requires via FAR Clause 52.236-6 Superintendence by the Contractor that you as the contractor have at all times on the job site a

Continues on page 279

superintendent satisfactory to the CO. Most government solicitations require that proposals include the name and resume of the superintendent, and they expect to see that person on the job. If there is to be a substitution at any time during the project, then you must submit the name and resume in writing to the CO for approval. Generally, this person must have at least the same or more experience.

FAR Clause 52.236-6 Superintendence by the Contractor.

As prescribed in 36.506 , insert the following clause:

Superintendence by the Contractor (Apr 1984)

At all times during performance of this contract and until the work is completed and accepted, the Contractor shall directly superintend the work or assign and have on the worksite a competent superintendent who is satisfactory to the Contracting Officer and has authority to act for the Contractor.

(End of clause)

16.0 Differing Site Conditions

A differing site condition or changed condition may be defined as a physical condition encountered in performing the work that was not visible and known to exist at the time of bidding and is materially different from conditions believed to exist at the time of bidding. This changed condition is one of the major causes of disputes in the construction industry. The use of this FAR clause actually places the risk of differing site conditions on the government. As the contractor, you must show that the physical condition encountered was one that a reasonably intelligent contractor, experienced in the particular field of work involved, could be expected to discover upon a reasonable site investigation.

To receive compensation, you must be careful to follow the notification procedures in this clause. The work must be stopped, and the CO must be promptly notified, in writing, and given sufficient time to inspect and evaluate the conditions. If the CO finds that the condition constitutes a "differing site condition," you must "Request an Equitable Adjustment" in accordance with DFARS Clause 252.243-7002.

FAR Clause 52.236-2 Differing Site Conditions.

As prescribed in 36.502 , insert the following clause:

Differing Site Conditions (Apr 1984)

(a) The Contractor shall promptly, and before the conditions are disturbed, give a written notice to the Contracting Officer of-

(1) Subsurface or latent physical conditions at the site which differ materially from those indicated in this contract; or

(2) Unknown physical conditions at the site, of an unusual nature, which differ materially from those ordinarily encountered and generally recognized as inhering in work of the character provided for in the contract.

(b) The Contracting Officer shall investigate the site conditions promptly after receiving the notice. If the conditions do materially so differ and cause an increase or decrease in the Contractor's cost of, or the time required for, performing any part of the work under this contract, whether or not changed as a result of the conditions, an equitable adjustment shall be made under this clause and the contract modified in writing accordingly.

(c) No request by the Contractor for an equitable adjustment to the contract under this clause shall be allowed, unless the Contractor has given the written notice required; *provided*, that the time prescribed in paragraph (a) of this clause for giving written notice may be extended by the Contracting Officer.

(d) No request by the Contractor for an equitable adjustment to the contract for differing site conditions shall be allowed if made after final payment under this contract.

(End of clause)

17.0 Site Investigations and Conditions Affecting the Work

FAR Clause 52.236-3 Site Investigations and Conditions Affecting the Work is almost always included in a federal government construction solicitation. You will be required to make a site visit to ascertain exactly what the existing conditions are. Such a requirement does not automatically nullify the effect of a differing site conditions clause if one is present and does not necessarily obligate you to discover hidden conditions at your peril. The federal courts have held that the adequacy of the site investigation is measured by what a reasonable, intelligent contractor, experienced in the particular field of work involved, could be expected to discover—

not what a highly trained expert might have found.

Documents that are presented at the site investigation are also considered part of the site investigation. The federal courts have held that a review of these documents, i.e. as-built drawings, soil boring logs, dredging reports, carry the same importance as a site investigation even if they are only made available to the contractor at the site. Although there appears to be no court decision dealing with this issue, it is imperative that you request a copy of the documents upon award of the contract. If the request is denied, then you should always notify the CO of a change under the "Differing Site Conditions" clause.

Attending the site visit is mandatory in the eyes of the federal courts in order to collect damages for changed site conditions. The federal courts have held that any claims for damages that are based on defective design or specifications that could have been reasonably seen during a site visit will be denied.

FAR Clause 52.236-3 Site Investigation and Conditions Affecting the Work.

As prescribed in 36.503 , insert the following clause:

Site Investigation and Conditions Affecting the Work (Apr 1984)

(a) The Contractor acknowledges that it has taken steps reasonably necessary to ascertain the nature and location of the work, and that it has investigated and satisfied itself as to the general and local conditions which can affect the work or its cost, including but not limited to (1) conditions bearing upon transportation, disposal, handling, and storage of materials; (2) the availability of labor, water, electric power, and roads; (3) uncertainties of weather, river stages, tides, or similar physical conditions at the site; (4) the conformation and conditions of the ground; and (5) the character of equipment and facilities needed preliminary to and during work performance. The Contractor also acknowledges that it has satisfied itself as to the character, quality, and quantity of surface and subsurface materials or obstacles to be encountered insofar as this information is reasonably ascertainable from an inspection of the site, including all exploratory work done by the Government, as well as from the drawings and specifications made a part of this contract. Any failure of the Contractor to take the actions described and acknowledged in this paragraph will not relieve the Contractor from responsibility for estimating properly the difficulty and cost of successfully performing the work, or for proceeding to successfully perform the work without additional expense to the Government.

(b) The Government assumes no responsibility for any conclusions or interpretations made by the Contractor based on the information made available by the Government. Nor does the Government assume responsibility for any understanding reached or representation made concerning conditions which can affect the work by any of its officers or agents before the execution of this contract, unless that understanding, or representation is expressly stated in this contract.

(End of clause)

18.0 Use and Possession Prior to Completion

FAR Clause 52.236-11 Use and Possession Prior to Completion authorizes the government to take possession of a facility or any part of a facility prior to project acceptance. The government does this for many reasons; however, the most common are that they may have work to be included in the facility prior to being occupied by the user or the user has an overriding requirement to use the facility.

The government will make a list (punch list) of items remaining to be completed prior to taking possession and these must be completed prior to final project acceptance. All other loss or damage after the government takes possession is the government's responsibility.

FAR Clause 52.236-11 Use and Possession Prior to Completion.

As prescribed in 36.511 , insert the following clause:

Use and Possession Prior to Completion (Apr 1984)

(a) The Government shall have the right to take possession of or use any completed or partially completed part of the work. Before taking possession of or using any work, the Contracting Officer shall furnish the Contractor a list of items of work remaining to be performed or corrected on those portions of the work that the Government intends to take possession of or use. However, failure of the Contracting Officer to list any item of work shall not relieve the Contractor of responsibility for complying with the terms of the contract. The Government's possession or use shall not be deemed an acceptance of any work under the contract.

(b) While the Government has such possession or use, the Contractor shall be relieved of the responsibility for the loss of or damage to the work resulting from the Government's possession or use, notwithstanding the terms of the clause in this contract entitled "Permits and Responsibilities." If prior possession or use by the Government delays the progress of the work or causes additional expense to the Contractor, an equitable adjustment shall be made in the contract price or the time of completion, and the contract shall be modified in writing accordingly.

(End of clause)

19.0 Schedules

FAR clause 52.236-15 Schedules for Construction Contracts mandates the requirement for project schedules and section 01 32 01 describes in detail the requirements for them. The government puts a high level of importance on properly done schedules. The requirements are such that only a true professional scheduler should attempt to create and update schedules for the government. Currently the government uses Primavera Version 6, and it is highly recommended that any software chosen be compatible with this software. Government personnel are highly trained in the use and analysis of schedules and will perform a very detailed review of all schedules. The government uses the schedule for progress payments and to ensure that the contract can be completed on time.

Five types of schedules are required:

- Preliminary Project Schedule, which includes all activities up to 90 calendar days after NTP;
- Initial Project Schedule, which includes all activities including design and construction;
- Design Package Schedule, which is a FRAGNET schedule extracted from the current Preliminary, Initial, or Updated Schedule, which covers all activities associated with that design package;
- Updated Schedule is submitted as may be requested by the CO but no less than monthly and is an update of the current schedule;
- FRAGNET Schedule is used to document changes to the schedule caused by specific events such as a change order request. These are submitted as required.

The progress schedule is a cost-loaded schedule, and because of this, great care should be exercised to balance the cost and duration of each activity in order to make it a useful tool for completing the project.

FAR Clause 52.236-15 Schedules for Construction Contracts.

As prescribed in 36.515 , insert the following clause:

Schedules for Construction Contracts (Apr 1984)

(a) The Contractor shall, within five days after the work commences on the contract or another period of time determined by the Contracting Officer, prepare and submit to the Contracting Officer for approval three copies of a practicable schedule showing the order in which the Contractor proposes to perform the work, and the dates on which the Contractor contemplates starting and completing the several salient features of the work (including acquiring materials, plant, and equipment). The schedule shall be in the form of a progress chart of suitable scale to indicate appropriately the percentage of work scheduled for completion by any given date during the period. If the Contractor fails to submit a schedule within the time prescribed, the Contracting Officer may withhold approval of progress payments until the Contractor submits the required schedule.

(b) The Contractor shall enter the actual progress on the chart as directed by the Contracting Officer, and upon doing so shall immediately deliver three copies of the annotated schedule to the Contracting Officer. If, in the opinion of the Contracting Officer, the Contractor falls behind the approved schedule, the Contractor shall take steps necessary to improve its progress, including those that may be required by the Contracting Officer, without additional cost to the Government. In this circumstance, the Contracting Officer may require the Contractor to increase the number of shifts, overtime operations, days of work, and/or the amount of construction plant, and to submit for approval any supplementary schedule or schedules in chart form as the Contracting Officer deems necessary to demonstrate how the approved rate of progress will be regained.

(c) Failure of the Contractor to comply with the requirements of the Contracting Officer under this clause shall be grounds for a determination by the Contracting Officer that the Contractor is not prosecuting the work with sufficient diligence to ensure completion within the time specified in the contract. Upon making this determination, the Contracting Officer may terminate the Contractor's right to proceed with the work, or any separable part of it, in accordance with the default terms of this contract.

(End of clause)

20.0 Suspension of Work

A suspension of work is a form of delay caused by the owner's purposeful interruption of the work. You can generally recover damages under this clause for costs generated by (1) delays in making the site available, (2) delays in issuing change orders, and (3) delays caused by defective plans and specifications. The suspension of work must be from the CO and must be in writing. To claim under this clause, you must notify the CO in writing within 20 days of the act or failure to act.

FAR Clause 52.242-14 Suspension of Work.

As prescribed in 42.1305(a), insert the following clause in solicitations and contracts when a fixed-price construction or architect-engineer contract is contemplated:

Suspension of Work (Apr 1984)

(a) The Contracting Officer may order the Contractor, in writing, to suspend, delay, or interrupt all or any part of the work of this contract for the period of time that the Contracting Officer determines appropriate for the convenience of the Government.

(b) If the performance of all or any part of the work is, for an unreasonable period of time, suspended, delayed, or interrupted (1)by an act of the Contracting Officer in the administration of this contract, or (2)by the Contracting Officer's failure to act within the time specified in this contract (or within a reasonable time if not specified), an adjustment shall be made for any increase in the cost of performance of this contract (excluding profit) necessarily caused by the unreasonable suspension, delay, or interruption, and the contract modified in writing accordingly. However, no adjustment shall be made under this clause for any suspension, delay, or interruption to the extent that performance would have been so suspended, delayed, or interrupted by any other cause, including the fault or negligence of the Contractor, or for which an equitable adjustment is provided for or excluded under any other term or condition of this contract.

(c) A claim under this clause shall not be allowed-

(1) For any costs incurred more than 20 days before the Contractor shall have notified the Contracting Officer in writing of the act or failure to act involved (but this requirement shall not apply as to a claim resulting from a suspension order); and

(2) Unless the claim, in an amount stated, is asserted in writing as soon as practicable after the termination of the suspension, delay, or interruption, but not later than the date of final payment under the contract.

(End of clause)

21.0 Changes

FAR Clause 52.243-4 Changes is used to authorize changes as the CO deems necessary. The CO can specifically make changes:

In the specifications (including drawings and designs)

In the method or manner of performance of the work

In the government-furnished facilities, equipment, materials, services, or site

Directing acceleration in the performance of the work

Any other written or oral order (which, as used herein includes direction, instruction, interpretation, or determination) from the CO that causes a change will be treated as a change order if you give the CO written notice stating:

The date, circumstances, and source of the order and

That the contractor regards the order as a change order.

Except as otherwise provided in this FAR clause, no order, statement, or conduct of the CO should be treated as a change or entitle you as the contractor to an equitable adjustment.

If any change causes an increase or decrease in your cost of, or time required for, the performance of any part of the work under the contract, whether or not changed by any such order, the CO will make an equitable adjustment and modify the contract in writing. However, except for an adjustment based on defective specifications, no adjustment for any change under paragraph B will be made for any costs incurred more than 20 days before you give written notice as required (termed the notification period). In the case of defective specifications for which the government is responsible, the equitable adjustment will include any increased cost reasonably incurred by you in attempting to comply with the defective specifications.

You must assert your right to an adjustment under this clause within 30 days after (a) receipt of a written change order or (b) the furnishing of a written notice to the CO a written statement describing the general nature and amount of the proposal, unless this period is extended by the government. The request for adjustment may be included in the notice as discussed above. No proposal for an equitable adjustment will be allowed if asserted after the final payment under the contract. If a claim is still in dispute at the conclusion of the contract, the "Waiver of Claims" and "Release of Lien" should be qualified to reserve your right to get a final payment and prosecute the claim. The number of the claim (if known), the date, the amount, and reasons should all be stated on the "Waiver of Claims" that accompanies the final invoice.

(d) Failure to agree to any adjustment will be a dispute under the Disputes clause. However, nothing in this clause excuses the Contractor from proceeding with the contract as changed.

FAR Clause 52.243-4 Changes.

As prescribed in 43.205(d), insert the following clause: The 30-day period may be varied according to agency procedures.

Changes (June 2007)

(a) The Contracting Officer may, at any time, without notice to the sureties, if any, by written order designated or indicated to be a change order, make changes in the work within the general scope of the contract, including changes-

(1) In the specifications (including drawings and designs);

(2) In the method or manner of performance of the work;

(3) In the Government-furnished property or services; or

(4) Directing acceleration in the performance of the work.

(b) Any other written or oral order (which, as used in this paragraph (b), includes direction, instruction, interpretation, or determination) from the Contracting Officer that causes a change shall be treated as a change order under this clause; Provided, that the Contractor gives the Contracting Officer written notice stating-

(1) The date, circumstances, and source of the order; and

(2) That the Contractor regards the order as a change order.

(c) Except as provided in this clause, no order, statement, or conduct of the Contracting Officer shall be treated as a change under this clause or entitle the Contractor to an equitable adjustment.

(d) If any change under this clause causes an increase or decrease in the Contractor's cost of, or the time required for, the performance of any part of the work under this contract, whether or not changed by any such order, the Contracting Officer shall make an equitable adjustment and modify the contract in writing. However, except for an adjustment based on defective specifications, no adjustment for any change under paragraph (b) of this clause shall be made for any costs incurred more than 20 days before the Contractor gives written notice as required. In

Continues on page 289

the case of defective specifications for which the Government is responsible, the equitable adjustment shall include any increased cost reasonably incurred by the Contractor in attempting to comply with the defective specifications.

(e) The Contractor must assert its right to an adjustment under this clause within 30 days after (1) receipt of a written change order under paragraph (a) of this clause or (2) the furnishing of a written notice under paragraph (b) of this clause, by submitting to the Contracting Officer a written statement describing the general nature and amount of the proposal, unless this period is extended by the Government. The statement of proposal for adjustment may be included in the notice under paragraph (b) of this clause.

(f) No proposal by the Contractor for an equitable adjustment shall be allowed if asserted after final payment under this contract.

(End of clause)

22.0 Government Furnished Property (GFP)

The government may from time to time require that a contractor use government - furnished property or GFP. This may be done for several reasons, such as the government has a piece of equipment on hand they want to use, the equipment may be very specialized and/or proprietary to the government, or that the government will provide special designated funds, such as for furnishings. Whatever the reason, you need to be aware that this clause requires you to accept the property "as is, where is." You must inspect the equipment, test it if necessary to make sure it performs as required for its intended purpose, and make sure it is available at the time of installation. If shipping charges or taxes must be paid, i.e. state use/sales taxes, then you must include them in the bid. It is also important to understand that if the GFP is damaged or destroyed then you will be responsible to either fix or replace it. You should also verify that your builder's risk insurance covers this item.

FAR Clause 52.245-2 Government Property Installation Operation Services.

As prescribed in 45.107(b), insert the following clause:

Government Property Installation Operation Services (Apr 2012)

(a) This Government Property listed in paragraph (e) of this clause is furnished to the Contractor in an "as-is, where is" condition. The Government makes no warranty regarding the suitability for use of the Government property specified in this contract. The Contractor shall be afforded the opportunity to inspect the Government property as specified in the solicitation.

(b) The Government bears no responsibility for repair or replacement of any lost Government property. If any or all the Government property is lost or becomes no longer usable, the Contractor shall be responsible for replacement of the property at Contractor expense. The Contractor shall have title to all replacement property and shall continue to be responsible for contract performance.

(c) Unless the Contracting Officer determines otherwise, the Government abandons all rights and title to unserviceable and scrap property resulting from contract performance. Upon notification to the Contracting Officer, the Contractor shall remove such property from the Government premises and dispose of it at Contractor expense.

(d) Except as provided in this clause, Government property furnished under this contract shall be governed by the Government Property clause of this contract.

(e) Government property provided under this clause:

____

(End of clause)

23.0 Inspection of Construction

FAR clause 52.246-12 Inspection of Construction authorizes the government to inspect and re-inspect any item of completed work within reasonable limitations. You must give notice that you require an inspection under the contract terms and give the government proper notification—usually at least 48 hours unless otherwise specified in the contract. The government must make all inspections in a manner that will not unnecessarily delay the work.

The government can accept or reject the work. If the work is rejected, you must promptly correct it. The government can also charge you for any additional cost of re-inspection or test when work is not ready at the time you specified.

Paragraph (h) of the clause is probably the most important part. This tells you that if the government decides to examine already completed and covered work, then you must open it up for examination. If this examination reveals the work was nonconforming to the contract requirements, you will have to bear all costs incurred to correct the work and government's costs for re-examining the work. If the examination reveals that the work conforms to the contract requirements then the government must pay all your expenses for the additional services involved in the examination and reconstruction, including, if completion of the work was thereby delayed, a time extension. You must request an equitable adjustment from the CO citing the "Inspection of Construction" clause of the contract.

FAR Clause 52.246-12 Inspection of Construction.

As prescribed in 46.312, insert the following clause:

Inspection of Construction (Aug 1996)

(a) *Definition.* "Work" includes, but is not limited to, materials, workmanship, and manufacture and fabrication of components.

(b) The Contractor shall maintain an adequate inspection system and perform such inspections as will ensure that the work performed under the contract conforms to contract requirements. The Contractor shall maintain complete inspection records and make them available to the Government. All work shall be conducted under the general direction of the Contracting Officer and is subject to Government inspection and test at all places and at all reasonable times before acceptance to ensure strict compliance with the terms of the contract.

(c) Government inspections and tests are for the sole benefit of the Government and do not-

(1) Relieve the Contractor of responsibility for providing adequate quality control measures;

(2) Relieve the Contractor of responsibility for damage to or loss of the material before acceptance;

(3) Constitute or imply acceptance; or

Continues on page 292

(4) Affect the continuing rights of the Government after acceptance of the completed work under paragraph (i) of this- section.

(d) The presence or absence of a Government inspector does not relieve the Contractor from any contract requirement, nor is the inspector authorized to change any term or condition of the specification without the Contracting Officer's written authorization.

(e) The Contractor shall promptly furnish, at no increase in contract price, all facilities, labor, and material reasonably needed for performing such safe and convenient inspections and tests as may be required by the Contracting Officer. The Government may charge to the Contractor any additional cost of inspection or test when work is not ready at the time specified by the Contractor for inspection or test, or when prior rejection makes re-inspection or retest necessary. The Government shall perform all inspections and tests in a manner that will not unnecessarily delay the work. Special, full size, and performance tests shall be performed as described in the contract.

(f) The Contractor shall, without charge, replace or correct work found by the Government not to conform to contract requirements, unless in the public interest the Government consents to accept the work with an appropriate adjustment in contract price. The Contractor shall promptly segregate and remove rejected material from the premises.

(g) If the Contractor does not promptly replace or correct rejected work, the Government may-

(1) By contract or otherwise, replace or correct the work and charge the cost to the Contractor; or

(2) Terminate for default the Contractor's right to proceed.

(h) If, before acceptance of the entire work, the Government decides to examine already completed work by removing it or tearing it out, the Contractor, on request, shall promptly furnish all necessary facilities, labor, and material. If the work is found to be defective or nonconforming in any material respect due to the fault of the Contractor or its subcontractors, the Contractor shall defray the expenses of the examination and of satisfactory reconstruction. However, if the work is found to meet contract requirements, the Contracting Officer shall make an equitable adjustment for the additional services involved in the examination and reconstruction, including, if completion of the work was thereby delayed, an extension of time.

(i) Unless otherwise specified in the contract, the Government shall accept, as promptly as practicable after completion and inspection, all work required by the contract or that portion of the work the Contracting Officer determines can be accepted separately. Acceptance shall be final and conclusive except for latent defects, fraud, gross mistakes amounting to fraud, or the Government's rights under any warranty or guarantee.

(End of clause)

24.0 Warranty of Construction

All government contracts contain FAR Clause 52.246-21 Warranty of Construction. This clause requires that you warrant all construction for at least one year from the date of acceptance. This can be for the total project or for a portion. The warranty can be for longer time frames if there are manufacturer's extended warranties involved, such as for mechanical equipment. The one-year warranty time frame also runs from the date an item may have been fixed, such as an air-conditioning unit.

The more complex projects generally require a detailed warranty management plan that requires you to specify response times to fix various items depending upon the criticality of the item. There is also the requirement for a joint government/contractor four-month, nine-month, and final warranty inspection that will have to be held with a warranty list being developed. The performance bond is not released until this one- year period is reached and all items needing correction have been completed.

You also have a responsibility to fix any latent defects and defects caused by design. The time limitation is dependent upon the statute of limitations and the statute of repose of the state in which the project was constructed. However, if a defect is caused by government-furnished equipment or design, then you are not responsible for correcting the defect. This can be very important because an RFP is a government-furnished design.

FAR Clause 52.246-21 Warranty of Construction.

As prescribed in 46.710(e) (1), the contracting officer may insert a clause substantially as follows in solicitations and contracts when a fixed-price construction contract (see 46.705 (c)) is contemplated, and the use of a warranty clause has been approved under agency procedures:

Warranty of Construction (Mar 1994)

(a) In addition to any other warranties in this contract, the Contractor warrants, except as provided in paragraph (i) of this clause, that work performed under this contract conforms to the contract requirements and is free of any defect in equipment, material, or design furnished, or workmanship performed by the Contractor or any subcontractor or supplier at any tier.

(b) This warranty shall continue for a period of 1 year from the date of final acceptance of the work. If the Government takes possession of any part of the work before final acceptance, this warranty shall continue for a period of 1 year from the date the Government takes possession.

Continues on page 294

(c) The Contractor shall remedy at the Contractor's expense any failure to conform, or any defect. In addition, the Contractor shall remedy at the Contractor's expense any damage to Government-owned or controlled real or personal property, when that damage is the result of-

(1) The Contractor's failure to conform to contract requirements; or

(2) Any defect of equipment, material, workmanship, or design furnished.

(d) The Contractor shall restore any work damaged in fulfilling the terms and conditions of this clause. The Contractor's warranty with respect to work repaired or replaced will run for 1 year from the date of repair or replacement.

(e) The Contracting Officer shall notify the Contractor, in writing, within a reasonable time after the discovery of any failure, defect, or damage.

(f) If the Contractor fails to remedy any failure, defect, or damage within a reasonable time after receipt of notice, the Government shall have the right to replace, repair, or otherwise remedy the failure, defect, or damage at the Contractor's expense.

(g) With respect to all warranties, express or implied, from subcontractors, manufacturers, or suppliers for work performed and materials furnished under this contract, the Contractor shall-

(1) Obtain all warranties that would be given in normal commercial practice;

(2) Require all warranties to be executed, in writing, for the benefit of the Government, if directed by the Contracting Officer; and

(3) Enforce all warranties for the benefit of the Government, if directed by the Contracting Officer.

(h) In the event the Contractor's warranty under paragraph (b) of this clause has expired, the Government may bring suit at its expense to enforce a subcontractor's, manufacturer's, or supplier's warranty.

(i) Unless a defect is caused by the negligence of the Contractor or subcontractor or supplier at any tier, the Contractor shall not be liable for the repair of any defects of material or design furnished by the Government nor for the repair of any damage that results from any defect in Government-furnished material or design.

Continues on page 295

(j) This warranty shall not limit the Government's rights under the Inspection and Acceptance clause of this contract with respect to latent defects, gross mistakes, or fraud.

(End of clause)

Alternate I (Apr 1984). If the Government specifies in the contract the use of any equipment by "brand name and model," the contracting officer may add a paragraph substantially the same as the following paragraph (k) to the basic clause:

(k) Defects in design or manufacture of equipment specified by the Government on a "brand name and model" basis, shall not be included in this warranty. In this event, the Contractor shall require any subcontractors, manufacturers, or suppliers thereof to execute their warranties, in writing, directly to the Government.

25.0 Value Engineering

Value Engineering is the analysis of the functions of a program, project, system, product, equipment, building, facility, service, or supply to improve performance, re- liability, quality, safety, and life-cycle cost. Note the broad range of analysis. Much more than just design! This process works on just about anything. And notice that the emphasis is not on cost-reduction. Cost is a measure of resource expenditure. It's good to spend just what you must for what you need.

The government uses the "Value Engineering Job Plan" (developed by the U.S. Army Corps of Engineers), a systematic approach in five phases that analyzes a project in terms of its functions. The five phases are:

1. *Information Phase,* in which documents are studied and the background, functions, and cost/worth of functions are identified.

2. *Speculation Phase*, which identifies what else can do what must be done. Free use of imagination (with no judgment) is essential.

3. *Analysis Phase*, in which alternative solutions in terms of quality with realistic judgment are ranked.

4. *Development Phase*, in which the details of the best alternatives are put into written proposals.

5. *Implementation Phase*, in which you try to sell proposals to the client and include accepted proposals in the project.

The process for value engineering was mandated by Public Law 104-106 National Defense Authorization Act, FY 1996, which amended the Office of Federal Procurement Policy Act to state: "Each executive agency shall establish and maintain cost-effective value engineering procedures and processes." This led to the creation of FAR Clause 52.248-3, Value Engineering—Construction, to implement the requirements of Public Law 104-106.

The process dictated by this FAR clause is very lengthy both in time and work. Although FAR Clause 52.248-3 Value Engineering allows you to share in the cost savings, the time involved to prepare the proposal can be one to four weeks, and government review time is allowed to be 45 days and possibly longer. There is also no guaranty that the CO will accept the value engineering change proposal (VECP), and therefore, you must proceed with the project as if no VECP had been proposed. The decision to propose a VECP must be made early in the project and must be taken into account so as not to slow the project down.

The VECP process is more commonly used on traditional design-bid-build projects and very seldom on design-build projects. This is because design-build projects by their very nature are performance based so the contractor has generally done his or her own value engineering just to win the bid.

FAR Clause 52.248-3 Value Engineering-Construction.

As prescribed in 48.202 , insert the following clause:

Value Engineering-Construction (Oct 2020)

(a) *General.* The Contractor is encouraged to develop, prepare, and submit value engineering change proposals (VECP's) voluntarily. The Contractor shall share in any instant contract savings realized from accepted VECP's, in accordance with paragraph (f) of this clause.

(b) *Definitions.* "Collateral costs," as used in this clause, means agency costs of operation, maintenance, logistic support, or Government-furnished property.

Collateral savings, as used in this clause, means those measurable net reductions resulting from a VECP in the agency's overall projected collateral costs, exclusive of acquisition savings, whether or not the acquisition cost changes.

Contractor's development and implementation costs, as used in this clause, means those costs the Contractor incurs on a VECP specifically in developing, testing, preparing, and submitting the VECP, as well as those costs the Contractor incurs to make the contractual changes required by Government acceptance of a VECP.

Continues on page 297

Government costs, as used in this clause, means those agency costs that result directly from developing and implementing the VECP, such as any net increases in the cost of testing, operations, maintenance, and logistic support. The term does not include the normal administrative costs of processing the VECP.

Instant contract savings, as used in this clause, means the estimated reduction in Contractor cost of performance resulting from acceptance of the VECP, minus allowable Contractor's development and implementation costs, including subcontractors' development and implementation costs (see paragraph (h) of this clause).

Value engineering change proposal (VECP) means a proposal that-

(1) Requires a change to this, the instant contract, to implement; and

(2) Results in reducing the contract price or estimated cost without impairing essential functions or characteristics; *provided*, that it does not involve a change-

(i) In deliverable end item quantities only; or

(ii) To the contract type only.

(c) *VECP preparation.* As a minimum, the Contractor shall include in each VECP the information described in paragraphs (c)(1) through (7) of this clause. If the proposed change is affected by contractually required configuration management or similar procedures, the instructions in those procedures relating to format, identification, and priority assignment shall govern VECP preparation. The VECP shall include the following:

(1) A description of the difference between the existing contract requirement and that proposed, the comparative advantages and disadvantages of each, a justification when an item's function or characteristics are being altered, and the effect of the change on the end item's performance.

(2) A list and analysis of the contract requirements that must be changed if the VECP is accepted, including any suggested specification revisions.

(3) A separate, detailed cost estimate for (i) the affected portions of the existing contract requirement and (ii) the VECP. The cost reduction associated with the VECP shall take into account the Contractor's allowable development and implementation costs, including any amount attributable to subcontracts under paragraph (h) of this clause.

Continues on page 298

(4) A description and estimate of costs the Government may incur in implementing the VECP, such as test and evaluation and operating and support costs.

(5) A prediction of any effects the proposed change would have on collateral costs to the agency.

(6) A statement of the time by which a contract modification accepting the VECP must be issued in order to achieve the maximum cost reduction, noting any effect on the contract completion time or delivery schedule.

(7) Identification of any previous submissions of the VECP, including the dates submitted, the agencies and contract numbers involved, and previous Government actions, if known.

(d) *Submission.* The Contractor shall submit VECP's to the Resident Engineer at the worksite, with a copy to the Contracting Officer.

(e) Government action.

(1) The Contracting Officer will notify the Contractor of the status of the VECP within 45 calendar days after the contracting office receives it. If additional time is required, the Contracting Officer will notify the Contractor within the 45-day period and provide the reason for the delay and the expected date of the decision. The Government will process VECP's expeditiously; however, it will not be liable for any delay in acting upon a VECP.

(2) If the VECP is not accepted, the Contracting Officer will notify the Contractor in writing, explaining the reasons for rejection. The Contractor may withdraw any VECP, in whole or in part, at any time before it is accepted by the Government. The Contracting Officer may require that the Contractor provide written notification before undertaking significant expenditures for VECP effort.

(3) Any VECP may be accepted, in whole or in part, by the Contracting Officer's award of a modification to this contract citing this clause. The Contracting Officer may accept the VECP, even though an agreement on price reduction has not been reached, by issuing the Contractor a notice to proceed with the change. Until a notice to proceed is issued or a contract modification applies a VECP to this contract, the Contractor shall perform in accordance with the existing contract. The decision to accept or reject all or part of any VECP is a unilateral decision made solely at the discretion of the Contracting Officer.

(f) Sharing-

Continues on page 299

(1) *Rates*. The Government's share of savings is determined by subtracting Government costs from instant contract savings and multiplying the result by-

(i) 45 percent for fixed-price contracts; or

(ii) 75 percent for cost-reimbursement contracts.

(2) *Payment*. Payment of any share due the Contractor for use of a VECP on this contract shall be authorized by a modification to this contract to-

(i) Accept the VECP;

(ii) Reduce the contract price or estimated cost by the amount of instant contract savings; and

(iii) Provide the Contractor's share of savings by adding the amount calculated to the contract price or fee.

(g) *Collateral savings*. If a VECP is accepted, the Contracting Officer will increase the instant contract amount by 20 percent of any projected collateral savings determined to be realized in a typical year of use after subtracting any Government costs not previously offset. However, the Contractor's share of collateral savings will not exceed the contract's firm-fixed-price or estimated cost, at the time the VECP is accepted, or $100,000, whichever is greater. The Contracting Officer is the sole determiner of the amount of collateral savings.

(h) *Subcontracts*. The Contractor shall include an appropriate value engineering clause in any subcontract of $75,000 or more and may include one in subcontracts of lesser value. In computing any adjustment in this contract's price under paragraph (f) of this clause, the Contractor's allowable development and implementation costs shall include any subcontractor's allowable development and implementation costs clearly resulting from a VECP accepted by the Government under this contract, but shall exclude any value engineering incentive payments to a subcontractor. The Contractor may choose any arrangement for subcontractor value engineering incentive payments; *provided*, that these payments shall not reduce the Government's share of the savings resulting from the VECP.

(i) *Data*. The Contractor may restrict the Government's right to use any part of a VECP or the supporting data by marking the following legend on the affected parts:

These data, furnished under the Value Engineering-Construction clause of contract __________, shall not be disclosed outside the Government or duplicated, used, or disclosed, in whole or in part, for any purpose other than to evaluate a value engineering change proposal

Continues on page 300

submitted under the clause. This restriction does not limit the Government's right to use information contained in these data if it has been obtained or is otherwise available from the Contractor or from another source without limitations.

If a VECP is accepted, the Contractor hereby grants the Government unlimited rights in the VECP and supporting data, except that, with respect to data qualifying and submitted as limited rights technical data, the Government shall have the rights specified in the contract modification implementing the VECP and shall appropriately mark the data. (The terms "unlimited rights" and "limited rights" are defined in part 27 of the Federal Acquisition Regulation.)

(End of clause)

Alternate I (Apr 1984). When the head of the contracting activity determines that the cost of calculating and tracking collateral savings will exceed the benefits to be derived in a construction contract, delete paragraph (g) from the basic clause and redesignate the remaining paragraphs accordingly.

26.0 Default

FAR clause 52.249-10 Default authorizes the government to take over the work and terminate the contractor for default, and it allows the government to take over part of the work that has been delayed and to notify the sureties of this. The liability to the government includes the cost to complete the work and any damages to the government. These costs can all be recouped by the government from the contractor or the surety. However, this clause also states the following:

A. The Contractor's right to proceed shall not be terminated nor the Contractor charged with damages under this clause, if –

1. The delay in completing the work arises from unforeseeable causes beyond the control and without the fault or negligence of the Contractor. Examples of such causes include

a. Acts of God or of the public enemy,

b. Acts of the Government in either its sovereign or contractual capacity,

c. Acts of another Contractor in the performance of a contract with the Government,

d. Fires,

e. Floods,

f. Epidemics,

g. Quarantine restrictions,

h. Strikes,

i. Freight embargoes,

j. Unusually severe weather, or delays of subcontractors or suppliers at any tier arising from unforeseeable causes beyond the control and without the fault or negligence of both the Contractor and the subcontractors or suppliers; and

2. The Contractor, within 10 days from the beginning of any delay (unless extended by the Contracting Officer), must notify the Contracting Officer in writing of the causes of the delay. The Contracting Officer will ascertain the facts and the extent of delay. If, in the judgment of the Contracting Officer, the findings of fact warrant such action, the time for completing the work will be extended. The findings of the Contracting officer will be final and conclusive on the parties, but subject to appeal under the Disputes clause.

B. If, after termination of the Contractor's right to proceed, it is determined that the Contractor was not in default, or that the delay was excusable, the rights and obligations of the parties will be the same as if the termination had been issued for the convenience of the Government.

This clause is used to support a claim or contract extension whenever the above listed activities may occur and delay the work. Official weather data, daily reports, strike notices, etc., should be used as backup documentation. As stated above, notification within 10 days of the beginning of any delay is crucial.

FAR Clause 52.249-10 Default (Fixed-Price Construction).

As prescribed in 49.504(c)(1), insert the following clause:

Default (Fixed-Price Construction) (Apr 1984)

(a) If the Contractor refuses or fails to prosecute the work or any separable part, with the diligence that will insure its completion within the time specified in this contract including any extension, or fails to complete the work within this time, the Government may, by written notice to the Contractor, terminate the right to proceed with the work (or the separable part of the work) that has been delayed. In this event, the Government may take over the work and complete it by contract or otherwise, and may take possession of and use any materials, appliances, and plant on the work site necessary for completing the work. The Contractor and its sureties shall be liable for any damage to the Government resulting from the Contractor's refusal or failure to complete the work within the specified time, whether or not the Contractor's right to proceed with the work is terminated. This liability includes any increased costs incurred by the Government in completing the- work.

(b) The Contractor's right to proceed shall not be terminated nor the Contractor charged with damages under this clause, if-

(1) The delay in completing the work arises from unforeseeable causes beyond the control and without the fault or negligence of the Contractor. Examples of such causes include-

(i) Acts of God or of the public enemy,

(ii) Acts of the Government in either its sovereign or contractual capacity,

(iii) Acts of another Contractor in the performance of a contract with the Government,

(iv) Fires,

(v) Floods,

(vi) Epidemics,

(vii) Quarantine restrictions,

(viii) Strikes,

(ix) Freight embargoes,

Continues on page 303

(x) Unusually severe weather, or

(xi) Delays of subcontractors or suppliers at any tier arising from unforeseeable causes beyond the control and without the fault or negligence of both the Contractor and the subcontractors or suppliers; and

(2) The Contractor, within 10 days from the beginning of any delay (unless extended by the Contracting Officer), notifies the Contracting Officer in writing of the causes of delay. The Contracting Officer shall ascertain the facts and the extent of delay. If, in the judgment of the Contracting Officer, the findings of fact warrant such action, the time for completing the work shall be extended. The findings of the Contracting Officer shall be final and conclusive on the parties, but subject to appeal under the Disputes clause.

(c) If, after termination of the Contractor's right to proceed, it is determined that the Contractor was not in default, or that the delay was excusable, the rights and obligations of the parties will be the same as if the termination had been issued for the convenience of the Government.

(d) The rights and remedies of the Government in this clause are in addition to any other rights and remedies provided by law or under this contract.

(End of clause)

Alternate I (Apr 1984). If the contract is for dismantling, demolition, or removal of improvements, substitute the following paragraph (a) for paragraph (a) of the basic clause:

(a)

(1) If the Contractor refuses or fails to prosecute the work, or any separable part, with the diligence that will insure its completion within the time specified in this contract, including any extension, or fails to complete the work within this time, the Government may, by written notice to the Contractor, terminate the right to proceed with the work or the part of the work that has been delayed. In this event, the Government may take over the work and complete it by contract or otherwise, and may take possession of and use any materials, appliances, and plant on the work site necessary for completing the work.

(2) If title to property is vested in the Contractor under this contract, it shall revest in the Government regardless of any other clause of this contract, except for property that the Contractor has disposed of by bona fide sale or removed from the site.

(3) The Contractor and its sureties shall be liable for any damage to the Government resulting from the Contractor's refusal or failure to complete the work within the specified

Continues on page 304

time, whether or not the Contractor's right to proceed with the work is terminated. This liability includes any increased costs incurred by the Government in completing the work.

Alternate II (Apr 1984). If the contract is to be awarded during a period of national emergency, paragraph (b)(1) below may be substituted for paragraph (b)(1) of the basic clause:

(1) The delay in completing the work arises from causes other than normal weather beyond the control and without the fault or negligence of the Contractor. Examples of such causes include-

(i) Acts of God or of the public enemy,

(ii) Acts of the Government in either its sovereign or contractual capacity,

(iii) Acts of another Contractor in the performance of a contract with the Government,

(iv) Fires,

(v) Floods,

(vi) Epidemics,

(vii) Quarantine restrictions,

(viii) Strikes,

(ix) Freight embargoes,

(x) Unusually severe weather, or

(xi) Delays of subcontractors or suppliers at any tier arising from causes other than normal weather beyond the control and without the fault or negligence of both the Contractor and the subcontractors or suppliers; and

Alternate III (Apr 1984). If the contract is for dismantling, demolition, or removal of improvements and is to be awarded during a period of national emergency, substitute the following paragraph (a) for paragraph (a) of the basic clause. The following paragraph (b)(1) may be substituted for paragraph (b)(1) of the basic clause:

(a)

(1) If the Contractor refuses or fails to prosecute the work, or any separable part, with the diligence that will insure its completion within the time specified in this contract, including any extension, or fails to complete the work within this time, the Government may, by written notice to the Contractor, terminate the right to proceed with the work or the part of

Continues on page 305

the work that has been delayed. In this event, the Government may take over the work and complete it by contract or otherwise, and may take possession of and use any materials, appliances, and plant on the work site necessary for completing the work.

(2) If title to property is vested in the Contractor under this contract, it shall revest in the Government regardless of any other clause of this contract, except for property that the Contractor has disposed of by bona fide sale or removed from the site.

(3) The Contractor and its sureties shall be liable for any damage to the Government resulting from the Contractor's refusal or failure to complete the work within the specified time, whether or not the Contractor's right to proceed with the work is terminated. This liability includes any increased costs incurred by the Government in completing the work.

(b) The Contractor's right to proceed shall not be terminated nor the Contractor charged with damages under this clause, if-

(1) The delay in completing the work arises from causes other than normal weather beyond the control and without the fault or negligence of the Contractor. Examples of such causes include-

(i) Acts of God or of the public enemy,

(ii) Acts of the Government in either its sovereign or contractual capacity,

(iii) Acts of another Contractor in the performance of a contract with the Government,

(iv) Fires,

(v) Floods,

(vi) Epidemics,

(vii) Quarantine restrictions,

(viii) Strikes,

(ix) Freight embargoes,

(x) Unusually severe weather, or

(xi) Delays of subcontractors or suppliers at any tier arising from causes other than normal weather beyond the control and without the fault or negligence of both the Contractor and the subcontractors or suppliers; and

27.0 Indian Incentive

DFAR Clause 252.226-7001 Utilization of Indian Organizations and Indian Owned Economic Enterprises, and Native Hawaiian Small Business Concerns allows a contractor to obtain 5% of a subcontract's value if it is with a bona fide Indian, Native Indian, or Native Hawaiian subcontractor. The firm must be 51 percent owned by an Indian, Native Indian, or Native Hawaiian. The Indian and Native Indian firms need not be considered a small business concern; however, the Native Hawaiian firm must be.

Two things must happen to receive this money. First, the money must be available. A special account within the DoD budget, this money has normally been available in the past, but there is no guarantee it will be available. Second, the contractor must request the money as detailed in the clause. The request process is not difficult and can be very rewarding.

You should keep this incentive in mind whenever determining which subcontractor to use on a contract. You should aggressively pursue using Indian-owned subcontractors because the 5% obtained by using these firms will go directly to your profit margin.

DFARS Clause 252.226-7001 Utilization of Indian Organizations, Indian-Owned Economic Enterprises, and Native Hawaiian Small Business Concerns.

As prescribed in 226.104 , use the following clause:

UTILIZATION OF INDIAN ORGANIZATIONS, INDIAN-OWNED ECONOMIC ENTERPRISES, AND NATIVE HAWAIIAN SMALL BUSINESS CONCERNS (JAN 2023)

(a) *Definitions.* As used in this clause—

"Indian" means—

(1) Any person who is a member of any Indian tribe, band, group, pueblo, or community that is recognized by the Federal Government as eligible for services from the Bureau of Indian Affairs (BIA) in accordance with 25 U.S.C. 1452(c); and

(2) Any "Native" as defined in the Alaska Native Claims Settlement Act (43 U.S.C. 1601 et seq.).

"Indian organization" means the governing body of any Indian tribe or entity established or recognized by the governing body of an Indian tribe for the purposes of 25 U.S.C. Chapter 17.

Continues on page 307

"Indian-owned economic enterprise" means any Indian-owned (as determined by the Secretary of the Interior) commercial, industrial, or business activity established or organized for the purpose of profit, provided that Indian ownership constitutes not less than 51 percent of the enterprise.

"Indian tribe" means any Indian tribe, band, group, pueblo, or community, including native villages and native groups (including corporations organized by Kenai, Juneau, Sitka, and Kodiak) as defined in the Alaska Native Claims Settlement Act, that is recognized by the Federal Government as eligible for services from BIA in accordance with 25 U.S.C. 1452(c).

"Interested party" means a contractor or an actual or prospective offeror whose direct economic interest would be affected by the award of a subcontract or by the failure to award a subcontract.

"Native Hawaiian small business concern" means an entity that is—

(1) A small business concern as defined in Section 3 of the Small Business Act (15 U.S.C. 632) and relevant implementing regulations; and

(2) Owned and controlled by a Native Hawaiian as defined in 25 U.S.C. 4221(9).

(b) The Contractor shall use its best efforts to give Indian organizations, Indian-owned economic enterprises, and Native Hawaiian small business concerns the maximum practicable opportunity to participate in the subcontracts it awards, to the fullest extent consistent with efficient performance of the contract.

(c) The Contracting Officer and the Contractor, acting in good faith, may rely on the representation of an Indian organization, Indian-owned economic enterprise, or Native Hawaiian small business concern as to its eligibility, unless an interested party challenges its status or the Contracting Officer has independent reason to question that status.

(d) In the event of a challenge to the representation of a subcontractor, the Contracting Officer will refer the matter to—

(1)

(i) For matters relating to Indian organizations or Indian-owned economic enterprises:

U.S. Department of the Interior

Bureau of Indian Affairs

Attn: Bureau Procurement Chief

Continues on page 308

12220 Sunrise Valley Drive

Reston, VA 20191

Phone: 703-390-6433

Website: https://www.bia.gov/

(ii) The BIA will determine the eligibility and will notify the Contracting Officer.

(2)

(i) For matters relating to Native Hawaiian small business concerns:

Department of Hawaiian Home Lands

PO Box 1879

Honolulu, HI 96805

Phone: 808-620-9500

Website: http://dhhl.hawaii.gov/

(ii) The Department of Hawaiian Home Lands will determine the eligibility and will notify the Contracting Officer.

(e) No incentive payment will be made—

(1) While a challenge is pending; or

(2) If a subcontractor is determined to be an ineligible participant.

(f)

(1) The Contractor, on its own behalf or on behalf of a subcontractor at any tier, may request an incentive payment in accordance with this clause.

(2) The incentive amount that may be requested is 5 percent of the estimated cost, target cost, or fixed price included in the subcontract at the time of award to the Indian organization, Indian-owned economic enterprise, or Native Hawaiian small business concern.

Continues on page 309

(3) In the case of a subcontract for commercial products or commercial services, the Contractor may receive an incentive payment only if the subcontracted items are produced or manufactured in whole or in part by an Indian organization, Indian-owned economic enterprise, or Native Hawaiian small business concern.

(4) The Contractor has the burden of proving the amount claimed and shall assert its request for an incentive payment prior to completion of contract performance.

(5) The Contracting Officer, subject to the terms and conditions of the contract and the availability of funds, will authorize an incentive payment of 5 percent of the estimated cost, target cost, or fixed price included in the subcontract awarded to the Indian organization, Indian-owned economic enterprise, or Native Hawaiian small business concern.

(6) If the Contractor requests and receives an incentive payment on behalf of a subcontractor, the Contractor is obligated to pay the subcontractor the incentive amount.

(g) The Contractor shall insert the substance of this clause, including this paragraph (g), in all subcontracts exceeding $500,000.

(End of clause)

28.0 Government Rights

This clause grants the government unlimited rights to use all documents developed by the contractor and his or her designers for use on this project and to use at any time anywhere in the world. This clause supersedes all patent and copyright laws. In construction, these are generally used as a basis for standardization of facilities for the DoD throughout the world and sometimes used to ensure facility compatibility in facilities such as barracks, dining facilities, transportation facilities, and operations facilities. The contractor, and especially the designers, must understand this when they are preparing drawings and specifications especially if something unique that normally would be patented or copyrighted has been developed.

DFARS Clause 252.227-7022 Government Rights (Unlimited).

As prescribed at 227.7107-1 (a) use the following clause:

GOVERNMENT RIGHTS (UNLIMITED) (MAR 1979)

The Government shall have unlimited rights, in all drawings, designs, specifications, notes and other works developed in the performance of this contract, including the right to use same on any other Government design or construction without additional compensation to the Contractor. The Contractor hereby grants to the Government a paid-up license throughout the world to all such works to which he may assert or establish any claim under design patent or copyright laws. The Contractor for a period of three (3) years after completion of the project agrees to furnish the original or copies of all such works on the request of the Contracting Officer.

(End of clause)

29.0 Levies on Contract Payments

DFAR Clause 252.232-7010 Levies on Contract Payments is only used when the Internal Revenue Service issues a notice to the contractor that it is going to impose a levy on the contract payments for taxes owed. The IRS has full authority to make this levy on all contracts the contractor has. The clause states that the contractor must notify the PCO if the contractor feels that it will limit him or her from fulfilling the contract. The contractor must also send a copy of the notification to the administrative CO.

If you find yourself in this position, it's best to include in the letter a complete assessment of the effects on your ability to perform the remaining work due to this levy along with rationale and all supporting documentation. It is especially important to stress the effects on national security and subcontractors' ability to perform without getting paid. You need to understand that the PCO does not have to agree with the rationale and that he or she can direct you to proceed to complete the work and still allow the IRS to collect the levy. You will only get one chance to convince the PCO that the levy will affect the project so the rationale must be very strong. There is no notification time period stated in the clause, but you should notify the PCO as soon as you are notified by the IRS. Also, no appeal of the PCO's decision is allowed; his or her decision is final.

DFARS Clause 252.232-7010 Levies on Contract Payments.

As prescribed in 232.7102 , use the following clause:

LEVIES ON CONTRACT PAYMENTS (DEC 2006)

(a) 26 U.S.C. 6331(h) authorizes the Internal Revenue Service (IRS) to continuously levy up to 100 percent of contract payments, up to the amount of tax debt.

(b) When a levy is imposed on a payment under this contract and the Contractor believes that the levy may result in an inability to perform the contract, the Contractor shall promptly notify the Procuring Contracting Officer in writing, with a copy to the Administrative Contracting Officer, and shall provide—

(1) The total dollar amount of the levy;

(2) A statement that the Contractor believes that the levy may result in an inability to perform the contract, including rationale and adequate supporting documentation; and

(3) Advice as to whether the inability to perform may adversely affect national security, including rationale and adequate supporting documentation.

(c) DoD shall promptly review the Contractor's assessment, and the Procuring Contracting Officer shall provide a written notification to the Contractor including–

(1) A statement as to whether DoD agrees that the levy may result in an inability to perform the contract; and

(2)

(i) If the levy may result in an inability to perform the contract and the lack of performance will adversely affect national security, the total amount of the monies collected that should be returned to the Contractor; or

(ii) If the levy may result in an inability to perform the contract but will not impact national security, a recommendation that the Contractor promptly notify the IRS to attempt to resolve the tax situation.

(d) Any DoD determination under this clause is not subject to appeal under the Contract Disputes Act.

(End of clause)

Chapter 8
Modification Proposals

1.0 Chapter Description and Use

2.0 Modifications

2.1 Modification Price Guidelines

2.2 Modification Format and Profit Calculation

3.0 Indirect Cost Allowability

4.0 Equipment Pricing for Modifications

5.0 Subcontractor Cost or Pricing Data – Modifications

6.0 Modification Markup Meeting

7.0 Guidelines for Pricing Modifications

8.0 Schedules (FRAGNET)

1.0 Chapter Description and Use

This chapter describes the federal government's modification (change order) pricing process. This process must be followed whether it is used for REA or through the RFP process. In either case, the scope of work must be well defined before beginning this pricing process. This chapter details the federal government's modification price guidelines, format, and profit calculations; U.S. Army Corps of Engineers forms; costs allowable for overhead costs; requirements for subcontractor cost or pricing data and when this must be used; costs allowed for modifications and definitions for each; when and why to use a FRAGNET schedule.

The objective of this chapter is to give you the ability to prepare a complete modification price proposal ready to negotiate with the federal government.

2.0 Modifications

Change orders in government language are called modifications because they "modify" the contract. Modifications can be required for many different reasons, and the government will require that you give a complete cost breakdown along with full justification and a FRAGNET schedule if a time extension or extended overhead is requested. DFAR Clause 252.236-7000 Modification Proposals—Price Breakdown delineates what needs to be included as part of the modification proposal.

2.1 Modification Price Guidelines

The government has developed modification pricing guidelines in accordance with FAR requirements and court decisions. The different agencies have their own forms for accomplishing this, but for the purposes of this manual we will concentrate on the methods and forms used by the USACE. The USACE requires that a nonbinding agreement be made between them and you that sets out what the various factors pertaining to indirect costs will be. This system has proven to be very effective because it is agreed upon once at the beginning of the contract and is used throughout the life of the contract. Other agencies may have the agreement as part of the contract or may just define what can be included as part of a modification and what cannot.

The USACE guidelines, as shown in Modification Markup Meeting and Guidelines for Pricing Modifications, clearly define what is required and/or allowed for each factor. The same factors should be used for each subcontractor, but you may need to negotiate these factors separately. Profit factors will be calculated for each modification based upon the USACE's "Weighted Guidelines Profit Analysis" sheet included with the Modification Format and Profit Calculation section of this manual.

Field office overhead will normally be the most significant amount on any modification that may justify a time extension. It is important to include all items including those that may be provided for the government's use, such as an office trailer, furniture, cleaning services, etc.

Home office overhead is always a point of contention with the government, and unless you have an audited general and administrative (G&A) factor or overhead factor that has been performed in the past year, they will try to dictate the percentage. It is recommended that each firm have this audit performed at least once every year. This requirement also pertains to subcontractors.

2.2 Modification Format and Profit Calculation

The USACE has developed an Excel spreadsheet for costing modifications. This spreadsheet incorporates all the markups you agreed to in the modification markup meeting and includes the direct costs and profit as calculated using the "Profit Analysis" sheet. This spreadsheet should be used for all costing modifications and should also be a requirement for subcontractors.

You should include this spreadsheet in all subcontracts as this will ensure the subcontractors will give you their breakdown with the same information and in the same format you will have to give the government.

Profit analysis is a very subjective calculation. Naturally you want the highest profit you can attain, and the government wants the lowest. The government will allow a 7.5 percent profit on all modifications; however, the profit analysis could show a profit as high as 12 percent. Generally, the profit will calculate out to around 8 percent. Design-build contracts should have the higher profit margins as they carry the greatest risk.

Note: This format also takes into consideration all bond costs, taxes, equipment costs, labor, materials, etc.

DFARS Clause 252.236-7000 Modification Proposals--Price Breakdown.

As prescribed in 236.570(a), use the following clause:

MODIFICATION PROPOSALS--PRICE BREAKDOWN (DEC 1991)

(a) The Contractor shall furnish a price breakdown, itemized as required and within the time specified by the Contracting Officer, with any proposal for a contract modification.

(b) The price breakdown—

(1) Must include sufficient detail to permit an analysis of profit, and of all costs for—

(i) Material;

(ii) Labor;

(iii) Equipment;

(iv) Subcontracts; and

(v) Overhead; and

(2) Must cover all work involved in the modification, whether the work was deleted, added, or changed.

Continues on page 315

(c) The Contractor shall provide similar price breakdowns to support any amounts claimed for subcontracts.

(d) The Contractor's proposal shall include a justification for any time extension proposed.

(End of clause)

3.0 Indirect Cost Allowability

FAR clause 31.205, Selected Costs delineates what costs are allowed and disallowed in the home office overhead calculations. The government will require you to include an overhead factor in each contract modification based upon the cost principle in FAR clause 31.205. The government also will usually allow a home office overhead of 5% if you choose not to provide the information required by this clause.

The government allows contractors to use a home office overhead factor of more than 5% if the contractor has had an audit performed in accordance with FAR clause 31.205 within the last year by a CPA that certifies what the home office overhead factor is. This is highly recommended both for prime contractors and subcontractors. Specialty subcontractors generally have home office overhead costs that are very high due to equipment costs being included in this overhead.

4.0 Equipment Pricing for Modifications

The government requires you to use USACE pamphlet EP1110-8 for determining construction equipment ownership and operating costs in lieu of using actual costs for contractor-owned equipment. This is a very complicated process and generally yields very low rates. The government allows you to use rental equipment, and you can recoup 100 percent of the costs in the modification.

You should use rental equipment for all modification work if possible due to its being 100 percent recoverable. Profit/ overhead can be added to this.

You can download USACE pamphlet EP 1110-1-8, *Construction Equipment Ownership and Operating Expense Schedule*, online at http://www.usace.army.mil/inet/ usace-docs/eng-pamphlets/ep.htm.

5.0 Subcontractor Cost or Pricing Data—Modifications

FAR clause 52.215-13, Subcontractor Cost or Pricing Data – Modifications, is used whenever a modification is contemplated to exceed $750,000. As the contractor, you must require the subcontractor to submit the "Certificate of Current Cost or Pricing Data" along with the pricing for the modification. The certificate certifies that the data submitted was accurate, complete, and current as of the date of the agreement. The government uses this certification when an awarded subcontract already exists and there would likely be no way to change subcontractors, thus making the government rely on the pricing of only one subcontractor. The data required and the government's detailed review can sometimes make this a lengthy, drawn-out procedure.

If any additional contract time and/or extended overhead is justified, then the subcontractor and subsequently you need to include this in the modification. The "Certificate of Current Cost and Pricing Data" must also be included in every subcontract. The "Certificate of Current Cost and Pricing Data" must be completed and signed by the subcontractor but does not have to be signed by you. If the government later determines that the subcontractor either withheld cost or pricing data or significant information that could have changed the cost downward, then the subcontractor can be prosecuted in federal court.

FAR Clause 52.215-13 Subcontractor Certified Cost or Pricing Data-Modifications.

As prescribed in 15.408(e) (1), insert the following clause:

Subcontractor Certified Cost or Pricing Data-Modifications (Jun 2020)

(a) The requirements of paragraphs (b) and (c) of this clause shall—

(1) Become operative only for any modification to this contract involving a pricing adjustment expected to exceed the threshold for submission of certified cost or pricing data in Federal Acquisition Regulation (FAR) 15.403-4(a)(1) on the date of execution of the modification; and

(2) Be limited to such modifications.

(b) Before awarding any subcontract expected to exceed the threshold for submission of certified cost or pricing data in FAR 15.403-4(a)(1), on the date of agreement on price or the date of award, whichever is later; or before pricing any subcontract modification involving a pricing adjustment expected to exceed the threshold for submission of certified cost or pricing data in

Continues on page 317

FAR 15.403-4(a)(1), the Contractor shall require the subcontractor to submit certified cost or pricing data (actually or by specific identification in writing), in accordance with FAR 15.408, Table 15-2 (to include any information reasonably required to explain the subcontractor's estimating process such as the judgmental factors applied and the mathematical or other methods used in the estimate, including those used in projecting from known data, and the nature and amount of any contingencies included in the price), unless an exception under FAR 15.403-1(b) applies. If the threshold for submission of certified cost or pricing data specified in FAR 15.403-4(a)(1) is adjusted for inflation as set forth in FAR 1.109(a), then pursuant to FAR 1.109(d) the changed threshold applies throughout the remaining term of the contract, unless there is a subsequent threshold adjustment.

(c) The Contractor shall require the subcontractor to certify in substantially the form prescribed in FAR 15.406-2 that, to the best of its knowledge and belief, the data submitted under paragraph (b) of this clause were accurate, complete, and current as of the date of agreement on the negotiated price of the subcontract or subcontract modification.

(d) The Contractor shall insert the substance of this clause, including this paragraph (d), in each subcontract that exceeds the threshold for submission of certified cost or pricing data in FAR 15.403-4(a)(1) on the date of agreement on price or the date of award, whichever is later.

(End of clause)

Alternate I (Aug 2020). As prescribed in 15.408 (e) (2), substitute the following paragraphs (a), (b), and (d) for paragraphs (a), (b), and (d) of the basic clause:

(a) The requirements of paragraphs (b) and (c) of this clause shall—

(1) Become operative only for any modification to this contract involving aggregate increases and/or decreases in costs, plus applicable profits, expected to exceed the threshold for submission of certified cost or pricing data at FAR 15.403-4(a)(1); and

(2) Be limited to such modifications.

(b) Unless an exception under FAR 15.403-1 applies, the Contractor shall require the subcontractor to submit certified cost or pricing data (actually or by specific identification in writing), in accordance with FAR 15.408, Table 15-2 (to include any information reasonably required to explain the subcontractor's estimating process such as the judgmental factors applied and the mathematical or other methods used in the estimate, including those used in projecting from known data, and the nature and amount of any contingencies included in the price)—

Continues on page 318

(1) Before modifying any subcontract that was awarded prior to July 1, 2018, involving a pricing adjustment expected to exceed $750,000; or

(2) Before modifying any subcontract that was awarded on or after July 1, 2018, involving a pricing adjustment expected to exceed $2 million.

(d) The Contractor shall insert the substance of this clause, including this paragraph (d), in each subcontract that exceeds $2 million.

FAR Clause 15.406-2 Certificate of Current Cost or Pricing Data.

(a) When certified cost or pricing data are required, the contracting officer shall require the contractor to execute a Certificate of Current Cost or Pricing Data, using the format in this paragraph, and must include the executed certificate in the contract file.

Certificate of Current Cost or Pricing Data

This is to certify that, to the best of my knowledge and belief, the cost or pricing data (as defined in section 2.101 of the Federal Acquisition Regulation (FAR) and required under FAR subsection 15.403-4) submitted, either actually or by specific identification in writing, to the Contracting Officer or to the Contracting Officer's representative in support of ________* are accurate, complete, and current as of ________**. This certification includes the cost or pricing data supporting any advance agreements and forward pricing rate agreements between the offeror and the Government that are part of the proposal.

Firm ____

Signature ____

Name ____

Title ____

Date of execution*** ____________________________

*Identify the proposal, request for price adjustment, or other submission involved, giving the appropriate identifying number (*e.g.,* RFP No.).

**Insert the day, month, and year when price negotiations were concluded and price agreement was reached or, if applicable, an earlier date agreed upon between the parties that is as close as practicable to the date of agreement on price.

Continues on page 319

***Insert the day, month, and year of signing, which should be as close as practicable to the date when the price negotiations were concluded, and the contract price was agreed to.

(End of certificate)

(b) The certificate does not constitute a representation as to the accuracy of the contractor's judgment on the estimate of future costs or projections. It applies to the data upon which the judgment or estimate was based. This distinction between fact and judgment should be clearly understood. If the contractor had information reasonably available at the time of agreement showing that the negotiated price was not based on accurate, complete, and current data, the contractor's responsibility is not limited by any lack of personal knowledge of the information on the part of its negotiators.

(c) The contracting officer and contractor are encouraged to reach a prior agreement on criteria for establishing closing or cutoff dates when appropriate in order to minimize delays associated with proposal updates. Closing or cutoff dates should be included as part of the data submitted with the proposal and, before agreement on price, data should be updated by the contractor to the latest closing or cutoff dates for which the data are available. Use of cutoff dates coinciding with reports is acceptable, as certain data may not be reasonably available before normal periodic closing dates (*e.g.*, actual indirect costs). Data within the contractor's or a subcontractor's organization on matters significant to contractor management and to the Government will be treated as reasonably available. What is significant depends upon the circumstances of each acquisition.

(d) Possession of a Certificate of Current Cost or Pricing Data is not a substitute for examining and analyzing the contractor's proposal.

(e) If certified cost or pricing data are requested by the Government and submitted by an offeror, but an exception is later found to apply, the data shall not be considered certified cost or pricing data and shall not be certified in accordance with this subsection.

6.0 Modification Markup Meeting

The U.S. Army Corps of Engineers has developed a Modification Markup Meeting form that is intended to clarify what modification markups need to be used in future modifications. This method has proved to be very successful and eliminates disputes during modification negotiations.

CHECKLIST

Contract: ____________________________ Date: ___________________________

Contractor: ____

Contractor Representative(s): ____

Government Representative(s): ____

The following worksheet contains a non-binding agreement between Contractor and Government representatives on the modification process. This agreement does not discuss direct costs. The contractor (and subcontractors) will provide proposals in sufficient detail for government cost verification. The contractor will separately provide a proposal template reflecting agreed markups.

1. **Direct Labor.** The contractor agreed to submit hourly (Davis-Bacon at a minimum) wages, with a separate markup for fringe benefits/labor burden.

2. _____apply _____% average labor burden applied to related trades OR

3. _____ the contractor provided backup to support separate markups for each trade

4. **Direct Supervision.** We agreed the contractor may not add costs for salaried supervisors; they belong in field overhead percentage. For hourly paid supervision (job foremen), we agreed to:

5. _____ % (normally 15%) applied to direct labor OR

6. _____ charge hourly based on level of required effort.

7. **"Contingencies."** We allow contingencies to the extent we expect the contractor to bear a higher level of risk. For example, we might pay a percentage waste on lumber and concrete. However, we do not pay for unsubstantiated contingency markups. We agreed to no separate percentage markup for:

_____ Safety (if required, itemize as a direct cost)

_____ Miscellaneous material (allocated to Small Tools & Consumables)

_____ Material Handling

_____ Warranty

_____ As-built drawings (for a reasonable number of changes without significant design effort)

_____ Estimating, negotiating, and scheduling changes

8. **Small Tools & Consumables.** The contractor will apply _____ % (typically 0-3%) to direct labor for small tools and consumables. By accepting a percentage, the contractor will not submit itemized proposals for wire nuts, tape, etc.

9. **Field Overhead (FOOH).** FOOH only applies if a mod extends time due solely to Government action. To establish a baseline for possible extending overhead costs, the contractor provided bid documentation to support $_____/workday FOOH prorated straight-line over the intended project duration—or (rarely used) _____% applied to all changes regardless of time extension. The actual FOOH daily rate, if required for a time extension, will depend on the stage of construction. To support a time extension, the contractor must submit a schedule analysis to prove a mod affects the critical path. The same requirements apply to subcontractors requesting FOOH.

10. **Project Management.** We agreed the itemized cost for project management belongs in Field Office Overhead (FOOH). See Item 5.

11. Home Office Overhead (HOOH or G&A). The contractor has accounting records to support _____ % (typically 4-5%) G&A. The G&A rate does not include unallowable or unallocable costs per FAR 31.205.

12. **Profit.** FAR requires a method to calculate profit on each change. The corps uses the Weighted Guidelines Method, where profit varies from 3% to 12% dependent on weight of seven factors. Using this method, average profit would calculate to 7.5%. We encourage all contractors to use the corps method to calculate profit. The government can furnish an Excel spreadsheet for profit calculations.

13. Bond, Insurance, B&O. We prefer to only pay for one bond. The government expects the contractor to set up a bond arrangement that has subcontractors share in the prime's bonding cost.

_____The contractor will use a combined rate of _____% or

_____The contractor will apply separate rates of _____% bond, _____ insurance, _____B & O.

The contractor _____does _____does not require separate bonds from subcontractors. If so, separate bond applies to these subcontractors:

____

____

14. **Extended Overhead.** We allow costs for extended FOOH, to the extent a contractor can prove damage and delays caused solely by the government. (We allow HOOH overhead as a percentage markup on all changes.) To receive compensation, the contractor must provide detailed justification with before and after (approved) schedules to document time-related costs. The government will not pay for concurrent delays. If weather or contractor actions contribute to time growth, the contractor will not receive monetary compensation but may receive additional time.

15. **Credit Modifications.** Contractors must return overhead, profit, insurance, and bond on credit modifications. We recognize that a contractor cannot recover sunk costs for FOOH. Consequently, we expect the contractor to return G&A, bid-climate profit, bond, insurance, and B&O. The contractor agreed to these rates for credit mods:

$ ____ FOOH

_____ % G&A

_____ % profit (typically 5%)

_____ % bond/insurance/B&O (typically 2%)

16. **Release Language.** FAR requires that we insert a contractor release statement in each modification. The release statement, in effect, requires the contractor to acknowledge that the modification represents full accord and satisfaction for the scope of work and its effects on the schedule and contractor's operations. We do not see a need for or accept blanket contractor reservations attached to the modification. New events, such as unanticipated effects on unchanged work or the impact and ripple of a multiplicity of changes, stand on their own merit and do not belong in a reservation of rights.

____

Government Representative

____

Contractor's Representative

7.0 Guidelines for Pricing Modifications

The government has pricing restrictions and traditions that may differ from your experience with other companies or state and local governments. Before you submit a modification proposal, I recommend you review your pricing structure against the following guidelines, which address typical areas that cause delays to successful negotiations. The guidelines were developed by the U.S. Army Corps of Engineers to explain what can be included in modifications. They should be used in conjunction with the Modification Markup Meeting. The list is as complete and well defined as any list the government uses.

As-built Drawings Markup. Typically, not allowed. Federal boards determined contractors must include an allowance for annotating modifications to as-built drawings in the original bid. The only exception involves a contract with an unusually large number or difficult changes that exceed those in a normal contract.

Bond, Insurance, B&O Tax. We allow actual costs. Unlike the state, we allow B&O as a separate markup, if not already included in your overhead percentage. Normally we will only pay for one bond. The government expects the contractor to set up a bond arrangement that has subcontractors share in the prime's bonding cost.

Contingencies. Typically, not allowed as an unsubstantiated markup. We consider contingencies a factor evaluated to establish the profit percentage based on who assumes the risk.

Credit Modifications. Federal boards determined contractors must return overhead, profit, insurance, and bond on credit modifications. We expect you to return bid-climate markups.

Direct Equipment. Do not submit "price book" rates for owned equipment. You may not charge more than rates in EP 1110-1-8 Construction Equipment Ownership and Operating Expense Schedule, available online at http://www. usace.army.mil/inet/usace-docs/eng-pamphlets/ep.htm. Clearly separate owned from rental equipment. If you use rental equipment, you pay sales tax based on where you use the equipment, not on where you rented it. We generally allow actual (relative to Blue Book rates) for rental equipment. You may not charge separately for any vehicles, such as pickups, carried under your field or home office overhead percentage.

Direct Labor. Do not submit "price book" labor rates. Use actual hourly wages paid (Davis-Bacon minimum), with a separate markup for fringe benefits and labor burden. In your first proposal, submit a breakdown to verify the components of your labor markup.

Direct Material. Provide detailed lists of all planned material, with actual direct costs for each component. As with labor, avoid "price book" material costs. Calculate tax based on where you will install the material, not the point of purchase. In lieu of detailed lists, we usually will accept vendor quotes, if you have three sources to verify competitive pricing. List all discounts. (Failure to disclose discounts to deliberately mislead the government is fraud.)

Direct Supervision. States generally allow 15% labor markup for supervision. We allow a percentage labor markup for supervision by working foremen provided you have no direct hours in the proposal for the effort. Either list actual hours or use a percentage markup, never both. You may not add costs for salaried supervisors; they belong in your field overhead percentage.

Estimating, Scheduling, and Negotiating Fees. Typically, not allowed. Federal boards determined contractors must include an allowance for modifications in the original bid. The exception involves a contract with an unusually large number of difficult changes that exceed expectations of a normal contract.

Extended Overhead. We allow costs for FOOH to the extent a contractor can prove damage and delays caused solely by the government. To receive compensation, you must provide detailed justification with before and after (approved) schedules to document time-related costs. The government will not pay for concurrent delays. If weather or contractor actions contribute to time growth, you will not receive monetary compensation but may receive additional time.

Material Handling. We consider delivery costs included in your material price. We consider uncrating and handling costs included in your labor price. This office typically rejects percentage markups for material handling.

Miscellaneous Material. Not allowed. We consider this a contingency already covered by an allowance for small tools and consumables.

Overhead. We expect you to list actual HOOH (general and administrative expenses or G&A) on each proposal. FAR Part 31.205 addresses allowable overhead costs. You must reduce the G&A percentage for unallowable costs such as advertising, charities, contributions, donations, recruiting, bad debts, entertainment, fines, penalties, interest, and federal income tax. For small sub- contractors, we typically allow 5% G&A. Any subcontractor or prime receiving pass-through costs typically receives G&A and reduced profit. Special note: An October 1996 ASBCA decision determined a contractor may NOT add a percentage to modifications for FOOH. The board held that a contractor normally does not incur additional FOOH costs to administer modifications that do not extend contract time. The government will only allow FOOH as a daily rate to the extent your schedule proves the government has sole responsibility for the time extension.

Profit. Per FAR, you must use a method to calculate profit on modifications. The government uses the USACE Weighted Guidelines Method, where profit varies from 3% to 12% dependent on seven weighted factors. Using this scale, average conditions would equate to 7.5% profit.

Project Management. Boards consider project management part of either home or field overhead. We will not allow separate payment for project management unless you can clearly prove your job costing system excludes project managers from overhead.

Safety. The government typically does not allow a separate markup for safety. The government considers safety already included in either your labor burden or FOOH. The government will allow direct safety costs for one-time applications related specifically to a modification. For example, if we extend a roof, we will allow costs to extend roof barriers. We would not, however, pay for portable barriers you intend to reuse on other projects.

Small Tools & Consumables. We typically allow up to 3% of labor for prime or subcontractor trades that use small tools and consumables. We will not allow separate markups for both small tools and consumables. We also will not allow percentage markups on proposals that contain detailed breakdowns for consumables such as nails, wire nuts, tape, etc.

Subcontracts. Provide breakdowns in the same detail as pricing by the prime. Exclude FOOH unless the subcontractor requires a time extension.

Technical Submittals. Boards consider the effort to engineer field changes part of either home or field overhead. We will not allow separate payment for preparing submittals unless you can clearly prove your job costing system excludes engineering from overhead.

Travel. We expect contractors to use local trades and avoid travel expenses. When you can justify bringing in outside workers or specialists, travel and subsistence may not exceed rates established by GSA for federal employees; i.e. no first-class accommodations or first-class travel.

Warranty Markup. Not allowed. (Manufacturers already provide warranties on equipment and material.) This means a contractor markup for warranty would equate to a contingency for poor workmanship.

8.0 Schedules (FRAGNET)

Whenever a change is contemplated by the government or a REA or claim is submitted by the contractor, a "Fragmented Network Analysis" (FRAGNET) should be submitted with the request to show the impact on the critical path of the schedule. The FRAGNET schedule must clearly show the as-planned and as-built critical paths and the effect that the change had. The government then needs to determine whether the delay is:

Non-excusable – It's the Contractor's problem to straighten out.

Excusable, but non-compensable – It is neither the contractor's nor the government's fault, i.e. excessive rainfall, union strike, etc.

Excusable and Compensable – Not the contractor's but the government's fault. Contractor has the burden to prove this.

The government will not consider a time extension or time-related costs for a REA or claim unless a FRAGNET schedule is submitted along with the REA or claim. The ASBCA will not entertain a claim based on delay unless the FRAGNET is submitted with the claim and clearly shows the government was at fault.

Chapter 9
Claims

1.0 Chapter Description and Use

2.0 Requests for Equitable Adjustment

3.0 Documentation Required for a Claim

4.0 Notifications

5.0 Contracting Officer's Final decision

6.0 Armed Services Board of Contract Appeals

1.0 Chapter Description and Use

This chapter deals with the federal claims process and its requirements. It defines what a "Request for Equitable Adjustment" is; what constitutes a REA or claim and how it must be processed; documentation required by you as the contractor in order to prove your REA or claim; a notice checklist; what the CO's "Final" decision means and when it must be obtained; and what the Armed Services Board of Contract Appeals is and what authority it has. This chapter is not meant to be a law class but instead give you direction as to the process, documentation required, and notice requirements so that you can set up procedures to be able to identify potential claim situations and to understand what will be required to avoid a claim.

You should engage the services of a competent and experienced construction law attorney if a claim is to be filed. Federal construction law is very different from state construction law, so the choice of an experienced federal construction attorney will increase your chances of winning a federal claim.

The objective of this chapter is to enable you to determine what the REA and claim process entails and how to set yourself up to avoid claims by being thoroughly prepared to handle them. A thorough understanding of the process and the details should enable you to be able to avoid claims. Remember, the burden of proof is on you, so you must be able to present all the documentation necessary to prove your case.

2.0 Requests for Equitable Adjustment

As the contractor, you can submit a REA in accordance with DFAR 252.243-7002 Requests for Equitable Adjustment at any time and for any reason. If you feel this is being required by the government to perform work not required by the contract, you should file a REA. Special attention should be given to the notification requirements (see *Notifications Checklist)*, which can be done via letter or e-mail and then followed with the REA later. Quite often, after the notification is given, an RFP for a contract modification will be issued by the CO.

When submitting a REA, care should be taken to provide the certification required in the DFAR clause as well as all necessary documentation. The documentation must be complete and clearly support the reasons and costs associated with the REA. Remember, you may get only one chance to present your case for the REA.

Cost and pricing data and certification may be required in accordance with FAR clause 15.403-4 in certain circumstances if the contract modification is greater than $750,000. This means that all data used in pricing the contract modification must be submitted to the government and that the contractor certifies that this data is correct to "the best of his knowledge and belief" at the time the proposal is prepared.

DFARS Clause 52.243-7002 Requests for Equitable Adjustment.

As prescribed in 243.205-71, use the following clause:

REQUESTS FOR EQUITABLE ADJUSTMENT (DEC 2022)

(a) The amount of any request for equitable adjustment to contract terms shall accurately reflect the contract adjustment for which the Contractor believes the Government is liable. The request shall include only costs for performing the change and shall not include any costs that already have been reimbursed or that have been separately claimed. All indirect costs included in the request shall be properly allocable to the change in accordance with applicable acquisition regulations.

Continues on page 329

(b) In accordance with 10 U.S.C. 3862(a), any request for equitable adjustment to contract terms that exceeds the simplified acquisition threshold shall bear, at the time of submission, the following certificate executed by an individual authorized to certify the request on behalf of the Contractor:

<table>
<tr><td colspan="3">I certify that the request is made in good faith, and that the supporting data are accurate and complete to the best of my knowledge and belief.</td></tr>
<tr><td colspan="3"></td></tr>
<tr><td></td><td></td><td></td></tr>
<tr><td></td><td>(Official's Name)</td><td></td></tr>
<tr><td></td><td></td><td></td></tr>
<tr><td></td><td>(Title)</td><td></td></tr>
</table>

(c) The certification in paragraph (b) of this clause requires full disclosure of all relevant facts, including□

(1) Certified cost or pricing data, if required, in accordance with subsection 15.403-4 of the Federal Acquisition Regulation (FAR); and

(2) Data other than certified cost or pricing data, in accordance with subsection 15.403-3 of the FAR, including actual cost data and data to support any estimated costs, even if certified cost or pricing data are not required.

(d) The certification requirement in paragraph (b) of this clause does not apply to

(1) Requests for routine contract payments; for example, requests for payment for accepted supplies and services, routine vouchers under a cost-reimbursement type contract, or progress payment invoices; or

(2) Final adjustments under an incentive provision of the contract.

(End of clause)

3.0 Documentation Required for a Claim

The two basic elements of any claim are entitlement and quantum. The entitlement portion establishes the factual and contractual basis supporting your right to recover from the federal government. The quantum portion requires that you state a sum certain under the Contract Disputes Act and the "Disputes" clause.

The entitlement portion requires that you show how the federal government injured you by its actions, such as a misinterpretation of a specification. You must describe and prove that you had to perform extra work and experienced a delay due to this action.

The quantum portion of a monetary claim requires you to describe the amount of money and time to which you are entitled and must relate the "cause to affect" action relating the federal government's actions to the cost incurred. The relation of cause and effect can be very difficult as it normally requires issues of scheduling, cost accounting, and support for estimates.

As a matter of routine, you should set policies and procedures that will provide ad- equate documentation should a claim situation arise. This same documentation will normally be required if a REA is contemplated. Contracting officers will tell you that "documentation, documentation, documentation" are the three key words to remember for a successful REA or claim. These can include daily reports, correspondence (mail, e-mail, faxes, telephone logs, RFIs, etc.), documentation of verbal or written directives, quality control reports, subcontractor daily reports, daily inspection reports, design clarifications, submittal registers, etc. Schedules may need to be submitted, especially if time is a factor in the claim. The schedule should be a FRAGNET schedule that clearly supports your claim to time impact. Make sure you follow the rules for preparing a FRAGNET schedule according to the rules of law. Proof that notifications were provided in the proper time frame will also prove critical.

I highly recommend that you employ a method to isolate all costs associated with a potential REA or claim as this will make it much easier to prove your case.

4.0 Notifications

Timely notifications to the government about what a contractor deems a change, a contracting officer's direction, or other circumstances are critical to protect the contractor's rights to file a claim. Notification requirements are included in the various FAR clauses but can be confusing and may not be readily apparent. The following Notice Checklist can be used to simplify this requirement.

Clause Reference	Subject Matter of Notice	Time Requirements for Notice	Writing Required	Stated Consequences of Lack of a Notice
Changes, FAR 52.243-4	Proposal for adjustment	**30 days** from receipt of a written change order from the government or written notification of a constructive change by the contractor	Yes	Claim may not be allowed. Notice requirement may be waived until final payment.
Constructive Changes, FAR 52.243-4	Date, circumstance, and source of the order and that the contractor regards the government's order as a constructive contract change.	No starting point stated, but notice within **20 days** of incurring any additional costs and/or time due to the constructive change fully protects the contractor's rights	Yes	Costs incurred more than **20 days** prior to giving notice cannot be covered, except in the case of defective specifications.
Differing Site Conditions, FAR 52.236-2	Existence of unknown or materially different conditions affecting the contractor's cost and/or time	From the time such conditions are identified, notice must be furnished **"promptly"** and before such conditions are disturbed	Yes	Claim not allowed. Lack of notice may be waived until final payment

Clause Reference	Subject Matter of Notice	Time Requirements for Notice	Writing Required	Stated Consequences of Lack of a Notice
Suspension of Work, FAR 52.212-12	(1) Of "the act or failure to act involved"...	(1) Within **20 days** from the act or failure to act by the CO (not including a suspension order)	(1) Yes	(1) Costs incurred more than **20 days** prior to the notification cannot be recovered
		(2) **"As soon as practicable"** after termination of the suspension, delay, or interruption.	(2) Yes	(2) Claim not allowed , but claim may be considered until final payment
Default, FAR 52.249-10	Causes of delay beyond contractor's control	**10 days** from the beginning of any delay	Yes	Contractor's right to proceed may be terminated and the government may sue for damages
Disputes, FAR 52.233-1	Appeal of any final decision by the CO	(1) **Boards of Contract Appeals - 90 days** from receipt of CO's final decision	(1) Yes - Notice of Appeal	CO's decision becomes final and conclusive
		(2) **U.S.Court of Federal Claims - 1 year** from receipt of CO's final decision	(2) Yes - Filing of Complaint	CO's decision becomes final and conclusive

5.0 Contracting Officer's Final Decision

The requirements for a CO's "Final" decision are contained in FAR clause 33.211 Contracting Officer's Decision. The decision must be based on review of the facts pertinent to the claim, assistance from legal and other services, (i.e. C.O.R.), coordination with the contract administration officer or CO and any other sources that may be necessary.

The written decision must include:

A description of the claim or dispute

A reference to the pertinent contract terms

A statement of the factual areas of agreement and disagreement

A statement of the Contracting Officer's decision with supporting rationale

Various paragraphs as required by the clause

The CO's final decision will generally not be given unless you specifically request it in writing. If you are contemplating requesting a claim, this decision is mandatory prior to filing the claim. By requesting this decision, you are forcing the government to answer formally with its rationale. This sometimes can have the effect of overturning a previous decision, such as a decision rendered by the administrative contracting officer (ACO). If a REA is denied, it is highly recommended that you request a CO's "final" decision.

The CO has sixty days in which to respond to this request if the certified claim is less than $100,000 and can take more than sixty days if the certified claim is more than $100,000, but the CO must render a decision in a "reasonable time."

FAR Clause 33.211 Contracting officer's decision.

(a) When a claim by or against a contractor cannot be satisfied or settled by mutual agreement and a decision on the claim is necessary, the contracting officer shall-

(1) Review the facts pertinent to the claim;

(2) Secure assistance from legal and other advisors;

(3) Coordinate with the contract administration officer or contracting office, as appropriate; and

(4) Prepare a written decision that shall include-

(i) A description of the claim or dispute;

(ii) A reference to the pertinent contract terms;

(iii) A statement of the factual areas of agreement and disagreement;

(iv) A statement of the contracting officer's decision, with supporting rationale;

(v) Paragraphs substantially as follows:

"This is the final decision of the Contracting Officer. You may appeal this decision to the agency board of contract appeals. If you decide to appeal, you must, within 90 days from the date you receive this decision, mail or otherwise furnish written notice to the agency board of contract appeals and provide a copy to the Contracting Officer from whose decision this appeal is taken. The notice shall indicate that an appeal is intended, reference this decision, and identify the contract by number.

With regard to appeals to the agency board of contract appeals, you may, solely at your election, proceed under the board's-

(1) Small claim procedure for claims of $50,000 or less or, in the case of a small business concern (as defined in the Small Business Act and regulations under that Act), $150,000 or less; or

(2) Accelerated procedure for claims of $100,000 or less.

Continues on page 335

Instead of appealing to the agency board of contract appeals, you may bring an action directly in the United States Court of Federal Claims (except as provided in 41 U.S.C.7102(d), regarding Maritime Contracts) within 12 months of the date you receive this decision"; and

(vi) Demand for payment prepared in accordance with 32.604 and 32.605 in all cases where the decision results in a finding that the contractor is indebted to the Government.

(b) The contracting officer shall furnish a copy of the decision to the contractor by certified mail, return receipt requested, or by any other method that provides evidence of receipt. This requirement shall apply to decisions on claims initiated by or against the contractor.

(c) The contracting officer shall issue the decision within the following statutory time limitations:

(1) For claims of $100,000 or less, 60 days after receiving a written request from the contractor that a decision be rendered within that period, or within a reasonable time after receipt of the claim if the contractor does not make such a request.

(2) For claims over $100,000, 60 days after receiving a certified claim; provided, however, that if a decision will not be issued within 60 days, the contracting officer shall notify the contractor, within that period, of the time within which a decision will be issued.

(d) The contracting officer shall issue a decision within a reasonable time, taking into account-

(1) The size and complexity of the claim;

(2) The adequacy of the contractor's supporting data; and

(3) Any other relevant factors.

(e) The contracting officer shall have no obligation to render a final decision on any claim exceeding $100,000 which contains a defective certification, if within 60 days after receipt of the claim, the contracting officer notifies the contractor, in writing, of the reasons why any attempted certification was found to be defective.

(f) In the event of undue delay by the contracting officer in rendering a decision on a claim, the contractor may request the tribunal concerned to direct the contracting officer to issue a decision in a specified time period determined by the tribunal.

Continues on page 336

(g) Any failure of the contracting officer to issue a decision within the required time periods will be deemed a decision by the contracting officer denying the claim and will authorize the contractor to file an appeal or suit on the claim.

(h) The amount determined payable under the decision, less any portion already paid, should be paid, if otherwise proper, without awaiting contractor action concerning appeal. Such payment shall be without prejudice to the rights of either party.

6.0 Armed Services Board of Contract Appeals

The Armed Services Board of Contract Appeals (ASBCA) is an administrative law court authorized by 41 U.S.C. SECT 601, *et seq.* originally set up in 1962 and revised in 1979 to hear contractors' appeals of contracting officers' decisions. The board reports directly to the Secretary of Defense. The court decisions are based in U.S. public law and are binding on the parties involved.

The Armed Services Board of Contract Appeals has 36 rules under the *Rules of the Armed Services Board of Contract Appeals* that must be strictly adhered to. Rule 1 is "Appeals, How Taken," which explains when an appeal must be filed and how and where it must be filed. Appeals have been dismissed just for being sent to the wrong office. Rule 2 is "Notice of Appeal, Contents of" and tells what must be included in the appeal, such as what paperwork must be included and who must get it. You and your attorney must learn these rules and comply with them explicitly.

A review of numerous ASBCA decisions indicates that the court is adamant about proper notifications, proper certifications, and adequate backup documentation for a contractor to prove a claim. Many decisions have been handed down dismissing a case based solely on a small technicality. These decisions have clearly shown that the contractor must have adequate documentation to prove a claim and that all notifications, certifications, and other ASBCA rules have been adhered to.

Before deciding to file a claim, you should be aware that only 17 percent of claims cases brought before the ASBCA are decided in favor of the contractor and that legal fees required to process and pursue the claim cannot usually be recouped.

Refer to the ASBCA rules, decisions, etc., at www.docs.law.gwv.edu/asbca

Commonly Used Government Acronyms

ACASS	Architect Contract Appraisal Support System
ACO	Administrative Contracting Officer
A/E	Architect/Engineer
AIS	Automated Information System
ASBCA	Armed Services Board of Contract Appeals
BAFO	Best and Final Offer
BOD	Beneficial Occupancy Date
BOSC	Base Operating Support Contract
BRAC	Base Realignment and Closure
CADD	Computer Aided Design and Drafting
CAO	Contract Administration Office
CCASS	Construction Contract Appraisal Support System
CCD	Contract Completion Date
CCN	Contract Change Notice
CCP	Contract Change Proposal
CFE	Contractor Furnished Equipment
CFM	Contractor Furnished Material
CFR	Code of Federal Regulations
CLIN	Contract Line Item Number
CO	Contracting Officer
CONUS	Continental United States
COR	Contracting Officer's Representative
COE	Corps of Engineers
COTR	Contracting Officer's Technical Representative
C/PD	Cost/Pricing Data

CPM	Critical Path Method
CQC	Contractor Quality Control
CSI	Construction Specifications Institute
DA	Designer Approval
DCAA	Defense Contract Audit Agency
DFARS	Defense Federal Acquisition Regulation Supplement
DFAS	Defense Finance and Accounting Service
DoD	Department of Defense
DOR	Designer of Record
ECD	Estimated Completion Date
EFA	Engineering Field Activity
EFD	Engineering Field Division
EIC	Engineer in Charge
EO	Executive Order
FAR	Federal Acquisition Regulation
FDR	Final or Formal Design Review
FFP	Firm-Fixed-Price
FOOH	Field Office Overhead
G&A	General and Administrative
GAO	Government Accountability Office
GE	Government Estimate
GFE	Government Furnished Equipment
GFM	Government Furnished Material
HAZCOM	Hazard Communication
HAZMAT	Hazardous Material
HOOH	Home Office Overhead
HUB	Historically Underutilized Business
IDIQ	Indefinite Delivery Indefinite Quantity

IFB	Invitation for Bid
IG	Inspector General
IGCE	Independent Government Cost Estimate
IQC	Indefinite Quantity Contract
ITP	Integrated Test Plan
ITR	Initial Technical Review
KO	Contracting Officer (Also CO)
LD	Liquidated Damages
MILCON	Military Construction (Appropriation)
MIL-HDBK	Military Handbook
MILSPEC	Military Specification
MOD	Modification
MOU	Memorandum of Understanding
MSDS	Material Safety Data Sheet
NAICS	North American Industry Classification System
NAVFAC	Naval Facilities Engineering Command
NBC	Nuclear, Biological, and Chemical
NTE	Not to Exceed
OBE	Overcome By Events
O&M	Operation and Maintenance
OMB	Office of Management and Budget
OPR	Office of Primary Responsibility
OSHA	Occupational Safety and Health Administration
OTP	Operational Test Plan
PCO	Procuring Contracting Officer
PDR	Preliminary Design Review
P&L	Profit and Loss
PL	Public Law

POC	Point of Contact
POP	Period of Performance
PW	Public Works
PWS	Performance Work Statement
QA	Quality Assurance
QAE	Quality Assurance Evaluator
QC	Quality Control
QCS	Quality Control System
RFB	Request for Bid
RFI	Request for Information
RFP	Request for Proposal
RFQ	Request for Quotation
RMS	Resident Management System
SADBU	Small and Disadvantaged Business Utilization
SAM	System for Award Management
SBA	Small Business Administration
SDBUP	Small Disadvantaged Business Utilization Program
SDVOSB	Service Disabled Veteran Owned Small Business
SECDEF	Secretary of Defense
SF	Standard Form
SIOH	Supervision, Inspection, and Overhead
SIPRNET	Secret Internet Protocol Router Network
SMDP	Standardized Military Drawing Program
SOC	Solutions Order Contract
SOP	Standard Operating Procedure
SOW	Statement of Work
SPEC	Specification
TBD	To be Determined or Developed

TFC	Termination for Convenience
TFD	Termination for Default
TM	Technical Manual
TO	Technical Order
TOC	Task Order Contract
TQM	Total Quality Management
UCA	Undefinitized Contract Action
UI	Unit of Issue
USACE	United States Army Corps of Engineers
U.S.C.	United States Code
USG	United States Government
VE	Value Engineering
VECP	Value Engineering Change Proposal
VOSB	Veteran Owned Small Business
WIP	Work in Place
WOSB	Woman-Owned Small Business

Government Contracts Glossary

Acquisition

The acquiring of supplies or services by the federal government with appropriated funds through purchase or lease.

Affiliates

Business concerns, organizations, or individuals that control each other or that are controlled by a third party. Control may include shared management or ownership; common use of facilities, equipment, and employees; or family interest.

Best and Final Offer (BAFO)

For negotiated procurements, a contractor's final offer following the conclusion of discussions.

Business Information Centers (BICs)

One-stop locations for information, education, and training designed to help entrepreneurs start, operate, and grow their businesses. The centers provide free on-site counseling, training courses, and workshops and have resources for addressing a broad variety of business startup and development issues.

Certificate of Competency

A certificate issued by the Small Business Administration (SBA) stating that the holder is "responsible" (in terms of capability, competency, capacity, credit, integrity, perseverance, and tenacity) for the purpose of receiving and performing a specific government contract.

Certified 8(a) Firm

A firm owned and operated by socially and economically disadvantaged individuals and eligible to receive federal contracts under the Small Business Administration's 8(a) Business Development Program.

Contract

A mutually binding legal relationship obligating the seller to furnish supplies or services (including construction) and the buyer to pay for them.

Contracting

Purchasing, renting, leasing, or otherwise obtaining supplies or services from nonfederal sources. Contracting includes the description of supplies and services required, the selection and solicitation of sources, the preparation and award of contracts, and all phases of contract administration. It does not include grants or cooperative agreements.

Contracting Officer

A person with the authority to enter into, administer, and/or terminate contracts and make related determinations and findings.

Contractor Team Arrangement

An arrangement in which (a) two or more companies form a partnership or joint venture to act as potential prime contractor; or (b) an agreement by a potential prime contractor with one or more other companies to have them act as its subcontractors under a specified government contract or acquisition program.

Defense Acquisition Regulatory Council (DARC)

A group composed of representatives from each military department, the Defense Logistics Agency, and the National Aeronautics and Space Administration and is in charge of the Federal Acquisition Regulation (FAR) on a joint basis with the Civilian Agency Acquisition Council (CAAC).

Defense Contractor

Any person who enters into a contract with the United States for the production of material or for the performance of services for national defense.

Electronic Data Interchange

Transmission of information between computers using highly standardized electronic versions of common business documents.

Emerging Small Business

A small business concern whose size is no greater than 50% of the numerical size standard applicable to the Standard Industrial Classification code assigned to a contracting opportunity.

Equity

An accounting term used to describe the net investment of owners or stockholders in a business. Under the accounting equation, equity also represents the result of assets with less liabilities.

Fair and Reasonable Price

A price that is fair to both parties, considering the agreed-upon conditions, promised quality, and timeliness of contract performance. "Fair and reasonable" price is subject to statutory and regulatory limitations.

Federal Acquisition Regulation (FAR)

The body of regulations is the primary source of authority governing the government procurement process. The FAR, which is published as Chapter 1 of Title 48 of the Code of Federal Regulations, is prepared, issued, and maintained under the joint auspices of the secretary of Defense, the administrator of General Services Administration, and the administrator of the National Aeronautics and Space Administration. Actual responsibility for maintenance and revision of the FAR is vested jointly in the Defense Acquisition Regulatory Council (DARC) and the Civilian Agency Acquisition Council (CAAC).

Full and Open Competition

With respect to a contract action, "full and open" competition means that all responsible sources are permitted to compete.

Intermediary Organization

Organizations that play a fundamental role in encouraging, promoting, and facilitating business-to-business linkages and mentor-protégé partnerships. These can include both nonprofit and for-profit organizations: chambers of commerce; trade associations; local, civic, and community groups; state and local governments; academic institutions; and private corporations.

Joint Venture

In the SBA Mentor-Protégé Program, an agreement between a certified 8(a) firm and a mentor firm to perform a specific federal contract.

Mentor

A business, typically large, or other organization that has created a specialized program to advance strategic relationships with small businesses.

Negotiation

Contracting using either competitive, or other-than-competitive proposals or discussions. Any contract awarded without using sealed bidding procedures is a negotiated contract.

North American Industrial Classification System

The standard used by federal statistical agencies in classifying business establishments for the purpose of collecting, analyzing, and publishing statistical data related to the U.S. business economy.

One-Stop Capital Shops

OSCSs are the SBA's contribution to the Empowerment Zones/Enterprise Communities Program, an interagency initiative that provides resources to economically distressed communities. The shops provide a full range of SBA lending and technical assistance programs.

Partnering

A mutually beneficial business-to-business relationship based on trust and commitment and that enhances the capabilities of both parties.

Prime Contract

A contract awarded directly by the federal government.

PRO-Net

SBA's Procurement Marketing Access Network, or PRO-Net, is a "virtual" one-stop procurement shop. The database offers an electronic search engine for contracting officers and serves as a marketing tool for small businesses that register with the system. It contains the profiles of thousands of small firms.

Protégé

A firm in a developmental stage that aspires to increasing its capabilities through a mutually beneficial business-to-business relationship.

Request for Proposal (RFP)

A document outlining a government agency's requirements and the criteria for the evaluation of offers.

SCORE

The Service Corps of Retired Executives is a 12,400-member volunteer association sponsored by the SBA. SCORE matches volunteer business-management counselors with present prospective small business owners in need of expert advice.

Small Business

A business smaller than a given size as measured by its employment, business receipts, or business assets.

Small Business Development Centers (SBDC)

SBDCs offer a broad spectrum of business information and guidance as well as assistance in preparing loan applications.

Small Business Innovative Research (SBIR) Contract

A type of contract designed to foster technological innovation by small businesses with 500 or fewer employees. The SBIR contract program provides for a three-phased approach to research and development projects: technological feasibility and concept development; the primary research effort; and the conversion of the technology to a commercial application.

Small Disadvantaged Business Concern

A small business concern that is at least 51% owned by one or more individuals who are both socially and economically disadvantaged. This can include a publicly owned business that has at least 51% of its stock unconditionally owned by one or more socially and economically disadvantaged individuals and whose management and daily business is controlled by one or more such individuals.

Standard Industrial Classification (SIC) Code

A code representing a category within the Standard Industrial Classification System administered by the Statistical Policy Division of the U.S. Office of Management and Budget. The system was established to classify all industries in the U.S. economy. A two-digit code designates each major industry group, which is coupled with a second two-digit code representing subcategories.

Subcontract

A contract between a prime contractor and a subcontractor to furnish supplies or services for the performance of a prime contract or subcontract.

Index

Accounting and Appropriation Data, 27
Acquisition Methods, iv, 1, 20, 128
Acquisition Process, 19
Additional Requirements, 250
Affirmative Action Programs, 12
Amendments, iv, 1, 25, 29, 73
Anti-Terrorism/Force Protection (AT/FP), vi, 130
Apprentices and Trainees, viii, 155, 199, 201, 203, 209
Bid Feasibility, 30
Bid Protest, 76
Bidder Eligibility, v, 30, 70
Bidding, xi, 3, 18, 20, 21, 31, 32, 33, 37, 43, 49, 72, 212, 279
Bonding Capacity, 31, 32
Bonds, 24, 31, 51, 67, 79, 80, 137, 271, 273, 275, 322
Business Strategy, 19
Buy American Act, viii, 36, 156, 210, 211, 212, 213, 234
Change Order, xiii, 42, 47, 50, 52, 53, 57, 65, 67, 76, 95, 284, 286, 287, 288, 289, 312, 331
Claims, x, 40, 42, 50, 57, 65, 67, 76, 88, 95, 157, 173, 174, 184, 193, 251, 258, 259, 262, 270, 271, 274, 281, 287, 306, 307, 327, 332, 334, 335, 336
Clause Inclusion, viii, 155, 171
Competition, v, 3, 19, 20, 30, 32, 33, 38, 65, 70, 71, 72, 277, 278, 344
Competitive Negotiation, 20, 21
Computer Software, 11
Construction Contracting, iii, xi, xii, xiii, xiv, 2
Construction Documents, 103
Contract Administration, 23, 27, 50, 262, 333, 334, 337, 343
Contract Administration Data, 23, 27
Contract Award, 19, 23, 79, 93, 127, 159, 161, 163, 164, 168, 185, 188, 213, 226, 235, 240, 241, 248, 274, 275, 345, 346
Contract Clauses, iv, vii, 1, 23, 27, 90, 92, 155, 210
Contract Performance, 84, 89, 90, 91, 93, 150, 176, 182, 185, 189, 192, 290, 309, 344
Contract Termination, 210
Contract Terms, 34, 132, 184, 269, 290, 328, 329, 333, 334
Contract Types, 88, 89
Contract Work Hours, 199, 206, 209
Contracting Officer, vi, x, 20, 23, 77, 78, 79, 80, 81, 82, 88, 89, 94, 95, 96, 105, 106, 107, 146, 147, 148, 151, 160, 166, 174, 175, 176, 181, 182, 183, 184, 185, 186, 187, 189, 190, 191, 192, 193, 198, 199, 204, 205, 206, 210, 214, 219, 220, 224, 225, 226, 232, 233, 235, 237, 239, 241, 246, 247, 248, 255, 256, 257, 259, 265, 267, 268, 270, 271, 275, 276, 277, 278, 279, 280, 283, 285, 286, 288, 289, 290, 291, 292, 293, 294, 295, 298, 299, 301, 303, 307, 308, 309, 310, 311, 314, 318, 319, 327, 330, 333, 334, 335, 336, 337, 339, 343, 346
Contracting Officer's Representative, vi, 88, 96, 337
Cost Overruns, 54

Cost-Reimbursement Contracts, v, 88, 89, 91, 299
Davis-Bacon Act, viii, xii, 155, 199, 201, 205
Department of Defense (DoD), iii
Design-Bid-Build, xiii, 32, 89, 100, 137, 296
Design-Build, xiii, 32, 89, 98, 99, 100, 101, 102, 103, 108, 128, 130, 133, 137, 138, 144, 166, 296
Differing Site Conditions, ix, 156, 279, 280, 281, 331
Disadvantaged Business Enterprise, 6
Disaster Response Registry, 9
Disputes, ix, 156, 199, 210, 262, 267, 268, 269, 279, 288, 301, 303, 311, 319, 330, 332
EM 385-1-1 Safety Manual, vii, 144, 152
Environmental Compliance, 60
Equipment Pricing, x, 312, 315
Evaluation Criteria, v, 30, 31, 32, 33, 73, 76
FAR Clauses, vii, 76, 104, 155, 158, 210
Federal Acquisition Regulation (FAR), 12, 19, 162, 173, 214, 216, 221, 228, 316, 318, 329, 343, 344
Federal Construction Projects, xiii
Federal Contracts, 8, 13, 99, 149, 168, 173, 342
Federal Government Rules, xi, xiii
Federal Procurement, 7, 98, 296
Financial Information, 7, 39
Fiscal Year, 5, 7, 13, 173, 184, 186, 190, 198
Fixed Price with Economic Price Adjustment, 21, 90
Fixed-Price Contracts, v, 88, 89, 90, 93, 299
Force Majeure, 36, 37, 50, 51
General Conditions Costs, xi
General Contractor, iii, 32, 141
Government Furnished Property (GFP), ix, 157, 289
Indefinite-Delivery Contracts, v, 93
Inspector Qualifications, vii, 141
Joint Venture, 11, 32, 39, 41, 71, 83, 86, 169, 173, 343, 345
Labor Standards, 13, 208, 209, 210
Liquidated Damages, viii, 34, 50, 51, 62, 66, 155, 166, 172, 198, 199, 339
Liquidated Damages Clause, 166
Management Risks, v, 30, 32, 37
Miller Act, ix, 156, 271, 272, 273, 274
Modification Proposals, x, 312, 313, 314
Negotiation, 1, 20, 21, 22, 92, 345
Notice to Proceed, 24, 127, 134, 138, 298
Operations Facilities, iii, 309
Past Performance, 4, 17, 21, 22, 184
Pay Determination, viii, 155, 201
Payment Bonds, ix, 25, 79, 156, 257, 271, 272, 274, 275
Payment Requests, viii, 156, 252
Performance Bonds, 79, 275
Preconstruction Submittals, vii, 133, 137
Predecessor Entity, 6
Preliminary Design, 339
Prevailing Wages, viii, xii, 155, 199
Price Evaluation Preferences, viii, 155, 168
Price Proposal, 21, 312
Procurement Process, 344
Progress Payments, viii, 156, 251, 255, 256, 257, 258, 284, 285
Project Manager, iii, 63, 64, 68, 201, 325
Project Risk, 54
Proposal Preparation, v, 30, 70, 99
Quality Assurance, 27, 134, 340
Quality Control Manager, vii, 108, 133, 140, 142
Quality Control Plan, vii, 98, 133, 134, 135
Request for Proposal (RFP), 346
Risk Management, v, xi, 30, 31, 33, 35
Safety Manual, 144, 145, 151, 152
Safety Program, vii, xiii, 144, 145
Scope of Work, 49, 51, 312, 322

Sealed Bidding, iv, 1, 20, 21, 167, 215, 345
Shop Drawings, vi, 97, 99, 100, 105, 106, 131, 139, 167
Site Investigation, ix, 157, 279, 280, 281, 282
Small Business Subcontracting Plan, viii, xii, 83, 87, 155, 170, 171, 173, 181, 197, 198
Small Business Utilization, 31
Solicitation, iv, 1, 15, 18, 20, 21, 22, 23, 24, 25, 26, 27, 28, 29, 31, 33, 34, 35, 70, 71, 73, 74, 75, 76, 79, 80, 81, 102, 131, 132, 133, 146, 157, 166, 167, 168, 169, 170, 172, 178, 180, 187, 194, 196, 211, 214, 261, 275, 280, 290, 343
Specifications and Drawings, vi, 97, 98, 100, 105, 131
Subcontracting, 19, 83, 86, 171, 172, 173, 174, 175, 176, 177, 178, 179, 182, 183, 184, 185, 186, 187, 188, 189, 190, 191, 192, 193, 194, 195, 196, 198, 199, 276, 277
Submittal Register, vii, 133, 137, 138, 330
Surety Bonds, v, 30, 79, 271
Suspension of Work, ix, 104, 157, 285, 286, 332
Taxpayer Identification Number (TIN), 5, 252, 260
Time-and-Materials Contracts, 94
U.S. Army Corps of Engineers, viii, xiii, 134, 144, 145, 146, 156, 252, 295, 312, 319, 323
Unique Entity ID, iv, 1, 3, 4, 5, 18, 179, 195, 196
Value Engineering, ix, 42, 157, 295, 296, 299, 341
Wage Determination, viii, 155, 200, 201, 202, 203, 204, 207
Warranty of Construction, ix, 157, 293
Work Hours, viii, 53, 155, 201

www.ingramcontent.com/pod-product-compliance
Lightning Source LLC
LaVergne TN
LVHW060023210926
848481LV00013B/3782
9798349616150